HARVARD EAST ASIAN SERIES

24

POLITICAL THOUGHT IN
EARLY MEIJI JAPAN
1868-1889

---

*The East Asian Research Center
at Harvard University
administers projects designed
to further scholarly understanding
of China, Korea, Japan,
and adjacent areas.*

POLITICAL

THOUGHT

IN

EARLY MEIJI

JAPAN

1868-1889

Joseph Pittau, S.J.

HARVARD UNIVERSITY PRESS
CAMBRIDGE, MASSACHUSETTS

1967

© Copyright 1967 by the President and Fellows of Harvard College

All rights reserved

Distributed in Great Britain by Oxford University Press, London

Preparation of this volume was aided by a grant from the Ford Foundation. The Foundation is not, however, the author, owner, publisher, or proprietor of the publication and is not to be understood as approving by virtue of its grant any of the statements made or views expressed therein.

Library of Congress Catalog Card Number 65–22065

Printed in the United States of America

PREFACE

No period of Japanese history has been more thoroughly examined or debated than the first two decades of the Meiji era. However, there has not yet been any detailed analysis of the political ideas of early Meiji Japan published in a Western language.

My main purpose is to examine the political concepts of the articulate elite of early Meiji Japan and to see what kind of state the Meiji leaders envisioned as they built the new nation and discussed the pros and cons of a representative constitutional government. Although economics, religion, and technology, constellations of personalities with their private ambitions and differing backgrounds, and fortuitous circumstances all played important roles in the change of the political system in the first half of the Meiji period, only passing reference will be made to these factors insofar as they explain the political ideas of the Meiji leaders.

Until just a few years ago it was generally assumed that the Meiji leaders wanted to build and actually did build an absolute state, with only a façade of constitutionalism. Today one notices among Japanese and foreign scholars the tendency to re-examine these past assumptions.

For the most part I have based my research on new materials only recently made available by the Japanese Government and private collectors. The great bulk of these new materials has been collected and patiently examined by Inada Masatsugu in his work *Meiji kempō seiritsu shi* (History of the framing of the

Meiji Constitution). I found other still unpublished documents in the National Diet Library very useful, particularly in compiling Chapters V and VI.

A word of thanks is due to those who have encouraged and helped to guide me in the writing of this book. The Superiors of the Japanese and New England Provinces of the Society of Jesus have been most generous in allowing me time and funds to pursue my graduate work at Harvard. To Professors Benjamin Schwartz and Albert Craig I owe my original interest in the phenomenon of the modernization of Japan. Their teaching and direction have inspired this research. For suggesting many fruitful lines of investigation I am deeply grateful to Professor Johannes Siemes of Sophia University and to Professor Inada Masatsugu of the Tokyo University of Education. Special thanks go to Professor John Nissel and Mr. Michael Gallagher, both of Sophia University, for their patient revision of my English. I am also indebted to Professors Gino Piovesana, Joseph Roggendorf, John Blewett, Joseph Bartoli, and many others who contributed in various ways to the writing of this book. I remain however, solely responsible for errors of fact or interpretation and for the translations not otherwise acknowledged.

J. P.

Tokyo
July 1966

CONTENTS

POLITICAL THOUGHT
IN EARLY MEIJI JAPAN
1868-1889

INTRODUCTION

In the unfolding of ideas within history there often emerges a contradiction between the whole system of a certain political philosopher, on the one hand, and parts selected by politicians to incorporate into a living system, on the other. The exigencies of time and place often impel politicians to be selective in their day to day applications of a system to the concrete reality.

A similar contradiction emerges also between the original presentation of a political system and its later rationalization. In later rationalizations there appears the tendency to interpret the past in terms of the present. What was intended to be but one part is often mistaken for the whole. While parts of the theories of Rousseau and Hegel have been used as a basis of defending totalitarian systems of government, these thinkers themselves probably never envisaged that their ideas would develop along modern totalitarian lines.

The Meiji leaders of Japan set about to construct a form of government which eventually in the 1930's grew into a strongly authoritarian militaristic state. The Japanese political regime of the thirties was based on the theory of an imperial, absolutist, and antidemocratic system, often referred to as *kokutai*.

The purpose of this study is to examine and to evaluate whether the Meiji leaders intended to develop such an absolute system or whether such a system was wholly or in part a degeneration that differed from their original concept. In order to clarify the central point of discussion a summary exposition of the *kokutai* theory is presented here as an introduction.

Kokutai is a concept of fundamental importance in the study of Japanese political thought. Its literal translation is "substance" or "body of the nation." Usually it is translated as "national polity" or "national entity." It can be used to mean the entire social and political structure of the nation or, in a restricted sense, a basic government policy framed to meet certain internal and external situations. The term can be also used in the sense of "national honor." Usually, however, *kokutai* signifies the permanent and fundamental constituents of the Japanese national, and particularly the imperial, system.[1] This notion stresses the absolute homogeneity of Japanese culture, characterized by the link of loyalty and love between the people and the emperor.

The official interpretation of the *kokutai* theory was presented by the Ministry of Education in the book *Kokutai no hongi* Fundamentals of the national polity), issued in 1937.[2] It was an authoritative and comprehensive statement rejecting directly all theory that tended to weaken the absolute powers of the emperor. Thus, in the thirties, the *kokutai* became the metaphysical foundation of a Japanese state commanded by the imperial throne, whose mission was to bring a higher civilization to the Far East. It was an organic theory of the state used to justify a repressive, militaristic, antiforeign political system. There is nothing equivocal in this statement of the *Kokutai no hongi:* "Our country is established with the Emperor, who is a descendant of Amaterasu Omikami, as her center, and our ancestors as well as we ourselves constantly behold in the Emperor the fountainhead of her life and activities. For this reason, to serve the Emperor and to receive the Emperor's great august Will as one's own is the rationale of making our historical 'life' live in the present; and on this is based the morality of the people."[3]

The *kokutai* theory involved a characteristic relation between the emperor and his subjects: it was not only a political subjection, but a moral and quasi-religious devotion, which made the political community a state and at the same time a family and a church. The nation became an extension of the family, and the emperor was considered not only the repository of all sovereign power, but also the paterfamilias to whom filial piety and devotion were due. As expressed in the idea of the *kokutai,* the sovereign emperor was the embodiment of absolute values and, therefore, the ultimate source of both ethics and power. Consequently the actions of the emperor, that is, the state, were not subject to any moral judgment other than that which the state itself chose to pass. This absoluteness of the national polity, a union of ethical and political authority, overwhelmed the Individual's freedom. The emperor was to be obeyed blindly without any reservation:

Loyalty means to reverence the Emperor as [our] pivot and to follow him implicitly. By implicit obedience is meant casting ourselves aside and serving the Emperor intently. To walk this Way of loyalty is the sole Way in which we subjects may "live," and the fountainhead of all energy. Hence, offering our lives for the sake of the Emperor does not mean so-called self-sacrifice, but the casting aside of our little selves to live under his august grace and the enhancing of the genuine life of the people of a State . . . An individual is an existence belonging to a State and her history which forms the basis of his origin, and is fundamentally one body with it.[4]

This community—the state—as something absolute, transcended all forms of political factionalism and antagonism and denied all possible pluralism. It was united at the center by and in the emperor, on whom converged all loyalty. The duty of the citizen was not only loyalty, but also filial piety, because "our country is a great family nation, and the Imperial Household is the head family of the subjects and the nucleus of national life."[5] This mingling of loyalty and filial piety was a characteristic of national ethics in Japan.[6]

In the *kokutai* ideology we find a combination of two diverse elements: the European organic concept of society and the Japanese traditional Confucian idea of family morality. This combination is expressed in the words *kazoku kokka* (family-nation or family-state).[7] The organic concept of the state was formed in Europe as an antithesis to the atomistic and mechanistic view of society held by eighteenth century exponents of natural rights. This theory insists that the state possesses an organic unity in which the whole is superior to its parts. The state, not the individual, becomes the end of political and social life.

In the final formulation of the *kokutai* the organic notion united with Confucian family morality, and this unification gave birth to the family-state concept, which considered the nation to be a kind of natural organism and loyalty to the state an extension of filial piety. The organic theory was used to affirm the primacy of the state and fundamental subjection of the individual to the political community. The notion of the family-state, on the other hand, was used to mitigate resistance to such a theory of absolute power of the state. Political relations were explained as relations existing within the family nation. Dominance and subservience were transmuted into benevolence and filial piety. The natural loyalty of every man to his family was sublimated into an awareness of his obligation of allegiance to the state.[8]

While in Western countries political allegiance was generally directed to some collective entity like the nation, the folk, or the party, in Japan the terminus of loyalty was the emperor. This was easily done, insofar as the Japanese nation was represented as a family in which the emperor and the people were all related by blood. The Japanese people were considered to be the twigs and branches of a mighty tree whose trunk was the imperial family. In Christian terms the *kokutai* might be said to be almost like a mystical body receiving life from the head and center, the emperor. This allegiance to the emperor, however, was not the allegiance shown to a charismatic leader. The emperor was not at the center because of his qualities, but because of the imperial institution. The emperor was the state, in the sense that he was a sublimated paterfamilias, the source of the nation's life and the seal of unity among all the members of the national family.[9]

This was the *kokutai* theory as presented in the 1930's. It was defended at the time as the unchanged and immutable basis of political and moral life in Japan. It was also officially held that the Meiji Constitution of 1889 and the political ideology of Meiji Japan explicitly professed the Japanese political system to be a family-state.

Our task, therefore, is to examine the various, often conflicting, currents of thought present in Meiji Japan and to attempt a comparison between the later formulation of the *kokutai* theory and the political theories of the Meiji leaders. Clearly, in Meiji Japan and in the Meiji Constitution there must have been some elements which could be used to justify the family-state ideology and thus canonize militarism and absolutism. Nonetheless the question arises: were these elements there in explicit form from the beginning, or were they read into these theories later? It is not enough to find the same term, *kokutai,* used in the period of the framing of the Meiji Constitution in order to affirm the continuity of ideology and values, for words can change meaning and acquire nuances. Was the idea implied in the *kokutai* of the 1930's—the emperor identified with the government, a ruler whose sovereignty suffered no limitations either from his people or from any other source—actually present in the Meiji Constitution itself? Do we have to accept the assumption of the thirties that the Meiji Constitution and the Meiji leaders built an absolute state based on the unchanged and unchangeable *kokutai?* These are the questions that confront us here.

That the answer is not a simple one is shown by some opinions expressed in the wake of the promulgation of the Meiji Constitution in February 1889. Though it is not true, as some people have stated, that at the time of the promulgation there was a conspicuous absence of criticism,[10] it can be said that the constitution was received with a sense of moderate optimism even by the leaders of the opposition. It is helpful to examine what the political leaders, the newspapers, and the magazines of the day had to say about the Meiji Constitution and the Meiji political system as it was envisioned by the Meiji leaders.

Three main themes recurred in editorials, speeches, and commentaries on the constitution. First, a sense of national pride was expressed in the fact that the constitution had been obtained without a bloody revolution, and that Japan was the first country in Asia to adopt a constitutional form of government.[11] Second, it was stated that the constitution marked the starting point of a real participation of the people in the affairs of the state. The powers given to the diet, the defense of the rights of the individual, and the independence of the courts were hailed as a clear negation of absolutism and of an irresponsible bureaucratic government. As Fukuzawa Yukichi, the great advocate of westernization and enlightenment and the founder of Keiō University, observed, the constitution was a powerful means to prevent arbitrariness in administration and to check the actions of officials.[12] Finally, some defects of the Meiji charter were clearly pointed out. Among these defects, contemporaries mentioned especially the fact that the constitution was one granted from above, not one arrived at through free discussion in a constituent assembly. They were also critical of the constitution's ambiguity in defining the responsibility of the cabinet.[13]

Ōkuma Shigenobu, the organizer of the Kaishintō (Progressive party) and the founder of Waseda University, expressed best the general reaction of his contemporaries on the political system emerging from the Meiji Constitution:

Introduction

There may be many different interpretations of the constitution, and criticism has even appeared in speeches and newspapers. But disapproval of the charter cannot be based only upon the letter of the constitution; the real problem lies in the way the constitution is applied in practice. It is not necessary to have it explicitly written down in the constitution that party cabinets should be established. If it pleases the emperor to entrust the party leaders with the formation of the cabinet, it is not difficult to have a party administration. In England they have arrived at the present form of party cabinets through historical development. So also in Japan through the progress of political parties it will be possible to reach the same political system as in England.[14]

Inoue Kowashi, the closest adviser to many of the prominent leaders of Meiji Japan and an important figure in the framing of the constitution, advised the opposition to concentrate its forces toward the goal of "taking advantage of the rights expressed in the constitution" instead of wasting its energy by attacking the charter.[15]

It was only later that the opinions on the Meiji Constitution and the Meiji political system crystallized in clear-cut definitions. In the beginning, at least, the Meiji Constitution did not appear as the embodiment of illiberalism, reaction, or absolutism. It was an ambiguous document. Because of its brevity the constitution had to be supplemented by other laws; therefore it could only be improved through new legislation and through the praxis of constitutional government. It did not occur to contemporaries that the Meiji Constitution had closed the door to a real form of limited government.

Which of these two interpretations, the absolutist interpretation of the thirties, or the interpretation of contemporaries, is closer to the actual ideals and plans of the leaders of early Meiji Japan?

7

I

ANTIFEUDAL NATIONAL UNIFICATION

With the battle of Toba Fushimi in January 1868, the issue of political power in Japan was virtually decided. The imperial forces, composed mainly of Satsuma and Chōshū troops, defeated the Tokugawa contingents. Although resistance by Tokugawa partisans continued into 1869, the first stage of the Meiji Restoration was accomplished in the spring of 1868. The Tokugawa regime had collapsed after two and a half centuries of political and military preponderance, and power had been transferred to the imperial court.[1]

The Tokugawa period, a long chapter in Japanese history, was followed, so to speak, by a blank page. Although in the last stage of the Tokugawa regime many plans had been proposed and discussed, no one could tell what the new era would be like. It was only later that the restoration of imperial authority appeared also as an imperial renovation.[2] The restoration was not meant to be a mere political settlement; it became a renovation or revolution in the political, social, and educational systems. The uncertain course was slowly and painfully mapped out in detail, and a national purpose was infused into what had been essentially a movement based on regional loyalties.[3] The simple fact of the restoration itself, however, was pregnant with vital consequences for the political ideology of the Meiji period. The restoration provided the fundamental principle of the new state: Japan was a monarchic system based on the unbroken line of emperors.

One may point out that all new nations and postrevolutionary societies face the crucial problem of legitimacy. The old order has been abolished and with it the set of beliefs that justified its system of authority. Meiji Japan did not face this crisis; at the moment of change the imperial system had remained intact to give sanction to the new administration.

During the Tokugawa period and even before the Tokugawa shogunate, the actual political power had not resided with the emperor. The legitimizing authority was always, however, implicitly or explicitly recognized as belonging to the imperial court. The Tokugawa *bakufu* dominated the country militarily and politically, yet the shogun never made the slightest move to usurp the throne. The shogun remained content with his theoretically secondary position.[4] The political thinkers of Tokugawa Japan were often ambiguous in their rationalization of the imperial powers; at times it seemed that they recognized in the emperor only sacerdotal and moral authority; at other times they attributed to him real secular power and upheld the opinion that his power had been usurped by the Tokugawa or that it had been delegated to the shogun.[5] But whatever the position reserved to the emperor in terms of actual political power, nobody denied that the emperor was at the center of the nation and very close to the heart of secular authority. After all, in the whole history of Japan there had been only one institution which had survived all vicissitudes of arms and which could be the principle of unity and continuity regardless of regionalism and pluralism.

In the last decades of the Tokugawa period especially, clearer propositions of the imperial power appeared in the theories of the Shinto-oriented School of National Studies (Kokugaku), the Mito School, and the loyalist movement.[6] Although the real political situation probably makes a misnomer of the "restoration," as the legal theorist Ishii Ryōsuke contends, in political theory the emperor was restored to his original position of actual ruler.[7] For an incipient political regime theories, even more than facts, are often crucial to its survival. In the moment of crisis in Japan, the imperial institution had remained, to serve as the link of continuity and legitimacy between the old and the new order. Politically impotent though he was, particularly at the beginning of the Meiji era, the emperor was there, and that was enough to focus the energies and the allegiance of the nation upon him as the rallying point.

But the imperial system was not enough to rationalize the new administration. Once the issue of the overthrow of the *bakufu* had been settled, the leaders of the new government were confronted with the pressing problem of defining the goals and ideals of the imperial renovation. The Charter Oath of April 1868 attempted the first declaration of the fundamental principles animating the new government:

1. Assemblies shall be widely convoked and all measures shall be decided by open discussion.
2. The government and the governed shall be of one mind, and the national economy and finances shall be greatly strengthened.
3. Civil and military officials as well as the common people shall achieve their aims and thus the people's minds shall not grow weary.
4. All absurd customs of olden times shall be abandoned, and all actions shall be based on international usage.
5. Knowledge shall be sought for all over the world, and thereby the foundations of the imperial rule shall be strengthened.[8]

Many of these promises were reminiscent of the proposals presented by many of the leaders in the last months of the Tokugawa era. They almost echo the eight-point plan prepared by Sakamoto Ryōma, a Tosa loyalist, to avert the necessity of force in overthrowing the *bakufu*.[9] These ideas were current everywhere in the closing days of Tokugawa Japan. Even Tokugawa Keiki in his letter of resignation giving up his position as shogun had hinted at the need for assemblies and unity of minds: "If national deliberations be conducted on an extensive scale, and the imperial decision then invited, and if the Empire be protected with united hearts and combined efforts, our country will hold its own with all nations of the world."[10]

The first three articles of the Charter Oath might well be taken as a statement of intention to set up a national parliament, to introduce democratic principles of government, and to adopt freedom and equality and the pursuit of happiness as the foundation of national life. The fourth article might be read as a promise to abolish all institutions not consistent with the doctrine of natural rights; and the fifth as the decision to adopt European philosophical beliefs and social practices.[11]

But many other interpretations are possible, and domestic political strife in Japan during the ensuing twenty years consisted largely of an argument over the interpretation of these five articles. It is useful, therefore, to try to discover what was in the minds of the Meiji leaders at the time when the Charter Oath was made public. Were they committed to some kind of constitutional, democratic government or were they attempting a compromise in order to gain time and collaboration from the daimyo?

The idea that it was the emperor's intention to establish representative legislative assembly can be easily discarded. The emperor was then only 16 years old and had spent his life in total seclusion in the imperial palace at Kyoto. The initiative for the oath came not from the emperor, but from the leaders of the restoration.[12]

The first draft of the oath was written by Yuri Kimimasa and reads as follows:

The Essentials for Deliberative Proceedings

1. The common people must be allowed to fulfill their aspirations so that there may be no discontent among them.

2. The samurai and common people must unite in vigorously promoting the economy and welfare of the nation.

3. Knowledge shall be sought throughout the world and thus shall be strengthened the foundations of the Imperial polity.

4. The office of domain representative must be conferred, for a fixed term, upon men of ability.

5. All matters of state must be decided by public decision and no discussion should be held in private.[13]

Fukuoka Kōtei, a samurai from Tosa,[14] made some corrections in this draft. He changed the title to "Council of Feudal Lords"; in article 1, "common people" was changed to read "all civil and military officials and the common people as well"; in article 2, "samurai and common people" became "all classes high and low"; in article 4, "representatives" became "imperial officers," and article 5 was revised to read "An assembly of feudal lords will be established and all matters of state shall be decided by public discussion."[15]

The third draft was prepared by Kido Takayoshi, the leader of the Chōshū loyalist movement. He cut and changed a few sentences of Fukuoka's draft, and added for the first time the following article: "Absurd customs of olden times shall be abandoned, and universal reason and justice shall be followed." In referring to "absurd customs" Kido was alluding to seclusionist and antiforeign thought; and "universal reason and justice" was a reference to international law.[16] Further changes brought the text of the document to the final form of the Charter Oath. In article 1, "an assembly widely convoked" is a revision of Fukuoka's "assembly of feudal lords." It is often contended[17] that even though the "feudal lords" clause was eliminated the revised form of the text still designated an assembly of feudal lords. But this interpretation is not based on a careful scrutiny of the text and the circumstances. The elimination of the "feudal lords" clause should be taken literally to mean that "an assembly widely convoked" would be established. Even the Seitaisho (Organic act),[18] promulgated on June 17, 1868, gave recognition to a lower house comprised of domain re-presentatives and to an upper house composed of senior and junior councilors.

It seems certain that the Charter Oath cannot be regarded as definitely promising an elective legislature and equal political and social rights for all subjects. But at the same time it should be pointed that the "widely convoked assemblies" were not restricted to assemblies of daimyo, but included also leaders of lower rank. The new government wanted the collaboration of all these leaders. The proclamation was issued when feudalism had not yet been abolished, and the most compelling problem was to reassure the leaders of the various han and to gain their loyalty.

In earlier periods of Japanese history the concept of settling matters by group discussion had not been completely unknown. Conferences, or *kaigi,* were part of the decision-making process in the Japanese tradition. Family councils, village councils, administrative councils in the Muromachi *bakufu* and even in the Edo *bakufu,* were customary institutions. But there appears to be no direct connection between these practices and the ideas associated with public assemblies after the restoration. The inspiration for this new kind of assembly came from abroad.[19]

In 1827 Aochi Rinsō, a physician and scholar of Dutch studies, wrote *Yochi shiryaku* (A brief description of the world), translated and adapted from W. S. Cramerus, *Algemeen Geographie* (Amsterdam, 1769), a Dutch book on world geography. *Yochi shiryaku* contained an explanation of the English Parliament and system of government. According to the historian Osatake Takeki, this was the first introduction of the idea of parliamentary government in Japan. In 1838 Elijah Coleman Bridgman, an American missionary in China, wrote in Chinese a book on the history of the United States, *Ta-mei lien-pang chih-lü eh* (A brief account of the American federation). This book was published in Japanese in 1861 under the title *Rempō shiryaku* (A brief account of the United States). In this translation for the first time appear the compounds *kokkai* (congress), Genrōin (Senate), and *shintōin* (house).[20] In 1865 the work of William Martin, an American missionary in China, was published in Japanese: *Bankoku kōhō* (International law). Martin's book was a Chineese translation of Henry Wheatons' *Elements of International Law* (Boston, 1863). *Bankoku kōhō* presented the terms "upper" and "lower house." Also in 1865 the first students sent by the *bakufu* to study abroad in the fields of social sciences and philosophy ended their foreign training and returned to Japan. At the behest of the *bakufu*, Nishi Amane and Tsuda Masamichi translated and circulated their lecture notes. They had studied in Holland under the direction of Professor Simon Vissering. Nishi published his notes under the title of *Bankoku kōhō* (International law), while Tsuda's were entitled *Taisei kokuhōron* (Public law in the West).[21]

These books, together with Fukuzawa Yukichi's *Seiyō jijō* (Conditions in the West), were probably the most influential works in the orientation of the Meiji leaders. *Taisei kokuhōron* (1868) explained in a detailed way the different forms of government and the theories on which these political systems were based.

Nishi Amane also presented a draft constitution. He proposed a threefold division of power into what he called the rights of the court, the rights of the *bakufu*, and the rights of the daimyo. Legislative power was vested in two houses—an upper house composed of leading daimyo and a lower house made up of samurai from each han. Legislation would be submitted to the *bakufu* which would retain "executive power over the whole country." The *bakufu* would present laws to the court for sanction, but the court would not have the power to veto. In this way, after returning the government to the emperor through the principle of the separation of powers, the *bakufu* could protect its real authority.[22]

These were some of the works which presented to the Japanese intellectuals the new theories of parliamentary government, the separation of powers, and constitutionalism. The Charter Oath and the Seitaisho stand in the middle between the old tradition of solving problems through conferences and the new ideals of parliamentary government. It seems that at least in the beginning there was no clear commitment to a popularly elected assembly. The general public was neither experienced nor interested in political forms; and it is most improbable that the government then in power wanted to set up bodies of popular representatives to allow the ignorant masses to decide national policies and to break down all existing class divisions by decree.

Despite the proclamation of the Charter Oath, the ideas it expressed were merely an abstract outline, and there was a need to present them in more concrete fashion. The Seitaisho was promulgated for this purpose. It had been jointly worked out by Fukuoka and Soejima Taneomi, a junior councilor from Hizen. Even more than the Charter Oath, the Seitaisho demonstrated the new tendencies of the Meiji leaders. The first goal was the centralization of authority and administration: "All power and authority centers in the Dajōkan [Council of state]."[23] The han were thus subordinated to the new central government in order to obviate the difficulties of divided government. But at the same time there emerged in the Seitaisho a tentative separation of the legislative, administrative, and judicial powers and the beginnings of an electoral system. Divided into three parts, the Dajōkan was parceled out so that the Legisltaive Council was responsible for making law; the Administrative Council and the departments of Shinto, Finance, Military Affairs, and Foreign Affairs were responsible for executing the laws; and the Department of Justice was responsible for administering judicial matters.[24] These principles were presumably adopted from the American concept of the division of powers.[25]

The other important feature of the Seitaisho in connection with constitutional developments was its reference to appointments of officials. According to its provisions, government officials would be changed upon completion of four years' service and they must be appointed by ballot.[26] Whether or not the ballot was used in 1868 is uncertain, but it was used in the election of major government officials in 1869. The reason for having an election at this time was perhaps, as Ishii Ryōsuke points out, to rid the government of sinecures and to follow up the barons' surrender of their feudal holdings with the completion of the basic form of national government.[27] Afterward, with the promulgation of the Government Officials' Order[28] in August 1869, no further appointment of officials by ballot was made, although this type of voting was kept on for a time in local districts.

Leaders like Kido Takayoshi, Ōkubo Toshimichi, and Iwakura Tomomi, who represented the three main groups of the restoration—Chōshū, Satsuma, and the court— had come to realize that the abolition of the han system was essential for the modernization of Japan, and that it was necessary to centralize governmental power and functions under one supreme authority. They saw as their first task the achievement of real centralization and unification under a single source of authority and power. For the time being constitutionalism appeared as a secondary goal. They understood that constitutionalism could be only a refinement of ordinary government. In any society there is always some sort of government, no matter how inadequate, but only a firmly established government is capable of being constitutionalized. Even in the evolution of the Western world, unification and centralization had had to precede constitutionalism.[29]

Thus we can now understand the implication of the term

"public opinion" (*kōron*), used in the first article of the Charter Oath. "Public" did not mean democratic, or of the people, but did mean "national" as opposed to "private." Since the feudal system was based on the autonomy and sectionalism of each han, it was natural that the new political system, which intended the destruction of the old feudal regime, should be based on a universal principle. Feudalism meant "particular good," "sectional interests," "private opinion." The new regime emerging from the ruins of the old had to represent the "common good," "the national interest," or, in a word, the *public opinion* of the whole nation.

It was in this sense that Ōkubo stated that a decree to have the force of law should be admitted as reasonable by everyone. Otherwise a decree could not be supported. In the beginning the principle of public opinion was not based on the universality of representation of the emperor. On the contrary, the universality of the imperial power was based on the political will of public opinion. Thus the emperor was the ruler of all Japan because he had the support of the whole people. If these ideas were brought to their logical conclusion, government by the emperor would be changed into the rule of public opinion, and real constitutional government would emerge.

Public opinion was essentially a principle of rationalization of national unity against the private opinion of the *bakufu* or the han. Though in the Seitaisho the separation of powers was stated, the fundamental aim was the establishment of a single center of power and authority. Separation of powers means essentially "weak government," limited by checks and balances in order to protect civil liberties, but the goal of the Meiji leaders was certainly not weak government; they wanted a strong central government with the exclusion of the pluralistic feudal system. Public opinion meant public power, under the control of a monistic regime, representing the whole nation and excluding various centers of private power. In opposition to public opinion stood the "private opinion" of the independent administrations of the various han.

In the public-opinion principle we can distinguish two aspects: a positive one, which leads to the respect for the opinion of the people, and a negative one, which tends to freeze and paralyze the old traditional power of the han in a mechanism called "assembly" (*kaigi*), authorized by the emperor and based on the principle of national unity. For the Meiji leaders the negative aspect, rather than the positive one, was of paramount importance.

This emphasis on the public, or universal, aspect is a basic prerequisite of modern nationalism: modern nations necessarily tend to monopolize public power and to destroy centers of autonomous, or private, power.[30] Especially after the emergence of a new government as a result of revolution the people, or public opinion, become the way of legitimating the new leadership. This ideology, however, does not seem necessarily to lead to democratic attitudes.

The trend toward centralization was also strongly expressed in the memorial presented to the emperor by the four western lords, Shimazu of Satsuma, Mōri of Chōshū, Nabeshima of Tosa, and Yamanouchi of Hizen. The memorial was written by Kido Takayoshi,[31] and defended the central power of the imperial government: "It is now sought to establish an entirely new form of government. Care must, therefore, be taken to preserve intact both one central body of government, and one universal authority. The land in which your servants live is the land of the Emperor, and the people whom they govern are his subjects. Neither the one, therefore, nor the other can belong to your servants."[32] The two things essential for the well-being of the country were a central body of government and one universal authority. The Warring Period and the Tokugawa era were considered a negation of the fundamental principle of "one central government." If everything belonged to the emperor there could not be any shogun or daimyo claiming authority over land and people. The shogun and the daimyo were but "robbers" and usurpers.[33]

The spirit emerging in this document is one of strong anti-feudalism. The principle of centralization was upheld mainly as a means to destroy the feudal system of divided loyalties and divided energies. It is the kind of argument the *philosophes* had already used in France: only a strong central government could secure liberty for the general people against the nobles, the clergy, and the established associations. The possible contradiction between liberty and enlightened despotism was not taken into account. In Kido's mind, too, a single centralized authority was not considered as being against the freedom of the people; on the contrary, it was seen as liberation from robbers and men of unprincipled character. Under the feudal system the "weak had become food for the strong"; the new centralized government would put an end to such a system of exploitation, and everybody would be equal under the emperor and under the laws of the central government.[34]

The effort toward centralization was made the more important because, in Kido's view,[35] the daimyo had become far more extravagant than under the *bakufu*, and their high-sounding phrases about the supreme moral obligation of loyalty to the emperor and morality in general were for the most part mere lip service. The daimyo were pressing selfish demands proportionate to their influence upon the court. Because the daimyo were only concerned with acquiring gain for themselves the situation on all sides had come to resemble "a collection of petty shogunates." At the beginning of 1868, Kido had already suggested to Sanjō Sanetomi and Iwakura Tomomi, two of the court leaders, that the "three hundred daimyo should be made to surrender their subjects all at one time," and "immediately unifying the energies of the empire thereby, we must utilize the resources of the entire country, including naturally the armed forces and the government, to strengthen the nation."[36]

A complete abolition of the han system was not a simple operation. It was only in 1871 that the imperial edict announcing the abolition of the han system and the creation of prefectures was proclaimed. The edict is but a repetition of the principle of centralized government: "In order to preserve the peace of Japanese subjects at home and to stand on equal footing with countries abroad at this present time of reform, We deem it necessary that the government of the country be centered in a single authority, so as to effect a reformation in substance as well as in fact . . . All this is for the purpose of doing away with superfluity, for issuing in simplicity, for removing the evil of empty forms and in order to avoid the grievance caused by many centers of government."[37]

Hans Kohn, the well-known historian of modern nationalism, has written that nationalism is "inconceivable without the ideas of popular sovereignty preceding—without a complete revision of the position of the ruler and the ruled, of classes and castes."[38] Rupert Emerson, also a historian of nationalism, wittily comments on this statement of Kohn's, "On the face of historical record no statement as uncompromisingly sweeping as this can be sustained . . . and yet it has more than a germ of fundamental truth."[39]

The heart of the argument is the proposition that the rise of nationalism is normally associated with deep-running social ferment and changes that disrupt the old order of society and speed the process of social mobilization. The social scientist Karl Mannheim has called this process "the fundamental democratization of society . . . the stirring into action of those classes who formerly played a passive part in political life."[40] In this sense the reforms introduced by the Meiji leaders can be called democratic. These reforms carried the program of unification and centralization a step forward. They systematically attacked the old feudal order and the old institutions.

In the process of Japanese modernization we can distinguish two fundamental themes: one concerned with social status, and the other with economic matters. In the realm of social status there was a leveling of the traditional class system with a view to giving all Japanese a position of equality. The samurai class, which had enjoyed a special status in the feudal era, was deprived of its privileges and was placed on a nearly equal footing with the commoner. The titles of the nobility were discarded and its privileges reduced.

In this process of eliminating status distinctions the edict on conscription issued in December 1872 and the conscription order announced in January of the following year were of particular importance because they destroyed the prerogatives of the military aristocracy. These two acts of government resulted in a system of universal conscription.[41] The leader responsible for the revolutionary changes in the military organization was Yamagata Aritomo.[42] He has often been considered the conservative par excellence, the archbureaucrat and authoritarian, the fountainhead of reactionary conservatism. But Yamagata, like the other Meiji leaders, was many things at different times: a revolutionary agitator against the *bakufu,* an innovator, and a conservative. He was an innovator as one of the architects of the military reform. His major contribution to the emergence of the new centralized state was in the development of a modern army and later of an efficient and centralized bureaucracy. The compulsory military service for all, without any distinction between *shizoku* (ex-samurai) and commoners, was one of the most effective measures destroying the feudal past.

The announcement concerning the army reorganization issued on the same day as the Imperial Edict on National Conscription, December 28, 1872, expressed also a strong sense of antifeudalism and egalitarianism:

Antifeudal National Unification

Those who have worn the two swords during the Tokugawa regime have been known as bushi [samurai] and in their bearing they have been obdurate; they have lived at the expense of others, and in extreme cases they have put people to the sword; their crime being regarded by officials as no offense . . . No such practices prevailed in ancient Japan. At the time of the Restoration, the domains surrendered their land patents, and in 1871 the prefectural system of ancient times was reinstated. After living a life of idleness for generations, the samurai have had their stipends reduced and they have been authorized to take off their swords so that all strata of the people may finally gain their rights to liberty. By these innovations the rulers and ruled will be placed on the same basis, the rights of the people will be equal, and the way will be cleared for the unity of the soldier and peasant. Therefore neither the samurai nor the common people will have the status to which they were accustomed in the past. Nor will there be any distinction in the service they render to their country, for they will all be alike as subjects of the Empire.[43]

Cutting across class lines in taking recruits from all segments of the population, the conscription order ended the monopoly on military service which had been held by the samurai, and it ended their claim to privileges arising from the bearing of arms.

Yamagata equated national security with military power, but he was also quite aware of the fact that modern military power is based upon strong economic development and drastic social changes. Economic development and a rising level in the people's welfare and education were essential preconditions for a strong army. He warned against premature and reckless military adventures, and stood against all social privileges for the *shizoku,* even when Ōkubo and Iwakura were vacillating during the Satsuma Rebellion.[44] It was because of the reorganization introduced by Yamagata that the government could pass the first great trial of the rebellion.

The part played by the reorganized national military force in shaping the character of Japanese political life cannot be underestimated. A new sense of national unity and devotion emerged from the training received in military service. Another reform, too, helped to build a new unified country: this was the educational reform.

In 1871 the government had established the Ministry of Education for the control of all matters related to education. In 1872 the Code of Education was promulgated.[45] This code laid the foundation of state-controlled compulsory education. The plan was ambitious, providing for universities, middle schools, elementary schools, normal schools, and technical schools on a large scale; and the statement of policy that accompanied it made it clear that education was to be organized along Western lines.[46] Education was not founded, however, on a nationalistic, anti-individualistic spirit. The Education Code was accompanied by a sort of preamble, which is worth quoting at length in order to understand the motivation of the Meiji government in the first years of power.

The only way in which an individual can raise himself, manage his property and prosper in his business and so accomplish his career, is by cultivating his morals, improving his intellect, and becoming proficient in arts; the cultivation of morals, the improvement of intellect and proficiency in arts cannot be attained except through learning. This is the reason why schools are established; from language, writing and reckoning for daily use to knowledge necessary for officials, farmers, merchants, and artisans and craftsmen of every description, to laws, politics, astronomy, medicine, etc., in fact for all vocations of men, there is none that is not acquired by learning. Every man only after studying diligently, each according to his capacity, will be able to increase his property and prosper in his business. Hence knowledge may be regarded as the capital for raising one's self; who then can do without learning? . . .

Although a long time has elapsed since there have been schools, through their being improperly administered, people have made the mistake of thinking that learning is a matter for those above samurai rank; and farmers, artisans and merchants, as also women—these have no idea of what learning is and think of it as something beyond their sphere. Even among those of samurai rank, it is said that their learning is for the sake of the State; and since they do not realize that it is the basis on which they have to raise themselves, they run into mere sentence-reciting and phrase-making and fall into ways of empty theorizing and vain talking; so that although their discourses sound profound, they cannot be carried into practice. All this is due to a long and continued bad custom; and this is why many people fall into poverty, bankruptcy and loss of their homes. Men must, therefore, acquire learning and in learning must not mistake its true purpose.

Now a system of education has been determined by the Education Code, and various regulations will be published in due course. It is intended that henceforth universally (without any distinction of class or sex) in a village there shall be no house without learning and in a house no individual without learning . . .

Owing to the long continued bad habit of regarding learning as a matter for those above samurai rank, there are not a few who consider that since their learning is for the sake of the State, they need not learn unless they are supplied by the State not only with expenses necessary for study, but also with food and clothing, and so by neglecting learning they spoil their whole life. This is a great mistake; henceforth such a vicious custom must be done away with, and people in general leaving all else aside must make every effort to apply themselves to learning.[47]

This passage on the principles which were to guide the new educational system reveals more than anything else the intentions of the Meiji leaders. Theirs was an endeavor to have a system of educational equality. Education had to be universal, not the monopoly of any one class. Everybody must receive elementary education, at least, without distinction of class, occupation, or sex, and as far as higher education was concerned, equal opportunity was to be given to all according to capability. In fact the new educational system was to effect a revolution, something equivalent to the abolition of the han system; it was a break away from the old feudal system, in which the upper classes monopolized the advantages of education.

The second guiding principle, besides equality of education, was a utilitarian view of the purpose of education. Education was to be obtained by each individual for his own sake, as necessary for maintaining or bettering his position. The state would consequently profit from this formation of the individual. The Meiji leaders were convinced that only through universal education could the country overcome the traditional divisions of classes and prepare Japan for reaching a high level of civilization. The utilitarian spirit shows itself in the fact that Japanese and Chinese classical studies were neglected.[48]

The third striking element of the preamble to the Education Code is the strong faith in progress through education. This faith is reminiscent of Condorcet's belief in the progress of humanity through enlightened education.[49] All evil, according to the preamble and to Condorcet, was due to the lack of a good educational system, and all good would come from a reformed method.

The system adopted in the Code of Education was modeled on French practice, and, besides centralizing control over education, it aimed at a high degree of standardization. This was in harmony with the general attitude of the new government toward all questions of administration. Yamashita Tokuji, in *Education in Japan,* writes: "The French system was followed because its strong policy of centralization attracted the attention of the Meiji Government, which desired to unify the education of the nation."[50]

The importance of the Education Code of 1872 did not rest solely on the somewhat grandiose scheme of more than 54,000 schools. It was in fact a code, a systematic body of laws regulating all details of educational structure, finance, and control.

Curricula were to be established by national regulation both of time and content, and national uniformity, by concurrent interpretation of the code, was to be maintained by government inspectors. Schools were to be financed by student fees, local taxation, and state subsidies. Private schools meeting certain standards were to be controlled through a licensing system.

Exceeding even the importance of these specific regulations, however, was the fundamental role the Education Code allocated to the Ministry of Education. Essentially, the duties of this ministry were to "control all affairs connected with education and learning." George Sansom's comment on this tendency toward centralization—"The new leaders had not been able to free themselves from that passion for regulating the life of the citizen which distinguished their feudal predecessors"[51]—is, to say the least, out of place. The motivation impelling the new leaders toward centralization of education was not a feudalistic sense of interference; it was based on the conviction that a modern nation needed an educated and united people. The control of education was proposed especially in order to stop the old schools of thought from preventing the modernization of the country and the introduction of Western techniques and Western ways.[52] After all, a centralized authoritarian government can be established without following the traditional pattern of authoritarianism.

The second part of the program for the unification of the country concerned economic matters.[53] Economic restrictions were eliminated and the peers, ex-samurai, and ex-soldiers were permitted in 1872 to engage in agriculture, industry, and commerce, except when holding public office. By the removal of these restrictions the feudal practice of identifying social rank with occupation was abandoned. Later, in the same year, the existing ban against the peasants' pursuit of trade as a subsidiary occupation was lifted, and these activities were left to the discretion of the individual.[54] In 1871 the government had already removed the prohibitions limiting cultivation to certain types of crops. The Land Tax Reform Regulations were promulgated on July 28, 1873. All land was to be valued—at its market value if it had recently changed hands, at an estimated value if not—and the owner was to pay an annual tax of 3 per cent of the land's value. The land tax reform gave Japan a modern system of taxation and provided the largest part of the government's revenue.[55] The decree on Regulations for the Commutation of Pensions, issued in December 1873, was another measure taken to shake off the past. The liquidation of pensions was not only an absolute financial necessity[56] but also a means of destroying re-emerging class distinctions.

The destruction of the past was only one preliminary step toward the building of a new economic system which would be the foundation of a strong country capable of competing with the West. The most farsighted leaders decided that internal reconstruction must precede foreign military adventures. Ōkubo, probably more than anybody else, was responsible for this policy.[57] His peace party thrust aside the Korean expansionist group in November 1873. Soon after this victory Ōkubo became Home Minister, charged, among other duties, with promoting economic development. Primarily this meant development of small-scale private enterprise.[58] Ōkubo carried out his industrial promotion duties effectively.

The arguments that Ōkubo advanced against the expansionist element in 1873 foreshadowed the economic emphasis of his future policies. In his memorial against the Korean war proposal, Ōkubo expressed opposition especially in economic terms. He summed up his thought in a seven-point document which, together with the Charter Oath and the Meiji Constitution, deserves to be called the fundamental document of Meiji Japan. We find here the philosophy which animated the leaders who were responsible for the emergence of the new Japan.

Antifeudal National Unification

In order to govern the country and protect the people it is necessary to have a flexible policy and to watch the world situation; always watching the situation we go forward or retreat. If the situation is bad we simply stop. The reasons why I say that it is too early to send a mission to Korea are as follows . . .

1. The basis of our government is not yet firmly established. We have made remarkable progress in abolishing the clans, etc.; if we look at the central part of Japan, everything seems accomplished, but if we look at the countryside, many people who oppose this will be seen. We have established a fortress and have good military equipment, so they dare not rise up against us. But if we reveal some weak point, they will be quick to take advantage. There is no special problem now, but we must look to the future . . .

2. Today government expenditures are tremendous, and income is below expense. Thus if we open fire and send several tens of thousands of men abroad we will incur enormous expense. This will require taxes or foreign loans or the issuance of paper notes and will lead to higher prices, social unrest and uprisings. Already we have a 5,600,000 yen foreign debt; even this is difficult to pay.

3. Our government has started to stimulate industries, but it will be several years before we get results . . . If we now begin an unnecessary war, spend a huge amount of money, shed blood, and worsen the daily life of the people, all these government works will burst like a bubble and we will lose several decades of time. We will regret it.

4. Regarding the foreign trade situation, each year there is a one million yen deficit . . . If we open fire without thinking of our economic and military power, our soldiers will have a bad time, and their parents will be in difficulty; they will cease to work well, and our national production will decrease.

5. In regard to the diplomatic situation, the most important countries for us are Russia and Britain . . . Relations with them are uncertain. I fear that Russia will interfere unless we secure our independence. If we open fire on Korea, Russia will fish out both the clam and the bird and get a fisherman's profit. Thus we should not begin a war in Korea now.

6. In regard to the Asian situation, Britain is especially powerful, watching with a tiger's eye. Our foreign loans depend on Britain. If there is trouble and we become poor, Britain will surely interfere in our internal affairs on that pretext. Look at India . . . observe carefully the process by which India became a colony. We must build our industry, our exports, etc. It is our most urgent business.

7. The Japanese treaties with Europe and America are not equal. This is harmful for our independence. Therefore we must do our best to revise them, or England and France will send armies on the pretext of an insecure internal situation . . . The first thing is to revise the treaties; the Korean business comes after that.

Conclusion. As I have said above we must not hurry to begin war. Of course, we cannot overlook the arrogant attitude of Korea, but we have no clear reason to attack Korea. Now it is argued, we should send our envoy and depending on his reception open fire or not. But we may be sure from experience that this reception will be cold; so this automatically means opening fire. Thus we must decide about sending an army before we send the envoy. If there is war we must have more than 100,000 soldiers, laborers, ships, etc. It will cost many times 10,000 yen. Even though we are victorious, the expense will be far beyond the profit. Also after the victory there will be uprisings over there. Even though we get all kinds of goods from Korea, they will amount to less than the expense. Also it is said that neither China nor Russia will intervene, but there is no proof. It is said that we cannot endure Korean arrogance, but this is an insufficient reason and it would be very bad to open fire without thinking of our security and our people's welfare. Therefore I oppose . . . [59]

Ōkubo's antiwar statement represents the basic ideology of the Meiji leaders. It has been defined as the internal-construction principle. It brings to mind immediately adjectives like "realistic," "rational," "careful," "cautious." These are indeed descriptive ingredients of government policy in general, not only in the Korean dispute but also in the determination of policy through the rest of the Meiji era. There is also an unenlightened side to the Meiji leaders,[60] but at least in the beginning their overriding preoccupation was to build a strong centralized government based on a modern army, universal education, and a well organized economy.

The first phase of the Meiji era (1868-1873) could be defined as the breach with the old order, part of which was the disruption of the traditional han and of the ties of status and custom. It could be called the negative aspect of the creation of a modern state. From this destruction of the past, however, a new positive aspect emerged, the sense of a national political community. The crumbling loyalty of the han was directed to the new community, the nation, in which the people could again find a social identity and in whose service they could gain dignity and purpose as they struggled to preserve their independence.

In this first period political theory was centered only on the problem of a unified state. There were as yet no discussions of fundamental problems, popular sovereignty versus imperial sovereignty, or parliamentary government versus an autocratic system. If the word "sovereignty" recurred in the early documents, it was a sovereignty over han autonomy and foreign encroachments. It was not a question of who was the repository of supreme power within Japan itself; sovereignty was synonymous with national unity and national independence. Thus the first cornerstone of modern Japanese political thought was the acceptance by all the articulate leaders of the idea that Japan must be a centralized country with one source of authority.

In this sense the Japanese leaders did not differ too much from the present leaders of the newly emerging countries, who are confronted with the lack of national unity which threatens disruption and is met by forced centralization.[61] The difference between Japan and the new countries consists in the fact that Japan already had a great number of elements which could easily work toward unity and social organization. Japanese leaders were eager to make the nation the military and econom-

ic equal of Western nations, as are the leaders of newly independent countries, who are no less patriotic. In the case of
Japan, however, it was an ethnically and culturally homogene-
ous country, with a deep sense of racial identity and traditions
of social and political order. Because of its geographic position,
Japan was from early times conscious of forming a different
state; its racial homogeneity helped to strengthen this consciousness.

The absence of language divisions also contributed to unification. The articulate elites spoke the same language and had the
same cultural formation. Religion too was a unifying factor, or,
at least, did not contribute to disruption. Religion never played
a significant role in the political life of Japanese society. Tokugawa society was already a secular society in all its manifesta-
tions. The Meiji leaders did not find any strong resistance to
their decisions from the established religions. These religions
had long since been transformed into obedient instruments of
the state during the Tokugawa period. In the first years of the
Meiji era an attempt was made to make Shinto part of the new
establishment. The newly established Department of Religion
(Jingikan) was theoretically given the highest position in the
new government structure, and the teaching of Shinto was
stimulated and revitalized throughout Japan, but this effort at
making religion a means of unifying the nation was short-lived
and ended in failure.[62]

Moreover, Japan had a well-developed class which provided
an exploitable social stratum to fill the ranks of an expert
officialdom: the samurai class represented a vast pool of trained
and uncommitted manpower which switched over easily from
the service of the *bakufu* to the service of the new regime.[63]
Despite the wholesale deprivation of traditional status and role
in these early years of Meiji Japan, the samurai remained the
leading class of the Japanese nation. And finally, the new Japan
was born when there was no worldwide division of nations into

different international blocs trying to upset political and economic development.

These advantages which the new Japanese nation profited from, as compared with most of the new states, point up rather than detract from the significance of the similarity of reactions. All states that have recently gained independence are faced with the problems of the internal and international challenge. The Meiji leaders had to face these same problems. Their ideology in this first period of the nation-building process was based on two principles. First, the new government had to be contralized and powerful enough to resist internal and external threats. Second, priority was to be given to internal construction, and whatever stood in the way of technological modernization had to be removed, including privileges of the samurai class itself. These two features of the new regime—centralized power and ruthless pragmatism—were the basic principles of the new political system. The best expression of these ideals is found in Kido's words: "A single rod, even though a stout one, may be broken by a young child, but if ten rods, though all are weak, are made into a bundle, they cannot be broken by a full grown man. They will maintain a weight of a thousand pounds without breaking."[64]

Immediately after the restoration it was still uncertain whether the complex balance of forces would swing back in the direction of sectionalism and division. It took all the energies of the Meiji leaders to tighten the controls over the whole nation. It was not possible for the leaders to look far ahead, and they had to proceed step by step, as was natural and indeed inevitable in times of commotion and uncertainty. The guiding principle of the Meiji leaders in their first trials was not a narrow adherence to a traditional conception of society, nor was it a clear commitment to any particular form of government. Their general aim was to establish a stable government and to develop the military and economic strength of their country so that it could face the internal and international future with confidence. Where the old and traditional forms got in the way of these goals, it was the old forms that gave way to make room for the new.

History shows us that in moments of rapid change it is easier to adopt a form of strong centralization without much respect for democratic ideals. To take a more moderate and liberal course would mean to slow down the pace of social change and to accept some kind of immobilism and reaction. And yet the traditional structure of values and orientations remained always, consciously or unconsciously, the basis of the political actions and political ideals of the Meiji leaders. The Confucian emphasis on loyalty, although originally thought of as a means to strengthen the *bakufu,* was also an extremely useful means for strengthening the new polity. The idea of loyalty to the shogun and the daimyo could be evolved into the idea of loyalty to the emperor. Thus Confucian ethical precepts could continue to have an appeal and could form the basis of the new commitment to the national administration.

Other pre-Meiji currents of thought were also influential. The loyalist movement to which many members of the ruling group had belonged, the Mito School, and the Shinto-oriented School of National Studies (Kokugaku), though ambiguous in their political theories, could always be used to rationalize a centralized government under the leadership of the court. The early Meiji regime was a *new* one insofar as the political institutions were concerned: the shogun, the daimyo, the han system had been abolished, and the "private" autonomy had been destroyed. But there were also *old* aspects: the imperial system was there with its legitimizing power and semireligious rationalization. In the first steps of the Meiji regime we find both continuity and change, continuity in the permanence of the imperial system, change in the suppression of the *bakufu* and han system; continuity in the value substructure, change in means and goals.

Can the tendency toward centralization be defined as traditional "oriental despotism"? The often-quoted slogan "Western technology and Eastern ideology" seems to be misleading. To define all authoritarian aspects of the Meiji leaders as deriving from old traditions does not take into account the fact that there are also modern forms of authoritarian governments. The formation of a new nation is such a complex phenomenon that to effect real change, such as large-scale social and political reforms as they were performed by the Meiji leadership, a high degree of governmental control is necessary lest society disintegrate into anarchy. This was the basic assumption of the Meiji leaders. When they were asking for a strong central government or for sovereign power united in the hands of the emperor, that is, in the Council of state, essentially they were applying the principles of modernization in a rapidly changing society.

To create a stable, representative decision-making process which provides a legitimate place for opposition—for the rights of those without power to advocate different opinions and overthrow those in office—is extremely difficult in any polity, and is particularly problematic in new states, which must be concerned with the sheer problem of national unity and national independence. Though we might not accept Nkrumah's political methods, we have to recognize that there is some truth in the statement of a Ghanian White Paper: "The strains experienced by an emergent country immediately after independence are certainly as great as, if not greater than, the strains experienced by a developed country in wartime."[65] David Apter describes the difficulties facing the new countries as follows: "New nations are plagued with almost the entire range of political problems known to man. They are beset by an accumulation of immediate and often mundane tasks such as building up adequate medical, health, education, transport, and other services, as well as improvement of housing, food supplies, and other basic necessities beyond the subsistence level."[66]

In addition to these problems and the danger of foreign encroachment, it is easy to see how debate, criticism, and opposition come to be regarded by those trying to push through this great revolution of building a new, modern nation as stultifying antiprogressive influences that deter the attainment of goals and wreak havoc with the tenuous basis of consensus and authority. Because of these very factors representation of political opposition in the decision-making process might not play the same role in newly emerging countries as in stable, industrialized countries. This, at least, was the rationalization of the Meiji political leaders, as well as the rationalization of the leaders of the new countries of today.

II

GRADUALISM VERSUS RADICALISM

The first years after the Meiji Restoration were characterized by a strong concern for national unity and power. More than anything else, chaos, anarchy, and a return to the old feudal system of political sectionalism had to be averted. Parliamentary government was not and probably could not be high on the list of problems to be solved. As long as feudal traditions were still strong and the challenge from the West was present, the first and only goal was to strengthen the central government in order to cope with internal disruption and external danger. Itagaki Taisuke himself, who from 1874 led the movement for representative government, in 1873 had stated that in order of importance the concentration of power in the central government preceded the establishment of a national assembly.[1]

Once the problem of feudalism was on the way to solution, the Meiji leaders felt the necessity of institutionalizing their administration in order to prevent arbitrariness and instability. If constitutionalism is defined as a system of government of effective and regularized restraints upon governmental action,[2] we must say that the Meiji leaders were in favor of such a system of government, a government of laws and not of men.

The theory advocated by all was summarized in the slogan *kummin dōchi* (joint rule by lord and subjects). Their program, though it was vague and not clearly defined, envisaged some kind of constitutional monarchy. The phrase *kummin dōchi* was used to express the relation which should exist between the emperor and the people. Although the two terms "ruler" and "people" are grammatically parallel, their relation is important: The emperor was to rule and lead, with the people following and assisting.

As early as 1872 the Meiji leaders were using this slogan to denote representative institutions within a constitutional monarchy. In a letter to Iwakura dated April 1872, Miyajima Seiichirō, a member of the Left Chamber, wrote that "it would be best for us to create a way for establishing the joint rule of sovereign and subjects [*kummin dōchi*]." And he added, "It is therefore natural that we should create an appropriate consitution which would take into consideration both the principle of monarchical rights and the principle of joint rule of sovereign and subjects [*kummin dōchi*]."[3]

Thus even before January 1874, when the leaders of the opposition presented their famous memorial advocating the establishment of a popular assembly, some plans were being formulated within the government concerning the enactment of a constitution and of joint rule. The discussion was not on the inevitability of a constitutional form of government, but on the type and timing of the constitution to be granted. It revolved around the problem of determining what phase Japan was in. Kido and Ōkubo thought that it was too early to have a perfect constitutional government, while Itagaki, once he had left the government and passed to the opposition, thought that Japan was ready for a constitutional system. This was the famous controversy between gradualism (*zenshinron*) and radicalism (*kyūshinron*), which divided the political and intellectual world of early Meiji Japan.

Before examining in detail the nature and the development of this controversy, it is necessary to clarify the reason for the fundamental agreement among the Meiji leaders, in or out of the government, about the need for a constitution. "The constitutional movement of Japan, unlike that of many other countries, was not inaugurated with the motive of arresting the power of the Sovereign nor of settling the problem of 'taxation and representation.' It was a logical sequel to the reform of the restoration—a reform largely based on the idea of Europeanisation of the country—whether or not the reformers were conscious of this from the first."[4]

The period from 1873 to 1877 has usually been designated as "the age of civilization and enlightenment," when all efforts were devoted to not falling behind in the race to be civilized and enlightened. There was in this movement much that was bizarre, but there was also involved a profound transformation in the manners and goals of private and public life.[5] The movement was essentially directed at establishing Japan as a country equal to the Western powers. In 1897 Ōkuma Shigenobu, then minister of foreign affairs, said in the House of Representatives:

If we enquire what points are practically most important in the foreign policy of the Meiji Era, we find that to attain an equal footing with other Powers, as declared in the Imperial Edict at the Restoration, has been the impulse underlying all the national changes that have taken place. It was perceived that in order to attain an equal footing with the Powers, it was necessary to change the national institutions, learning and education. Hence, the replacement of clans by prefectures took place, as well as coinage reform, enforcement of the conscription law, revisions of various other laws and promulgation of new ones, establishment of local assemblies, and the granting of local self-government— a step that led at length to the promulgation of the Constitution. This national policy, this so-called opening and development of the country, or, in other words, this principle of attaining an equal footing with the Powers was, I firmly believe, the motive that has enabled Japan to become a nation advanced in civilisation and respected by the world.[6]

Ōkuma's words were pronounced twenty-five years after the age of civilization and enlightenment and thus could be considered a *post factum* rationalization, but from the beginning the other Meiji leaders had alleged the revision of the treaties and Japan's aspiration to equality to the Western powers to be fundamental reasons for the codification of the government system of Japan. On October 16, 1871, Prime Minister Sanjō wrote a letter to Iwakura suggesting that a special mission be sent to countries having treaty relations with Japan. This letter is important to an understanding of some of the motives guiding the Meiji leaders in their endeavors. It expresses the sensitivity of the Japanese to their inferior international status and the injustices they felt at the hands of Western nations. It indicates also that the government clearly recognized the need for radical changes in legislation in order to achieve the desired revision of the treaties. Sanjō suggested that the mission should study foreign laws, customs, and institutions directly and recommend those which should be adopted by the Japanese.[7]

The study of foreign institutions occupied the attention of the government more and more, and increasing importance was attached to it. The emperor himself in an address to an assembly of nobles in November 1871 repeated this fundamental theme: "If we would benefit by the useful arts and sciences and conditions of Society prevailing among more enlightened nations, we must either study these at home as best as we can, or send abroad an expedition of practical observers, to foreign lands, competent to acquire for us those things our people lack, which are best calculated to benefit this nation."[8]

From this desire to revise the unequal treaties and to learn about foreign institutions and foreign things emerged the idea of the Iwakura Mission.[9] The Japanese wished to approach the problem of modernization of their country with great deliberation and care. Much of what had been done since 1868 had been based on expediency; there had been some administrative and legal reforms and some progress in the economic field, too. But modernization depended upon more than haphazard or day-to-day decisions. Principles, long-range goals, and specific reforms tied to specific ends needed to be enunciated, and this was part of the work of the Iwakura Mission.

It seems, then, that the first ideas of a reorganization of the political system did not wait for the demand for assemblies presented by the opposition in 1874. The mission was extremely important for later developments. Its leaders were the dominant figures in the government: Iwakura Tomomi, Ōkubo Toshimichi, and Kido Takayoshi. This mission was unique, for no country had ever before sent such a group of its foremost leaders and ablest administrators to journey abroad for an extended period of time, sacrificing a large proportion of its leadership when there were pressing economic, political, and social problems at home.[10]

Throughout the mission Kido took personal charge of the studies of law and government. He was conscientious but cautious; although the Japanese had to learn from the West, he believed that they should not adopt Western ways without careful consideration of Japan's special conditions. Kido wrote in his diary: "I am deeply concerned for the future of my beloved country and my people if we disregard the evils and abuses of the world, past and present, and eagerly borrow everything at random."[11]

Kido had not been a gradualist from the beginning. Not until 1873, five years after the restoration, did Kido emerge firmly and finally as the moderate reformer. He had been one of the Chōshū extremists who in 1862 had signed the blood oath. The signers had pledged to set free the suspects imprisoned after the unsuccessful assassination attempt on Andō Nobuyuki, a member of the *bakufu* Senior Council, and to kill high officials and foreigners.[12] Kido was a loyal disciple of Yoshida Shōin, who had said that "men of peace are all disloyal and unrighteous." Once the restoration had been carried out, Kido, as a reforming privy councilor in the Meiji government, would have moved with reckless haste, possibly igniting profeudal rebellion. He was against both Iwakura and Ōkubo because he felt that they were advocating "gradualism," and he was inclined to take radical measures to destroy feudalism completely and to expand in foreign military campaigns.[13] In succeeding years a steady stream of memorials to the emperor set forth Kido's rationale for opening Korea, by diplomacy if possible or by force if necessary. As late as the fall of 1872, Kido remained keenly interested in Korea as a field for Japanese expansion. The insults of Korea fully justified war, he wrote in his diary; whatever the expenses, Japan must force open Korea.[14]

What was the cause of Kido's change? After 1873 he sought to lead Japan cautiously toward constitutional monarchy and to do it by keeping peace with the profeudal classes in Japan and with foreign nations. Experience in power had probably mellowed his youthful extremism. But more than anything else the visit to America and Europe with the Iwakura Mission had evoked in Kido a keen awareness of contemporary trends in the West and a deep sense of admiration for Western methods.[15]

On his return from the grand tour he spoke clearly in favor of a constitutional form of government. His was the first voice to be heard advocating as the final goal of Japanese political progress a constitutional system with limited and defined powers. Kido's "Observations on Returning from the West" deserve close study not only for their intrinsic value as an exposition of liberal principles, but also for the revelation of the astonishing development of Kido's views during the journey through America and Europe.[16] This document shows the evolution of his thinking from an initial concern for centralized authority to one for the exercise of that authority according to law. What struck Kido most in the West were the constitutional processes which limited those in power and provided a sound basis for orderly change. The rise and fall of nations, he said, is determined by their fidelity to constitutional order:

Gradualism Versus Radicalism

This inquiry has convinced me that the history of all countries, great or small, enlightened or unenlightened, proves that the inquiry into the causes of their conservation or downfall resolves itself into the question of the state of vigour or decay, and the merits or faults, of their laws and constitutions. No matter how extensive their territory may be or how numerous their subjects, if a due control is not exercised over them by means of the laws and constitution, one man will basely follow his own selfish ends, while another will presumptuously turn right into wrong, and so the government will swarm with parasites and place hunters.[17]

Kido's analysis of Poland's tragedy demonstrates his principle that without a working constitution a country cannot be united internally and becomes a prey of foreign intervention. Without a constitution, that is, without clearly defined rights and duties, which constitute the essence of independence, no country can survive internal strife or occupation by foreigners. A constitution is necessary "to set on a firm basis the weal of the entire nation, which prevents officials from taking unauthorized steps merely on their own judgment." It is not enough to have a sovereign, and he must not hold power in an arbitrary fashion. For this reason it is necessary to have a parliament, whose duty it is to advise and consent and to check arbitrary proceedings on the part of officials. "Every citizen's object in life is to maintain all his rights and so preserve his natural liberty, and to assist in carrying on the government by bearing his part of the national burden; and therefore they (i.e., the rights and burdens) are specified exactly in writing and men bind themselves by a solemn promise to permit no infringement of them, but to act as mutual checks on each other in maintaining them."[18] But Kido was also very aware of the fact that the constitution had to be adapted to the degree of civilization the people enjoyed. He believed that Japan was not ready yet for an elective parliamentary form of government. Japan had to proceed by gradual steps in preparing such a constitutional system, for no nation ever attained to a perfect state of civilization in a single morning. But a constitution, if not yet a democratic one, remained the most urgent need of the moment.

Guided by these principles, Kido had, in 1872, while visiting Europe, instructed Aoki Shūzō, a student in Germany at the time, to compile a draft constitution. There are two versions of this draft constitution, one called "Dai Nihon seiki" (Japanese constitution), and the other "Dai Nihonkoku seiten" (Constitution of the Japanese nation), the second one being a revision of the first.[19] This draft can be called the first systematic attempt to formulate a constitutional charter.[20] In its exterior form the draft follows very closely the Prussian constitution.

In this draft we find the principle of equality and natural rights clearly stated and defended. All citizens "regardless of special standing based on lineage" were entirely equal before the laws of the land. Kido condemned partiality in the appointment of citizens to political office and all sorts of discrimination. The abuses of transmitting public offices by heredity were to be removed so that all people "may have the right to hold office according to their ability." The natural rights of each person, which were explained as "inherent rights conferred by heaven," were to be protected. These natural rights were listed as freedom from illegal arrest, search, and seizure of property; the right to a fair trial; freedom of speech, freedom of assembly; and freedom of petition and complaint to the government. The draft covered many aspects of Japanese life. Bigamy was forbidden regardless of the distinction between nobles and commoners, and "marriages between nobles and commoners may be made according to the wishes of each." The custom of adoption was to be abolished altogether because it was susceptible of great abuses. Adoption was simply a private transaction, often between the two family heads concerned, conceivably without regard to the will of the adoptee. There was no judicial control whatever, and adoption could be used to cover the sale of a human being for purposes of gain and exploitation.

The draft imposed compulsory education for all boys and girls beginning at the age of eight years. Freedom of education was guaranteed by the clause stating that "individuals and groups are free to establish private schools, and boys and girls may enter public or private schools according to their own convenience and wishes." In the first version of the draft constitution freedom of religion was not guaranteed. Article 18 reads: "In Japan Buddhism is the religion in which we principally have faith. Consequently, we shall prohibit belief in Christianity and other religions for the time being."[21] This decision was in consonance with the ideas expressed by Rudolf von Gneist, who wanted Buddhism as the religion of state.[22] But in the revised version this clause is changed and reads: "Belief in different religions depends on the voluntary choice of the citizens." Freedom of the press is not unconditional. Such freedom does not contain the right to slander the government or fellow citizens or to publish news items that disturb customs, arouse the people with seditious ideas and lead them into dangerous ways. These were the most important clauses under the heading "The Rights and Duties of the People." They were liberal enough and were a good start toward a recognition of the inalienable rights of the individual.

Even more important than the chapter on the rights and duties were the chapters on the powers of the emperor, the cabinet, and parliament. The third chapter deals with the affairs of the state. The first version of this chapter read in its introductory article: "All powers emanate from the whole Japanese nation, and they are to be exercised according to this constitution."[23] This article was a direct translation of article 25 of the Belgian constitution: "Tous les pouvoirs émanent de la nation. Ils sont exercés de la manière établie par la Constitution." It is interesting to note that this was a clear formulation of the principle of popular sovereignty. In the second draft this clause disappeared completely, and in its stead we read, "All the articles of the constitution are rules agreed upon between the emperor and the people. Thus, even the policies of the emperor and his officials shall be regarded as the result of harmony existing between the sovereign and his people, unless such policies are actually in violation of the purposes of laws."[24] The legislative power was to reside in the emperor and parliament.

There was no clear formulation about the repository of sovereignty, but the emperor, at least indirectly, appeared as the fountainhead of political power. The emperor had power to superintend the administration, to conduct foreign policy, and to command the army and navy; he appointed and dismissed officials, declared war and made peace, and concluded treaties. With regard to legislation the emperor had the right to veto all bills passed by parliament; moreover he was vested with the power to issue emergency ordinances, which had the force of law. However, an imperial ordinance required the countersignature of a minister, who bore personal responsibility to parliament for its provisions. When the government declared a national emergency the ministers of state as a body assumed responsibility for the announcement and were required to explain the circumstances to parliament when it reconvened.

While these powers resided in the emperor, they were to be exercised by his ministers, who actually managed the administration according to the constitution. Kido envisioned some sort of cabinet system headed by a prime minister, but it is not clear whether he limited the powers of this body by any comprehensive system of ministerial responsibility to parliament. Following the Prussian custom, the draft supported the principle of the division of responsibility between the civil government and the military; thus only army or naval officers could be appointed as ministers of the army and the navy.

Gradualism Versus Radicalism

The draft provided for a bicameral parliament: the Genrōin (senate), whose members are appointed by the emperor, and the Giin (Lower House), composed of elected members, were to share legislative power with the emperor. The parliament's role, however, was severely limited by the imperial power to veto and to issue emergency ordinances. The emperor could also dissolve parliament in an emergency. Besides legislative powers, the lower house also had financial responsibilities. In fact, the annual budget required the consent of the lower house. The annual expenditures of the imperial family were to be decided by law and paid out of tax revenues. The lower house determined what constituted the private property of the imperial family.

The ultimate constitutional system that Kido envisioned was a monarchic one based upon broad imperial powers. He thought in terms of a monarchy whose power would be clearly defined and limited by strict adherence to a constitution. In the final analysis, Kido regarded a constitution as a means of securing and maintaining harmony between the powers of the emperor's government and the "natural rights" of the people.

This draft cannot be said to represent a popular democratic constitution. It could rather be called an authoritarian document. But it represents a great declaration of fundamental rights which were advanced and progressive in many points. The guarantee of individual rights, the limitation of imperial power by the constitution, responsibility—though not clearly stated and defined—of the cabinet to parliament, the independence of the judiciary—all these clauses constituted a defense of popular liberties and a negation of unlimited arbitrary power in the hands of the emperor or the government. If we compare this draft with the Meiji Constitution, we find that Kido's document was much more liberal than the final one. Some trends which were later adopted in the Meiji Constitution were already visible in Kido's draft; namely, the power in the emperor

47

to issue emergency ordinances and to conduct foreign policy, the division between civil and military authority, and the general tendency toward centralized government. These limitations notwithstanding, Osatake is right in defining Kido's draft as "a solemn attempt at progressive and liberal legislation."[25]

In his diary, Kido concisely described his general ideas on the problem of constitutional government.[26] He said that a constitutional order like that of England was "too early" for Japan; hence, for the time being, it was necessary to frame a despotic constitution which would be the basis of a real popular constitution. In a letter to Itō Hirobumi, Kido repeated the same ideas.[27]

Ōkubo Toshimichi was also among those who advocated some kind of a constitution. While Kido's gradualism could be called a liberal one, Ōkubo's must be called a conservative one. In his "Opinion on Constitutional Government" submitted in November 1873 to Itō Hirobumi, minister of public works, and Terajima Munenori, minister of foreign affairs, Ōkubo described his position on the form of government Japan should adopt.[28] This document is quite long, and clarity and precision are not its most noticeable qualities.[29] In the introduction Ōkubo stated that both democracy and absolute monarchy were out of place in Japan. Democracy ideally is the best form of government, because it provides for the freedom of the people through the principles of administration by law and the responsibility of officials. But this system "cannot be applied to a people who are accustomed to long-standing practices based on old ways." Therefore democracy could not be the best form of government for Japan at that time. Ōkubo thought that also constitutional monarchy, based upon a contract between the people and the monarch, was not yet possible in Japan because "the people are unenlightened." Nevertheless, some kind of limits and checks had to be determined in order to avoid the

shortcomings of an absolute monarchy and to achieve the
necessary stability in the execution of domestic and foreign
policy. Governments not based on laws deriving from the
natural order could not survive for long:

> In view of this, we must establish a system of government in our
> country that is consistent with our conditions, customs, and tenden-
> cies. Since the Meiji Restoration, we have endeavored to study and
> learn from the rest of the world, and to make Japan superior to all
> nations . . . Since our forefathers founded the nation, Japan has not
> had a government that did not include the people; nor has it main-
> tained the country without a monarchy. Constitutional monarchy is
> a joint government of the ruler and the people; it is a limited mon-
> archy. It seeks to determine the powers of the monarch and the
> people must not think only of their interests . . . This shall be the
> foundation of our nation and the basis of our government.[30]

According to Ōkubo, limited monarchy was the best form
of government. But he was not consistent and did not state
clearly what the limitations of the imperial power should be
and how the rights of the people should be defended. He said
only that the new system of government "must maintain the
emperor's position for all ages to come and make the people
preserve their natural order."

It is difficult to say what the ideal form of government
Ōkubo had in mind was. He kept saying that the political system of a nation has to adhere to the old customs, the feelings of
the people, and the circumstances of a nation. The conclusions,
however, remain very obscure. In Ōkubo's mind an absolute
form of government dominated by men of ability was in keeping with Japanese tradition. He did concede that the Japanese
people were becoming more and more enlightened and concerned with politics, and that the establishment of a constitution was inevitable. He regarded constitutional monarchy as
the ultimate goal, but he did not think in terms of responsible

parliamentary government. Ōkubo was convinced that democratic representative government was not suitable to the customs and needs of Japan. He was extremely wary of possible encroachments upon the powers of the emperor and his ministers by parliament. He insisted that political power, at least for the time being, remain in the hands of a small group of dedicated leaders, assisting the emperor who was the source of all power. He was against arbitrary government, and he considered his plan as the middle road between representative government and arbitrary imperial absolutism. He would preserve the Dajōkan system as the nucleus of Japan's ultimate constitutional government and establish a legislative body, which would be only advisory and appointed.[31]

In fact, as home minister Ōkubo ruled with an iron hand. His practice in political leadership reflected his ideals, at least in the period of construction, of a strong authoritarian government which could serve as the vehicle for prompt execution of decisions. He wanted a constitution, but Japan should adopt a constitution only after laying the necessary foundation. The constitution to be adopted had to conform to "our country's geography, customs, and the sentiments of the people."

Against the gradualist view of people like Kido, Ōkubo, and other members of the ruling elite, an opposing group of leaders presented a memorial in January 1874 calling for the creation of a popularly elected assembly. The memorial was presented by a group of people who had held important positions in the Meiji government until October 1873. This group included, among others, Soejima Taneomi, former foreign minister, Gotō Shōjirō, Itagaki Taisuke, and Etō Shimpei, junior councilors in the Council of State. They had left the government in defeat over the Korean issue.[32] It seems that this memorial was originally drafted in English and then translated into Japanese.[33] The memorial starts with the following statement: "When we humbly reflect upon the quarter in which the governing power lies, we find that it lies not with the Crown (the Imperial House) on the one hand, nor with the people on the other, but with the officials alone."[34]

The fundamental criticism by the opposition was that the government did not share power with the people, the administration was arbitrary, and the power of officials was unlimited. The opposition recognized that the ruling group did not deny the eventual formation of a constitutional form of government and the establishment of a representative assembly; what they attacked was the principle of gradualism prevalent among the group in power. The memorialists warned that "if a reform is not effected the state will be ruined." In order to avert such a calamity they urged that a popular assembly be elected *immediately*. The argument in favor of giving the people a voice in the government was the strengthening of the country and the formation of a united feeling among all the members of the nation. "How is the government to be made strong? It is by the people of the empire becoming of one mind." The establishment of a council chamber chosen by the people would create a community of feeling between the government and the governed, and they would unite mutually into one body. Then and only then would the country become strong.[35]

From such ideas it seems that Itagaki and the opposition in general were favoring some kind of democracy by plebiscite, without the possibility of opposition and without consideration for the rights of the minority. Probably they were influenced by the English radicals, who thought that public discussion would necessarily bring about the best solution for all by promoting the greatest happiness of the greatest number.

Against the objections of the gradualists that the Japanese were not ready for a constitution, the memorialists responded that the reason why foreigners were so slow and gradual in developing a constitutional form of government was because they did not have any example before them. But now the

Japanese had such an example before their eyes and could imitate it. Just as in the technical sphere Japan was not waiting to invent all the new machines and use new methods of research but was adopting what had already been invented in other countries, so also in the political sphere Japan could without any gradualism adopt systems perfected in other nations.

The memorial is in a certain way a democratic document, but the term "democratic" needs some qualifications. As has been noted, there was no mention at all of the rights of the minorities, or defense of pluralism, which is the basis of real democracy. The kind of government advocated in this memorial seemed to be a Rousseauian democracy, with a general will binding all. The council-assembly was the means to achieve this general will, or "one mind," but if the rights of the minority were not defended, the rights of the individual would suffer. The real motivation for the establishment of a popularly elected assembly was not the defense of the civil liberties of the citizens, but "the strength of the empire." The memorialists conceded that the franchise need not be universal. Political rights would be given only to the samurai and to the richer farmers and merchants.[36]

Thus the regime advocated by Itagaki could be defined as a Rousseauian upper-class democracy. The memorial opened a strong debate not only among the political leaders but also among the most articulate elite of the day, the members of the Meirokusha (Meiji Six Society).[37] The Meirokusha, named for the year of its formation in 1873, was the nucleus of the movement for civilization and enlightenment. Many of the most influential and progressive thinkers and leading students of the West were members of the Meirokusha. Some of them—Katō Hiroyuki, for example, Mori Arinori, Tsuda Masamichi, and Nishi Amane—held official positions in the government. Others, such as Nakamura Masanao and Fukuzawa Yukichi, preferred to work outside government circles. All were concerned with the problem of modernization and progress in social, political, and educational fields. They discussed and disseminated their views through the organ of the society's journal, the *Meiroku zasshi*. The members of the Meirokusha were divided in their reaction to Itagaki's memorial. Mori Arinori, Nishi Amane, and Katō Hiroyuki were strongly opposed to the idea of the early establishment of a popular assembly; Tsuda Masamichi and Nishimura Shigeki were in favor of it; and Fukuzawa took a neutral position.

Mori was one of the most enthusiastic upholders of modernization and assimilation of Western culture. His enthusiasm can be seen in his exhortations to Japanese students studying in America. Speaking in New York, he explained the importance of bringing enlightenment to Japan and went on to advocate that, to reach this objective, the use of Japanese should be discontinued and English adopted as the national language. He also told the students that they should marry American women and return with them to Japan so as to improve the Japanese race.

Mori questioned also traditional marriage, which, by placing central importance on the linkage of two houses, resulted in the degradation of women. In his *Saishōron* (Essay on wives), published in 1874, Mori advocated monogamous marriage and the equality of men and women, stating that a married couple should love and protect each other with devotion and fidelity and not transfer their affections to another. Mori, however, was not an undiscriminating adulator of the West. He saw that if the ideal of a modern Japan was to be realized, westernization had to be selective.

When Soejima, Itagaki, Gotō, and others presented their memorial advocating the establishment of an elective assembly, Mori was critical of the idea and suggested that the petition was a political rationalization and political maneuver adopted by a group who had lost its fight to force the government into a "positive policy" toward Korea. Mori thus shed a veil of doubt over the objectives of the memorial, since "its motives are not clear." He made it clear that Itagaki and his group did not leave the government for the purpose of establishing a popular assembly, suggesting that it was because they had to withdraw that they petitioned for the establishment of a popular assembly. Their political activities were not motivated by the idea of freedom and popular rights; rather, they utilized the idea of freedom and popular rights for their political activities.[38]

Mori wrote that the people advocating the establishment of a popular assembly were people who had formerly, as state councilors, advocated a strong policy against Korea. During the period that they were among the "ins" in October 1873, the Press Law had come out. And in 1874 these same people were preaching the evil of "the locking up of public opinion." Yet this locking up of public opinion was passed through the votes of these same people. Furthermore, had their proposal to conquer Korea been implemented, would public opinion had been aroused by this? Was there not the danger that their vaunted popular assembly, too, would in practice become an officials' assembly? Mori's criticism was essentially political, but it gives a clear view of the circumstances in which the new regime and the new ideals were advocated.[39]

Nishi Amane's criticism was based on philosophical principles. Near the end of the first volume of his *Hyakuichi shinron* (New theory on the one hundred and one doctrines)[40] Nishi distinguishes between an a priori, or physical, principle and an a posteriori, or spiritual, principle. The physical principle is the principle of nature, that is, of the external world, the general natural law which governs human beings, animals, and plants. This principle is uniformly operative in every country. However, the spiritual principle is not as broad a principle, and applies only to human beings. It is the normative law, the moral law, the foundation of human society. This moral law, or spiritual principle, is based on the moral sense of each different people and nation. Nishi criticized those who wanted to transplant hastily and without adaptation Western-style political systems to Japan. He also criticized the concept of a social contract. He argued that the authors of the memorial spoke of the social contract as constituting a "universal principle," while history would seem to indicate the unique origins of all states. Nishi was not concerned so much about the rightness or wrongness of a popularly elected assembly, but rather about the defense of such an assembly through false principles.[41]

While Mori criticized the motives of the authors of the memorial and Nishi Amane their "false" premises, Katō Hiroyuki's position was that the establishment of a popular assembly was premature. Katō's political thought is of extreme importance for an understanding of the ideas of the time and their evolution. To put it bluntly, Katō could be called the prototype of the bureaucratic scholar at the service of the political master. From the last years of the Tokugawa era until his death in 1916 he was never out of office. He found himself always on the side of the "ins" and on the side of power. It would seem that when the government was progressive Katō followed a liberal course; when the government was conservative, he would find arguments for moderate policies; and, finally, when the government became reactionary, he too would assume a reactionary attitude.[42] Some have accused him of bureaucratic servility and weak opportunism in the face of power. Katō himself described his personality as that of *rōnin* of feudal times: the man born to serve and follow the master. However, it is rash to call him an opportunist without qualification. He was also a scholar with a deep sense of commitment to truth and with a desire to find a solution to the political and social problems facing Japan. Although he was an official, he always remained involved in the intellectual search for a true solution.

Katō's intellectual production started in 1861, at the age of twenty-six, when he wrote *Tonarigusa* (Neighboring vegetation).[43] According to his own memoirs, *Tonarigusa* was the first book to deal with the problem of constitutional government.[44] The "neighboring vegetation" purported to be China. The decline of the Ch'ing dynasty in China and the defeat at the hands of the West were not the consequence solely of deficiencies in military preparation. Katō, of course, was pointing at Japan, using China only as a symbol. The decline was rooted in the defects of the Chinese, that is, the Japanese, polity, and in the loss of unity among the people. He advocated a revolution and the introduction of constitutional monarchy based on the equality of rights of all and on the natural-rights theory. He rejected royal despotism as well as aristocratic absolutism, and felt that republicanism was too idealistic and would not be appropriate for modern "China." As he put it: "To my way of thinking, in order to reform the Ch'ing dynasty it would be well to adopt some system of constitutionalism. Of course the system of equal powers for all the people is a system which tends to elevate the man of virtue and ability and subordinate the ignorant to his rule, and it is probably the fairest. Since, however, it is not possible to establish a system like this at present, it is urgent for the Ch'ing dynasty to reform speedily by adopting the system of the division of powers and obligations between high and low, and in this way to replace evil customs from the past with good government."[45]

Tonarigusa could not be published at that time because of its anti-*bakufu* implications, and so was only circulated in manuscript. It is interesting to note that Katō was at that time already working as a clerk of the Tokugawa *bakufu*. In 1865 Katō wrote two other books, *Seiyō kakkoku seisui kyōjaku ichiran hyō* (General outline of the situation in the Western countries) and *Kōeki mondō* (Questions and answers on commerce), which were two liberal works introducing the political systems of Europe and America, with special emphasis on the equality of rights and on the representative assemblies.[46] In *Kōeki mondō* he attacked the point of view of the isolationists and advocated the necessity of commercial relations with other nations.

During the first years of the Meiji era, Katō produced the most liberal books in defense of the natural rights theory and of the constitutional system of government. In 1868 he published *Rikken seitai ryaku* (Principles of constitutional government), a short pamphlet of twenty-six pages. It was probably the most enlightened and the most valuable book on political theory of that period.[47]

Through this book Katō introduced to the Japanese intellectuals the terms of a constitutional form of government. *Kokken* was for the first time used by Katō, meaning "national constitution." Katō defined *kokken* as the fundamental law of the administration of the nation. He explained the general structure and the general outline of procedures and techniques for stability and for orderly change.[48] Katō also clearly divided the rights of the citizens into two categories, private and public.[49] Private rights (*shiken*) were those directly related to the person of the citizen and included habeas corpus, the right to private property, freedom of speech and opinion, freedom of religion, and equal rights under the law for all the citizens. Public rights (*kōken*) determined the right of every citizen to take part in the administration of the national government. Among the public rights the greatest and most important was that of every citizen to be elected and to elect others to public office.

In 1870 Katō's *Shinsei tai-i* (Outline of practical politics) was published. There he went into detail on various administrative techniques. Following Locke's terminology, he defined the scope of government as the defense of the people's rights to life, civil liberties, and property. The natural rights theory was the foundation of a constitutional system of government. In this work, we can see the influence of Johann Kaspar Bluntschli and other conservative Western authors. Katō was already leaning toward a gradualist position and expressing some reserves about the premature realization of the democratic constitutional government.[50] In the second part of *Shinsei tai-i,* especially, in the discussion of freedom and conservatism, he reached a position of compromise and gradualism.

In *Shinsei tai-i* we find an exposition of the dangers of communism and socialism. It was the first time that these two words had been mentioned to the Japanese world.[51] In 1874 Katō compiled *Kokutai shinron* (New theory on the national polity), which was published the following year. Here he went even further in his advocacy of natural rights:

> It has been taught that the true "Way of the Subject" is to submit, without questioning whether it is good or evil, true or false, to the Imperial Will and to follow its directives . . . This type of behavior has been characteristic of our national polity. It has been said that for this reason Japan's national polity is superior to that of any other country. This viewpoint is a base and vulgar one! . . . Our national polity is characterized by the mean and vulgar tradition of servility, the land held to be the private property of the Emperor alone. The Emperor and the people are not different in kind: the Emperor is a man; the people too are men. Within the same species there are only divisions between high and low; there is no such separation as between beasts and men.[52]

Katō did not, however, advocate a republican system of government. He distinguished between *kokutai* (the national polity) and *seitai* (the political or administrative system). The distinction he made was that the *kokutai* was the main objective, and that the political system was the way to attain it. To Katō, the national polity was the general theoretical concept that the state rested on; political systems differed from country to country in accordance with differing historical and social configurations. Therefore, the function of a political system in Japan would be only one method of attaining the objective of the *kokutai.*[53]

Katō's defense of the natural rights theory and his opposition to despotic forms of government in *Kokutai shinron* was essentially based on the refutation of the feudal system and of the position of the Kokugaku scholars of the time, whose view was that "people born in Japan exist only to serve the imperial will." Katō said that under this system the people lost their own will and ultimately became slaves of the imperial will. So, he commented, "the people of Japan will become as cattle and horses."[54] His advocacy of the natural rights theory was not directed against the views of the prominent Meiji leaders, but against the reactionary Kokugaku scholars, who wanted to turn the clock back to a feudalistic ethical code, and who were influential in certain sections of the government. Katō stressed the point that both the ruler and the ruled were human beings with the same nature and the same fundamental rights, and to agree with the Kokugaku scholars that the ruler was sublime and the people were base was vulgar and ridiculous.

Before Katō completed *Kokutai shinron,* he had translated part of Bluntschli's *Allgemeines Staatsrecht* and was acquainted with the writings of many conservative Western authors.[55] It was in this same period that he prepared the answer to Itagaki's memorial.[56] Katō accepted the great principle that the government is made for the people, not the people for the government. He also said that the final goal must be a deliberative assembly chosen by the people and a government run according to the wishes of the people. But he warned that it was extremely difficult to judge the appropriate moment to set up a new political system. Radicalism might cause great damage and suffering: "I fear that if, regardless of these facts (stupidity and ignorance of the great majority of the people), we proceed to establish in a sweeping way a deliberative assembly chosen by the people, the only fruit of such public discussion will be foolish ideas not worth consideration."[57]

Katō was thus an advocate of gradualism. The first step was

to prepare the nation for a constitutional form of government. Katō's main argument was based on two considerations. First the basic purpose behind the plan to establish a popular assembly, was to inaugurate a constitutional system. The question remained, however, whether the Japanese were really prepared to establish a working constitutional regime. No one in Japan could yet answer such simple questions as what a government was, what subjects were, or what right a government had to exact military service and levy taxes. The constitutional system must be appropriate to the conditions of the country; what was suitable for a civilized country could not be said to be appropriate for a backward people. Second, Katō felt that Japan should endeavor to educate the people and raise their standard of civilization before trying to establish an assembly. The only way to prepare the nation for a constitutional form of government was "by establishing schools and thus nourish the nation's intellect." Katō's gradualist attitude was expressed also in the introduction to his translation of Bluntschli's *Allgemeines Staatsrecht:* "This book which I have translated is not against public opinion but only argues against the willful and arbitrary spread of public opinion without reference to the temper of the times and without observing the customs and manners of different people."[58]

Within the Meirokusha there were also those who agreed with the memorial for the early establishment of a popular assembly. Nishimura Shigeki and Tsuda Masamichi pleaded the cause of the memorialists. Nishimura, an official of the Department of Education, was the first to argue in support of Itagaki and his group. Nishimura admitted that Soejima, Etō, Itagaki, and the other authors of the memorial had acted rashly in publishing the petition for a popular assembly. However, this was not enough to condemn them and their ideals; on the contrary, violence and passion could be the cause of much good. Nishimura distinguished between violence leading to good and violence leading to evil. The American revolution against England was an example of violence engendering good; the overthrow of the king of France by Robespierre and Danton was an example of violence leading to evil.[59] The theory of a popular assembly was defended as valid by the fact of the wealth and power of the countries of Europe and America. Therefore, the idea of a popular assembly in Japan was to be deplored for its lateness, not attacked for its prematureness.[60]

Tsuda, then secretary at the Department of Foreign Affairs, published his article in defense of a popular assembly in *Meiroku zasshi* of June 1874. He opposed the Peers' Assembly which the government was planning to establish in order to appease the people's rights movement. He argued that the aristocrats did not possess the superior knowledge necessary to become members of the upper house, and so to speak of a Peers' Assembly was a meaningless gesture. He also opposed the Assembly of Prefectural Governors because as representatives of the central government they could not be representatives of the people. The representative assembly should be chosen by an electorate comprising the ex-samurai and commoners, whose taxes came to 200 yen a year for city people and 50 yen for rural people. The individuals chosen by such an electorate would constitute the true representatives of the nation in the assembly.[61]

Fukuzawa Yukichi stood halfway between the gradualists and the radicals. He was one of the leading figures in the movement toward civilization and enlightenment. Since Fukuzawa towered above most of the other Meiji liberals in intellect and perceptivity, the direction and the impact of his thought and action should be given special consideration. His values and ideals represent one of the best expressions of early Meiji thought, both in its limitations and in its positive aspects.[62] At the root of his philosophy was a "relative" principle, which held that one group is not always right, and that any single idea, whether progressive or reactionary, becomes the enemy of civilization if pushed too far: "Light and heavy, long and short, good and evil, right and wrong, all these terms express a relative conception. Without 'light' there can be no 'heavy,' without 'good' there can be no 'evil.' When we say 'light' we understand lighter than 'heavy,' when 'good' we mean better than 'evil.' Thus without this relative principle we would not be able to discuss light or heavy, good or evil. Similarly, by relating one thing to the other we determine what is heavy or what is good."[63]

In the absence of this relative principle one finds the phenomenon of indulgence, which Fukuzawa criticized strongly: the use of abstract ideals to approach real problems. He called it "idleness of the human spirit." We find it in a political situation when that which was created as a means becomes an end in itself. The popular rights movement itself can become an example of indulgence if it sins by "ultrapoliticalism" and makes a fetish of devoting all its energy to overthrowing the government and acquiring political power.

The opposite of indulgence, said Fukuzawa, is the spirit of independence, initiative, and responsibility. The spirit of independence involved an entirely new outlook on the universe and a rethinking of some of the most unquestioned assumptions about man, nature, and values. In the civilized world the spirit of independence and of doubt had led to the discovery of truth and made progress possible. Indeed, "if we look for the origin of Western civilization, it comes down to one thing, doubt."[64] It was necessary to submit the old traditional truths to the scrutiny of the intellect; and it was also necessary to examine Western things and methods thoroughly before adopting them. Things must not be preserved only because they were old; at the same time things must not be adopted only because they were new and Western.[65]

The adoption of the modern civilization of Europe was the best possible means of making Japan strong and rich. However,

European civilization was not an end in itself: "At present the only duty of the Japanese people is to preserve the *kokutai*. To preserve the *kokutai* means the maintenance of independent political power. To maintain the independence of the nation, it is necessary to foster the education and knowledge of the people."[66] And this could be accomplished by introducing Western culture and Western civilization. Fukuzawa's central theme was the preservation of the *kokutai*,[67] which must be the ultimate aim of Japanese political thought and action. According to Fukuzawa, if the real independence of the country was not preserved, that is, if the Japanese lost their independent power of decision, then even if the unbroken line of emperors was preserved, the *kokutai* would be destroyed. The most important problem facing Japan in the specific historical period of the early Meiji era was how to preserve real independence in the face of the Western challenge. The civilization of modern Europe was the indispensable *instrument* by which to reach the *end* of the preservation of the *kokutai*. "The nation's independence is the aim, the nation's civilization is the means toward the aim."[68] Before speaking of progress and civilized forms of government it was necessary to preserve the independence of the Japanese nation. Only later could the other problems be solved.

It is wrong to regard Fukuzawa either as an undiscriminating adulator of the West or as a mere nationalist. For him, even the independence of Japan and the preservation of the *kokutai* were conditional in character. When he said that the independence of the country was the end and civilization the means, he always stressed the qualification "at present, in the present historical situation." His fundamental attitude remained always his sense of the "relative" value of movements and systems, which have to be judged according to differing specific circumstances. Such an attitude is sometimes interpreted as mere opportunism or lack of solid principles. In the case of Fukuzawa, it seems that this judgment is out of place. He never denied the existence of a universal truth. His attitude can probably be described best by saying that he was a pragmatic politician who, without forgetting the ideal, always had in mind the principle that politics is the art of the possible.

I have dealt at some length with Fukuzawa's ideological perspective because it is necessary to understand his position on the people's rights movement. At times he expressed a critical, almost sarcastic, attitude toward this movement, which demanded an early establishment of a popular assembly. He objected to the arguments presented by the opposition leaders in defense of the popular assembly. These leaders based their arguments on the example of the Western countries, on the principles of individualism and internationalism, and on natural rights. Fukuzawa answered that it was foolish to use such arguments because the European countries had reached such a stage only after many centuries of political development. Moreover, the principles of individualism and internationalism based on natural rights did not take into account the international situation, in which power, not natural rights, was the decisive factor. To force upon Japan a political system appropriate to the historical situation of the European countries was a great mistake. He accused the opposition leaders of "formalism" and of not understanding the real situation of the Japanese nation.

Fukuzawa defended the principle of "expediency." Yet he remained an advocate of liberalism, even though he felt that before reaching the stage of a popularly elected assembly the Japanese nation itself had to be built. He deplored the fact that Japan was only a government and not yet a nation.[69] The Japanese were not a nation because, historically, they had only been subjects. Japanese history had been the history of Japanese governments, with the people playing almost no part in the development of Japanese civilization. Progress for Japan would depend on the people becoming a nation by assuming the dual role of ruler and subject—by accepting duties and enjoying rights.[70]

Fukuzawa did not endorse revolution or sudden change. He felt that true progress in civilization depended on the spiritual development of the people alone: "A sudden blind upheaval can only replace violence by violence and stupidity by stupidity . . . there is nothing in the world as inhuman as civil disorder . . . Such evils as fathers and sons killing each other, brothers hating each other, arson and slaughter must not happen!"[71] He condemned as blind and stupid the successive peasant uprisings then taking place in Japan, which were more reactionary than progressive.[72] He believed in gradual progress, which would be followed by the enlightenment brought about by knowledge. Yet he did not subscribe to the kind of gradualism that was advocated by the ruling group;[73] he was a believer in a liberal form of government and was opposed to authoritarianism, and relied more on the intellectuals for the formation of a good nation than on the leadership of the government.

This great debate about gradualism and radicalism continued for several years. Katō Hiroyuki became more and more the spokesman of the gradualist-conservative position, while the people's rights movement was represented by people like Ueki Emori, Nakae Chōmin, and Ōi Kentarō.[74]

Ueki Emori was a young intellectual and the braintruster of Itagaki Taisuke. Much of his writing was concerned with the problem of liberty and the form of government that could defend and ensure liberty. His book *Minken jiyūron* (On popular rights and liberty), published in 1879, and later *Tempu jinkemben* (In defense of natural rights), published in 1883, were the best defense of a democratic form of government. In *Minken jiyūron* he wrote:

According to Rousseau, man is born free and can be called a free animal. Therefore, although there might be statements that civil freedom comes from social laws, it is nature which endows men with freedom. If people do not assume this natural endowment of freedom it is not only a great sin against nature but also a great disgrace to themselves. Disgrace does not reside merely in assuming things which should not be assumed, but also in not assuming things which should be assumed. To steal is a disgrace, to lie is a disgrace, to be an adulterer is a disgrace; for the people not to assume their natural right to freedom is similarly a great disgrace![75]

Ueki began with the assumption that the people formed the basis of the state because the state cannot exist without the people. For the state to be strong, therefore, the people must be energetic. The ancients were mistaken in thinking that if the people were obedient the state was well ruled. For the people to be energetic they must be self-reliant. Absolutism is contrary to the strength of the state because it does not prepare the citizens to be energetic and self-reliant. Absolutism is the certain means toward internal disorder, revolution, and weakness, and to prove it Ueki cited examples from Rome to China.

Thus Ueki felt that liberty and individual freedom are indispensable to the vigor and power of the state, and should be guaranteed by a constitution established by a conference between the people and their rulers to draw up a division of rights which are not to be transgressed. A written constitution would preserve peace and security and prevent disorder by providing for emergencies. When Lincoln was assassinated, Ueki said, there was no disorder because of the provisions of the constitution. Ueki understood one of the first elements of a constitutional government: that a good government is a complex system providing for orderly change. He insisted also that the constitution be discussed and drafted in a constitutional convention. He thought that a constitution or a democracy granted from above was not the real manifestation of popular rights.

Nakae Chōmin, often called the Rousseau of Japan, had studied in France, and on his return became one of the intellectual leaders of the people's rights movement. Nakae was against all extreme egalitarianism, but at the same time he was against absolutism and autocratic government. He defended a constitutional form of government, yet did not see any contradiction in democracy being granted from above. To him there was no essential difference between a democracy attained from below by the people, as in France and in England, and a constitutional form of government granted from above, as in Prussia, where the people were not permitted to decide for themselves the amount of freedom they could have and the limits to be imposed on the government; there was only a difference of degree.[76]

Ōi Kentarō was in the government until 1876, working as a junior secretary of the Genrōin, but even before leaving government service he had advocated an early constitution, against the government's position defending gradualism.[77] He stood also for a free ballot, opposing Itagaki's desire for a restricted ballot for the samurai.

The newspapers also played an active role in the debate on the popular assembly. With one or two exceptions the Japanese press had as its *raison d'être* the task of criticizing whatever the government did.[78] A synopsis of editorials which appeared in the mid-seventies will show the revolutionary radicalism of many of the newspapers.

In *Saifū shimbun* an editorial praised the example of Patrick Henry and proclaimed that, if the circumstances arose, his example should be followed and that it would be desirable to start a rebellion as the thirteen colonies of North America had done against England. Thus it would be possible to establish a republican form of government.[79] In another article the same newspaper advocated the natural rights theory and proclaimed: "Our government is tyranny, and our authorities are brutal; therefore we must destroy this government and punish the officials with death."[80] Other newspapers, too, asserted the right of revolution, and *Sōmō zasshi* of June 16, 1876, stated that liberty must be earned with blood. Assassination was defended as a means of obtaining liberty; the emperor and the other leaders were nothing but tools created for the purpose of protecting the rights of the people. Komatsubara Eitarō, a journalist of *Hyōron shimbun,* who later became minister of education, was sentenced to prison for two years for having written:

> In case tyrants suppress and abuse people by usurping their power, and no arguments nor public opinion have any effect upon their atrocious attitude, what can be done with them? Shall the whole nation be sacrificed for the benefit of a few despotic authorities, or shall the latter be sacrificed for the sake of the former? Even a child would not hesitate to give a reply in this fashion: "In such a case, the tyrants must be sacrificed as a natural punishment of Heaven upon them. Why should we neglect the welfare of the people for the sake of a few despots?"[81]

Yamawaki Ki, another journalist of *Hyōron shimbun,* wrote a violent article against the government authorities: "Heaven has bestowed on us freedom. Consequently if there are people who would not dare struggle to extend their freedom when they are bound by artificial barriers, they must be called sinners before God. It is a people's duty to overthrow a tyrannical government by raising the standard of liberty, sounding the drums of freedom, and casting a new government according to the will of the people . . . We must remember that true liberty grows only out of blood and death, not from empty table discussions."[82]

The newspapers often advocated the right of revolution against despotic governments. When rascals and wicked ministers oppressed the people, the only way left was to overthrow the government and punish the government officials. In the late seventies political narratives based on radical revolutionary philosophies made their appearance in newspapers, such as serial stories of the fall of the Roman Empire and of the American and the French revolutions.[83]

A cursory examination of these debates on gradualist and radicalism might suggest that there was an unbridgeable difference between the advocates of gradualism and the upholders of radicalism but on more careful consideration it is seen that some fundamental ideas were accepted by leaders both inside and outside of the government.

All of them had come into contact with Western ways of thinking, and all of them, though in differing degrees, accepted Western ideas of government. There were men like Kido, who rejected the past, but were cautious in introducing Western political institutions; men like Itagaki, who wanted to preserve some of the privileges of the samurai class, but at the same time were dedicated to constitutional ideals; and there were the bureaucrat-intellectuals, who took a middle position and attempted to make an eclectic synthesis of democratic and traditional systems. And yet, despite these cleavages and the sharp intellectual and political conflicts they provoked, the leaders of early Meiji Japan had many things in common. The core of agreement among them was their common background, their advocacy of civilization and enlightenment, and, above all, their common dedication to the task of preserving Japan's independence.

A vision of international politics governed by the "might is right" (*jakuniku kyōshoku*) principle led the spokesmen of the Meiji era to this agreement. Almost all of them must have observed that international society, particularly what Asia saw of it, was a jungle in which the strong devoured the weak. One can hardly chide any of them, whether government leaders or opposition leaders, for the espousal of *fukoku kyōhei* (enrich the country, strengthen the army). To understand the Meiji leaders' ideology it is important to consider the possible alternative to *fukoku kyōhei,* the leading concept of the period: a poor and divided country and a weak defense against the challenge of the West, the final result of which could easily be, at least so the Meiji leaders thought, the loss of independence, as had happened in other Asian countries, or the return to feudal times.

It cannot be denied that more antidemocratic and absolutist tendencies appeared later on. The early Meiji leaders, however, did not desire as the ultimate political ideal an absolute despotism; they only wanted a strong national state, an independent state. If authoritarian methods were used in the beginning, the explicit goal was a strong unified state, and centralized control and direction were only the means to achieve it. The documents of this early period reveal a mixture of liberal ideals and despotic methods. The real preoccupation of both the ruling group and the opposition seems to have been not so much absolute power or a solid democratic system as national strength and modernization. There emerges a picture of rival Japanese groups addressing themselves to the problem of national independence and national progress. The opposition, or "liberals," were in general large-minded and optimistic seekers after freedom and progress, confident that individual freedom would result in national freedom. The men in power were practical, cautiously progressive, but concerned above all else with Japanese security and the national interest, thoughtfully preparing Japan to stand as an equal with the Western powers.

The early stages of Japan's modernization were determined more by the defense of the integrity and unity of the state than by constitutional theories. Constitutionalism was accepted as the final goal, but the ruling elite felt that for the time being the Japanese people were not yet ready for a constitutional form of government: "It was the question whether the abler few should direct the many who were unstable, irrational and likely to be disorderly destructive."[84] Although these words were written about early nineteenth century America, and not about the Meiji leaders, they define quite well the attitude of the Japanese rulers.

Constitutionalism in its perfection may be conceived as a system of institutionalized opposition in which the people choose among alternative contenders for public office. It is very doubtful that the concession of a constitution and the opening of an assembly in the late seventies or early eighties would have resulted in a real constitutional system. It is not improbable that the result would have been a government even less democratic and less progressive than the Meiji government. As Robert Bellah puts it, "The real choice was not between the Meiji government and a democratic revolution as the means of modernization but between modernization brought by this kind of government or no modernization at all."[85]

III

TOWARD A CONSTITUTIONAL GOVERNMENT

The controversy over the establishment of a popular assembly was a lively one, and all the prominent leaders of the time took part in it. In this discussion, the problem of the character of the constitution to be enacted often came to the surface, but only indirectly. Natural rights, liberty, progress, and civilization came up as connected problems in the discussion of the convocation of a popular assembly. Only later, when the problem of centralization and strengthening of the country had already advanced toward a solution, did definite plans arise about the nature of the constitution. Concrete proposals for a charter and a general reorganization of the political system were being presented by the ruling group and by leaders outside of government.

With the death of Ōkubo, the first period of the Meiji government can be said to have come to an end. By the spring of 1878, the original triumvirate of the Meiji Restoration—Ōkubo, Kido, and Saigō Takamori—had ceased to exist. Kido had died on May 26, 1877; Saigō, the military genius of the restoration, had perished in September 1877 by his own hand in the last battle of the Satsuma Rebellion; and Ōkubo was assassinated on May 14, 1878, while on the way to his office. The assassination of Ōkubo marked the end of the era of centralization of power. It was time now to rationalize this concentration of power in the central government and to find more efficient ways to carry on the principles of the restoration.

In June 1878, the Genrōin presented a draft constitution, "Nihon kokken an" (Draft constitution of Japan).[1] The primary purpose of this draft was described in an accompanying memorial as the distribution of power between sovereign and subjects and the further division of the sovereign's power into the executive, legislative, and judicial branches so that each branch would have specific functions and responsibilities.[2] The hope was expressed that a government so constituted would bring great benefits not merely to a well-disciplined administration but to the nation at large.

On the whole the Genrōin's draft constitution made important concessions to democratic ideals, and clear checks and controls were established in order to limit the power of the central government and of the emperor. The powers of the emperor were not unlimited: he was first of all limited by the constitution, and then by parliament. The first article of the draft constitution read: "The Japanese Empire shall be governed by an imperial line unbroken for ages."[3] The emperor was thus put at the center of the Japanese nation, and his person was "sacred and inviolable." His power was vast: he had the power of administration, appointed and dismissed government officials, approved and proclaimed laws, had the supreme command of the army and navy, declared war and made peace, concluded treaties, summoned both houses of parliament, extended their sessions and ordered their adjournment. These were vast powers indeed, but there were also limitations of these powers. For instance, the draft constitution provided that "those treaties which would involve expenditures or a change in the national boundaries would require the approval of both houses of parliament."[4] Moreover, the annual income of the emperor would be decided by law, and the emperor would not have financial independence. With regard to changing the order of imperial succession, the draft required both houses to give their consent, and at the enthronement ceremonies the

74

emperor was to take an oath to "adhere to the constitution before a meeting of both houses."

It was in the matter of legislative power, especially, that the draft constitution made the greatest inroads on the absolute power of the emperor, for it provided that the legislative power was "divided between the emperor and the imperial parliament." The emperor had the right to initiate bills, and parliament had the right to discuss the return of them to the throne with its decisions. All bills required the consent of both houses, while the emperor had the ultimate power of veto. The only exceptions to this rule were budgetary and taxation measures, both of which simply required the consent of the lower house. Constitutional amendments required the consent of both houses expressed by at least a two-thirds majority.

Parliament was to consist of the Genrōin or Senate, and the House of Representatives. The Genrōin was to be an appointive body, while the House of Representatives was to be a popularly elected assembly whose members would serve a four-year term, with elections for half the total membership every two years. The draft constitution also contained a bill of rights for Japanese citizens which guaranteed individual rights and freedoms, with these rights and freedoms being qualified by the proviso "according to the law." Freedom of opinion and religion, the right of free assembly and association, the right of private secret communication, and freedom from unlawful arrest could therefore be modified and legislated out of existence.

This draft constitution was prepared after close analysis of many European and the American constitutions.[5] The only touch of Japanese tradition is found in the first article's words "an imperial line unbroken for ages," and in the rules of succession, which allowed illegitimate children of the emperor to reach the throne.[6] Otherwise, the draft follows the constitutions of constitutional monarchies in Europe. The idea of absolute imperial sovereignty was not defended: we can see that it was denied by the division of the legislative power between the emperor and parliament. The emperor was also limited by the constitution. The constitution was above both the emperor and parliament, for both had to submit to its terms. The people were not "subjects" of the emperor; according to the constitution, they had rights and duties, and all were equal under the law. Unlike the Meiji Constitution, this draft clearly defended a division of sovereignty between the emperor and the people. There were, it is true, also common points between the two documents, such as the presence of conditions in the enumeration of the fundamental rights of the people and the stress on the unbroken line of emperors; but on fundamental points they differed. The Genrōin's draft was by far more liberal and more democratic.[7]

According to Kaneko Kentarō,[8] an outstanding statesman of the Meiji period, this draft constitution was fashioned after the English tradition. Kaneko probably wanted to stress the point that this draft did not attribute total sovereignty to the emperor, following the English tradition of the "king in parliament." Or perhaps he wanted to point out the fact that the Genrōin's draft did not follow the American constitution nor the republican constitution of France. Miyazawa Toshiyoshi, a legal scholar of present-day Japan, contends that the Genrōin's draft was more in line with Belgian and Prussian constitutional models. The same interpretation is given also by the historian Inada Masatsugu. Close study of the different constitutions shows this interpretation to be the more likely one.[9]

Iwakura Tomomi, then minister of the Right, did not like the implicit democratic tendencies of the Genrōin's draft, which, according to his opinion, would destroy the traditional *kokutai*. He was also growing anxious over the agitation of the people's rights movement and the increasing number of memorials demanding the establishment of a national assembly. Thus in

1879 he petitioned the throne to order the junior councilors to report their views on a constitution so that those most suitable to the traditional Japanese patterns of government could be singled out by the emperor as the basis for a constitution, which was, of course, to be granted by the emperor.[10] Iawkura said that the matter was urgent, and the throne accepted Iwakura's petition.

As a result, the views of the junior councilors—Yamagata Aritomo, Kuroda Kiyotaka, Yamada Akiyoshi, Inoue Kaoru, Itō Hirobumi, Ōki Takatō, and Ōkuma Shigenobu—were presented to the emperor between December 1879 and March 1881. These opinions must be closely examined in order to understand the motives leading the ruling group in their endeavors toward a constitutional form of government.[11]

The first to submit his "Opinion on Constitutional Government" to the emperor was Yamagata Aritomo, the founder of the military system and civil service in Meiji Japan.[12] In his answer Yamagata showed a deep concern for the strength and independence of the Japanese nation, and at the same time he revealed a deep understanding of the different forces working in the nation.

Yamagata expressed his attachment to traditional values and his sadness at the decay of older customs and virtues. Yet he was not a narrow-minded adulator of the past; he was not looking backward to a *status quo ante*. He favored Western methods, and was aware of the need to adopt new laws based on Western legal systems, but he was equally alive to the tensions involved in the building of a new nation and to the dilemma between the new trends and the old society. He saw the modernization of Japan as a race with time: "There is not always enough time to make the necessary adjustments to such a sudden change."[13] The tempo of the revolution had been too fast for many people. It was natural that many felt alienated from the new regime. Yamagata was worried by the fact that an alienated people could not be the basis of a stable and strong government. The greatest challenge for a statesman was to direct popular sentiment and popular opinion to coincide with the government. It would seem that Yamagata was advocating some kind of totalitarian manipulation of the public opinion, but he did not; he said that in order to obtain this objective of harmony and unity between rulers and ruled the demands of the common people had to be taken into account, and that this required a constitution and a representative assembly.

Yamagata's analysis of the social and political changes of the Meiji era could be applied to the situation of many newly emerging countries of today: the restoration was a great achievement and much progress had been made, but the changes had been too rapid. There was not time for gradual adaptation and transformation. The old regime had been destroyed, but the new methods had not taken root yet. They were still superficial. Moreover, in a period of upheavals "there are some who have gained much happiness, but there are also many others who have lost their property, wealth and position."[14] A new Western system of laws had been introduced, but written law was not enough. Yamagata complained, "We have failed to realize that we must also govern society with good morals and customs."[15] The deterioration of the moral foundation of the country had to be stopped if a rash imitation of the West were not to undermine the social fabric. Yamagata wanted to find a solution to the fundamental problem facing the nation, the opposition between the new and the old, but how could a creative tension be brought about from this clash which could allow progress along the lines of the Western powers without destroying the national individuality and the Japanese way of life?

Yamagata advocated social and economic reforms as the first step toward national strength. Traditional class divisions and privileges were detrimental to rapid modernization, and Yamagata was one of the most forceful in stressing total equality and impartiality in the application of the laws. He felt the need of bringing the people into some kind of participation in the political affairs of the nation, but he was worried about popular discontent and division between the government and the governed. He thought that the only way to reach unity of purpose was to instill once again the traditional Japanese virtues; loyalty, discipline, and respect toward authority.

What Yamagata feared most was division. Division meant disruption of the advance of modernization, and political parties meant division, selfishness, and partisanship. The leaders of the political parties were first and foremost loyal to their factions, not to the country as a whole. Yamagata felt that the civil administrators must be above all factional politics, especially in times of great change.

We can now understand Yamagata's ideas on constitutional government. He felt that unless a united and determined cabinet seized unquestioned and total administrative authority, hopeless conditions would result. The duty of the cabinet was to provide the force which would enable the country to advance with strength and unity.

But at the same time Yamagata was convinced that a division of powers was necessary. The cabinet should not intervene in the legislative and judicial processes. Separation of powers had to be adhered to strictly. The powers of the emperor and the rights of the people also had to be defined clearly in the constitution. It would be in the popular assembly that the "powers of the emperor and the people are divided."[16] Yamagata was of the opinion that a popular assembly was an "inevitable development," and therefore he believed it best for the time being to open a single assembly composed of men selected from the prefectural assemblies on the basis of their learning and ability. The first duties of this assembly would be to discuss the provisions of a constitution and the particulars of legislation. After several years of trial, when it had become clear that the grant of the legislative prerogative would be suitable, a popular assembly should be organized.

Yamagata was truly convinced that in order to have a stable government the *governed* must have the right to participate in the national administration. He clearly advocated a division of powers and did not make the emperor the only repository of sovereignty. Even more than the emperor's fate it was Japan's fate as a strong and united nation that worried him: "If we gradually establish a popular assembly and firmly establish a constitution, the things I have enumerated above—popular enmity towards the government, failure to follow government orders, and suspicion of the government, these three evils— will be cured in the future."[17]

In February 1880, Kuroda Kiyotaka, a junior councilor and concurrently commissioner of the Colonization Bureau, sent his "Opinion on Constitutional Government."[18] He stated that the establishment of a popular assembly was premature. It should be preceded first of all by the completion of basic legislation, that is, by the formulation of the civil code and the penal code, and then by the improvement of the educational system and industrialization and increase in general production. Four months later Yamada Akiyoshi, a junior councilor and former minister of public works, presented his thoughts on the fundamental issues of government.[19] He did not see any "natural" reason or right on which the people could base their demand for a voice in government; however, the alternative evils of despotism were so great, in his estimation, that the people should be allowed to take part in the management of government. A constitutional form of government had to be established with care, based on an eternal foundation achieved through the consideration of traditional customs and values and of new circumstances. Yamada proposed that the people be allowed to participate in deliberating upon laws which affected their general rights, in the auditing of revenue collections and expenditure reports, and in the changing of local boundaries.[20] In consequence, a provisional constitution approved by the emperor should be given a trial for four or five years by both the Genrōin and the Assembly of Prefectural Governors. Yamada believed that after an investigation of the achievements under the constitution had been made, the constitution should be given definite form and promulgated.[21]

Inoue Kaoru, minister of foreign affairs, made several noteworthy suggestions.[22] He recognized the urgent necessity of establishing a national assembly and thus of reorganizing the government. He proposed that the government first establish an upper house composed of ex-samurai and nobles, partly elected and partly appointed, that would counterbalance a popularly elected lower house. He felt that the upper house, not the lower, should have the ultimate power to pass judgment on taxes and the budget. Regarding the drafting of the constitution, he recommended that the task be delegated to the upper house acting in consultation with the government. Final decision would be the prerogative of the emperor, if differences of opinions should arise among the upper house, the lower house, and the government. Inoue said also that without an imperial mandate on the national assembly and the constitution, it was doubtful whether the public mind could be quieted. Among the suggestions of Inoue the most extraordinary was his belief that the ideal form of government was a political system based on democratic parties. Following the example of the British and American systems, Japan too should endeavor to reach such a form of government, in which political parties peacefully alternated in running the state. This was probably the first time the official leadership expressed clearly the ideal of a democratic form of government based on political parties.[23]

The views of Itō Hirobumi, presented in December 1880, are of particular importance because of Itō's role in the formation of the Meiji Constitution.[24] Itō saw that the movement toward a change in the form of government stemmed from two causes. The first was the discontent of the many ex-samurai who had lost stipends, property, and special privileges and now were trying to regain some of the lost power by fomenting revolutionary ideas. The second cause was the spreading of European ideals and manners. Both of these were inevitable. The samurai class had suffered most during the restoration, and the government could hardly give everybody a job and compensation. European ideas and manners could not be rejected altogether, and sooner or later all nations would come under the influence of the ideas originating in Europe. It was impossible to alter world trends: "Today conditions in Japan are closely related to the world situation. They are not merely the affairs of a nation or province. The European concepts of revolution, which were carried out for the first time in France about one hundred years ago, have gradually spread to the various nations. By combining and complementing each other, they have become a general trend. Sooner or later, every nation will undergo changes as a result."[25] This is a good definition of the intellectural, cultural, and social interdependence of various nations in the late 1800's. Itō understood better than the European statesmen at the Conference of Vienna in 1815 that the new trends could not be ignored. He saw the only solution to this revolutionary situation in "discarding absolutist ways and sharing political power with the people."

Itō's position was a moderate one, dictated by the practical considerations of politics, where it is best to adopt methods that fit changing circumstances. He defended the necessity of adopting a conciliatory policy toward the new trends "so that we may control but not intensify the situation, and relax our hold over government but not yield it." He recognized the importance and even the necessity of some limitations on the administrative power of the government. Despotic government and lack of channels of communication between the people and the government could lead only to public agitation and unnecessary friction. Now a clear organization of government, well-established limits of power, and representative were indispensable for a smooth and effective system of government. If the Meiji leaders did not make some decisions in this direction, the opposition would be able to use public opinion against the government, and the peace of the nation would be disrupted.

As a practical plan Itō proposed, first, that the Genrōin be enlarged and its members be selected from the peerage. Second, extraordinary members of the Board of Audit should be selected from among the members of the prefectural assemblies in order to ensure public discussion of financial matters. And third, Itō desired that the emperor declare without reservation the aims of the nation, informing the people that the nation should advance gradually and that in due course he would share his legislative power with the people. The emperor should also announce the date of the granting of the constitution and the opening of parliament.[26]

Itō did not discuss the problem of where final sovereignty resided, but implicitly he made the emperor the repository of supreme power when he said that only the emperor had the right to decide whether to share his legislative power. At the same time, however, Itō said clearly that in modern states power must be limited and checked if one wanted to prevent revolution and agitation.

Ōki Takatō, the most conservative among the junior councilors, submitted his opinion in May 1881.[27] He divided the Western systems of government into absolute monarchies, constitutional monarchies, and republics. These systems could not be applied to the Japanese situation, however, because the Japanese nation, based on the imperial line, was unique in the world. Thus the Japanese constitution had to be unique. Ōki suggested a division of the constitution into two parts. One part, the law of the emperor, the *kokutai,* should contain those matters touching upon the very foundation of the empire—the emperor's position as the fountainhead of peace and happiness for the people—and it should also contain the charter for the Imperial Household. The other part, the *seitai,* or the system of administration, was to clarify the division of powers and the essentials of the administrative organization as well as the general principles of the assembly. The law concerning the emperor, according to Ōki, must be rigid, admitting of no change, because it was based on the immutable *kokutai* of the Japanese nation, while the second part could be modified according to circumstances.

Ōki's opinion is peculiar among all the other opinions because it espouses clearly and strongly the theory of the *kokutai.* The other leaders had their reservations about the immediate establishment of a full constitutional regime, but their reservations were based only upon expediency—Japan was not yet ready—and therefore they would have to advance slowly. Ōki, however, based his principles on the unique nature of the *kokutai.* He rejected all forms of foreign political systems, not because the Japanese people were not ready yet for such systems, but because the *kokutai* required different solutions.

By March 1881, all the junior councilors but Ōkuma Shigenobu had submitted their proposals to the emperor. Since Ōkuma was the only one among them who had not tendered his opinion, he was urged to do so by Prince Arisugawa, minister of the Left. Ōkuma took this opportunity to request that he be allowed to present his views in person to the emperor; denied this wish, he finally put them in writing.[28] His opinion had been prepared by two of his followers, Ono Azusa and Yano Fumio, both officials at the Ministry of Finance.[29] Ōkuma's opinion was divided into seven parts, the titles of which give us the central ideas of Ōkuma's proposal.

1. The date of the establishment of a parliament should be announced . . .

2. High officials should be appointed on the basis of popular support, i.e., the leader of the majority party should be asked to form the cabinet . . .

3. A distinction should be made between political party leaders, owing their jobs to election, and permanent civil servants . . .

4. The constitution should be established according to the emperor's will: careful consideration should be given to state clearly where power is vested and what are the rights of the people . . .

5. Elections for parliament should be held by the end of 1882 and parliament should be convened at the beginning of 1883 . . .

6. Administrative policies of the government should be clearly stated. Victory or defeat of a party is victory or defeat of its policies . . .

7. The essence of constitutional government is government by political parties . . .[30]

The novelty and importance of Ōkuma's report was the insistence on the necessity of government by political parties. We have seen that Inoue had already presented as the final ideal of government a constitutional system based on a two-party regime. But it was Ōkuma who stressed the necessity of the political parties to the point of defining constitutional government as government by political parties. Ōkuma pleaded for the English style of constitutional government. That is, he advocated that the cabinet be organized by the head of the political party having a majority in the national assembly and that the cabinet either resign or dissolve the assembly on a vote of no confidence.

His distinction between party officials and permanent civil servants was also based on the British system. Ōkuma spoke of permanent executive officials, among whom he included permanent, politically neutral officials, military, police, and judicial officers, and the three top-ranking ministers (the chancellor, the minister of the Left, and the minister of the Right). He was trying to give the three high-ranking ministers an advisory position like the Lord Keeper of the Privy Seal.[31] Under the party system, according to Ōkuma, each cabinet was required to define its policies and make them public. Constitutional government consisted in a contest of political principles between different parties.[32] The party supported by the majority of the people deserved to administer the government.

On the problem of sovereignty Ōkuma did not state his ideas clearly. He wished the constitution to be established by imperial sanction. He did not see the necessity of a constituent assembly which could defend the rights and interests of the people. He wanted the establishment of a committee in the cabinet with the task of framing the constitution. But at the same time Ōkuma asked that the constitution make it clear where power was vested and what the rights of the people were. His was essentially a granted constitution, but with clearly stated popular rights. These rights would, after all, be defined by the government. They were not natural rights.

The most controversial proposal was the fifth point of Ōkuma's opinion, in which he advocated the election of the House of Representatives at the end of 1882 and the convocation of the national assembly early in 1883. Being identified with the notion of radicalism and rapid progress, this article particularly invited the opposition of the other leaders.

Up to 1881 Ōkuma had never advocated government by political parties, and many hypotheses have been presented to explain his change.[33] On the fundamental problems of sovereignty, decision, and imperial power, Ōkuma agreed with other leaders. The constitution was not to be decided by a constituent assembly, but was to be granted by the emperor. Ōkuma regarded an imperial decreee as absolute, something which no citizen could or should challenge. The emperor remained very much in the center of his political thought: "The ultimate objective of constitutional government is the prosperity of the Imperial Household and the welfare of the people." He often repeated that the true function of government was to "work for the everlasting preservation of the dignity and prosperity of the Imperial Household and the happiness of the people."[34] Ōkuma, like Itō, Inoue, and Yamagata, was stressing the principle of the prosperity of the Imperial Household.

After these memorials of the junior councilors had been submitted to the throne, they formed the basis for a discussion between Sanjō, Arisugawa, and Iwakura.[35] In July 1881 Iwakura sent two documents to Sanjō and Arisugawa, the first presenting his "Opinion on the Constitution," and the second explaining the fundamental principles to be included in the future constitution.[36]

Iwakura's opinion on the constitution was divided into three parts. In the first part Iwakura compared the English and Prussian constitutional systems. He observed that although the purposes of constitutional government in the various countries of Europe were generally the same, methods and procedures differed according to the level of civilization, national polity, and customs. Japan, too, had to find the methods and procedures applicable to its own peculiar situation and its national polity.

In discussing England, Iwakura wrote: "The English Parliament has not only legislative power but also administrative. An English proverb says: Parliament can do everything but change men into women, and women into men."[37] The reason for parliament's great power, he said, was that the king, according to the customary law of England, did not exercise political power by himself, but entrusted it to the prime minister, who depended on a majority in parliament. Although sovereignty was nominally shared by the king and parliament, sovereignty in fact resided in parliament; as a French saying puts it, "Le roi règne et ne gouverne pas." Iwakura concluded his analysis of the British system by observing that it did not differ from the system Japan had enjoyed from the early Middle Ages up to the restoration, when the real political power resided in the military government and the emperor had no say in political matters.

In contrast to the English system, the Prussian system accepted a division in the exercise of legislative power between king and parliament, but the administrative or executive power resided solely in the hands of the king. This power was not transferred, and the king appointed the prime minister without any consideration of the majority or minority groups in parliament. The executive power was never subject to the control of the political parties in the national assembly.

Japan had to decide whether to adopt a system close to that of England or one close to that of Prussia. As Iwakura phrased the problem:

> If we plan to establish a constitutional government in our country and open a parliament, we will be creating something new. The problem is: shall we follow the English model and establish a party government, making the parliamentary majority responsible for the administration? Or shall we, following the principle of gradualism, grant only legislative power and reserve the executive power to the Emperor, according to the Prussian model? Today's decision between these two alternatives will establish a permanent foundation and determine the interests of the country for a hundred years. It is, therefore, an extremely important problem.[38]

Iwakura gave two reasons for not adopting the English system in Japan. First, in England the two-party system was already well developed and the two parties were mature enough to take the responsibility of governing the country, whereas in Japan there were no parties which could take over the government if the present leaders resigned. The small political parties would fight among themselves and the political arena would become a battlefield. The final solution would probably be the resort to arms. Second, there were not enough capable people in Japan to take over the duties of the administration in the case of a change of system. There would be chaos, and everybody would struggle for power.[39]

This kind of reasoning probably derives from the simple human inclination of those who have power to hold on to it. The contention that those who know best should be the custodians of power applies to the leaders of Meiji Japan. The claim of the educated few to manage the affairs of society until there has been gradual progress in the enlightenment of the masses is not, however, an exclusive characteristic of the Meiji leaders. In similar fashion white colonialists used the theory of the white man's burden, and postcolonial native leaders have clearly stated that without discipline, that is, whithout some kind of totalitarian regime, true freedom cannot survive.[40]

In the second part of his opinion Iwakura proposed the steps to be taken in case the Prussian system of government should be adopted: "There shall be a clear statement in the constitution that the emperor has the responsibility to select the ministers and officials of high rank."[41] The emperor would have the power to appoint and dismiss these ministers and high officials without being controlled by parliament. Even in the case of a lack of majority in parliament the cabinet would not have to resign or change its general policy. Cabinet responsibility would not be collective. If the ministers' responsibility were collective, then the cabinet would be subject to frequent changes. In order to prevent total domination of the national assembly over the cabinet Iwakura suggested that the constitution adopt a provision of the Prussian constitution, that the taxes of the previous year remain in force. This was a safety valve in case the assembly and the cabinet could not agree on the annual budget.

The third part of Iwakura's opinion described in more detail the provision concerning the annual budget, and criticized some of the draft constitutions. The document accompanying the opinion had the title "General Principles." In it Iwakura pointed out the fundamental principles which had to be embodied in the constitution:

1. The Constitution shall emanate from the Emperor and the policy of a gradual approach toward constitutional government shall prevail.

2. The Emperor shall have supreme command over the army and navy, declare war, make peace, conclude treaties, etc.; moreover, the Emperor will direct the national administration.

3. The organization of the cabinet shall not be subjected to the intervention of parliament. Except for those administrative affairs that are of fundamental importance to the state, for which all ministers shall be jointly responsible, each minister shall only be individually responsible for administrative affairs under his official jurisdiction. Ministers shall be responsible to the Emperor and not to parliament.

4. Parliament shall consist of two houses: an upper house composed of members appointed by the Emperor and members elected from among the ranks of peers and former samurai; and a lower house of popularly elected representatives.

5. The election law for the lower house shall include a property qualification for the suffrage, while the electors for the peerage and ex-samurai shall not be subjected to property qualifications.

6. All legislative bills shall be initiated by the government.

7. When parliament does not pass an annual budget bill, the government may execute the provisions of the budget of the previous year.

8. With regard to the rights of the citizens, constitutional provisions of other nations shall be consulted.[42]

Inasmuch as many of the principles enumerated above were embodied later in the Meiji Constitution of 1889, it is clear that Japan's fundamental law conformed to the essentials expressed by Iwakura in his "General Principles." It is interesting to note that, with the exception of the suggestion that only the government could initiate legislation, all the tenets of Iwakura's thought were incorporated in the Meiji Constitution. Thus eight years before the final formulation of the Meiji Charter the basic points had already been decided. The question arises how Iwakura had come to have these ideas and how the principles were formulated. The historians Suzuki Yasuzō and Inada Masatsugu[43] have traced the compilation of these documents with great detail. When Iwakura saw Ōkuma's opinion, he was startled at the radicalism of the proposals. He thought it necessary not only to refute Ōkuma's propositions, but also to determine in an unmistakable way the fundamental principles which had to be the guiding points in framing the constitution. For this reason he called Inoue Kowashi and entrusted him with the task of examining the constitutional problem. Inoue consulted Hermann Roesler, the German adviser on legal matters, and from their collaboration emerged Iwakura's "Opinion" and the "General Principles."[44]

The final results of the debate on gradualism and radicalism were the cancellation of the proposed sale of the Hokkaido development enterprises, the expulsion of Ōkuma from the government, and the imperial rescript in which the government promised to establish a parliament in 1890 and to prepare a constitution in the meantime. Since the establishment of the Colonization Bureau in 1869 for the purpose of opening Hokkaido to settlement and to economic development, the government had spent more than fourteen million yen on the project, promoting education, establishing agricultural industries and farming institutions, founding and laying out schools and towns. Early in 1881 the new government policy of turning over some of its industries to private hands had been inaugurated, and in addition the ten-year appropriation for Hokkaido was to expire in 1882. The scandal over the disposal of government property in Hokkaido erupted when the public learned that the newly formed Kansai Trading Company had been assured that the government properties in Hokkaido would be sold to them for the ridiculous price of 387,082 yen. Even the newspaper *Nichi nichi shimbun,* generally inclined to defend the official position, in this case strongly attacked the corruption of the bureaucracy. Under the pressure of public opinion the government canceled the sale.[45]

Ōkuma was forced out of the government because his proposals that the diet be opened by 1883 and that the government be based on political parties were viewed by the other junior councilors and ministers as too precipitous. Ōkuma's ouster from the government signaled the loss of the leading contender against the Satsuma-Chōshū monopoly of the principal posts in the government and the defeat of the advocates of parliamentary government along British lines.[46] The imperial rescript promising the establishment of a parliament was promulgated on October 12, 1881. Among other things it declared: "Systems of government differ in different countries, but sudden and unusual changes cannot be made without great inconvenience . . . We therefore hereby declare that We shall, in the twenty-third year of Meiji (1890), establish a Parliament, in order to carry into full effect the determination We have announced, and We charge Our Faithful subjects bearing Our commission to make, in the meantime, all necessary preparations to that end."[47]

On October 21, 1881, a special bureau was established in the Dajōkan to assist in drafting laws and regulations, its special task being to act as a consultative committee on laws pertaining to the framing of the constitution.[48] Itō Hirobumi was selected as chairman, with Tanaka Fujimaro as his deputy; members included Saionji Kimmochi, Inoue Kowashi, Itō Miyoji, Hirata Tōsuke, and Kiyoura Keigo. On March 3, 1882, the emperor ordered Itō to lead a mission to Europe to observe and study the different constitutional system in order to collect material for the formulation of the Japanese constitution.[49]

The opinions that have been examined so far were those of the ruling group who had direct political control of the decision-making process. Motoda Eifu, a bureaucrat of the Imperial Household, often stood in open opposition to the ruling group. For about twenty years he was the tutor and unofficial adviser of Emperor Meiji. He more than anyone else was responsible for the important role played by traditional ideas in the crystallization of moral and educational thought in the later part of the Meiji era. Only his ideas on the constitution will be discussed here.

Motoda's political creed was based essentially on Confucianism. He advocated the establishment of a national assembly, but he justified it purely on the basis of expediency. In a proposal he made to the emperor in June 1879 concerning the framing of a constitution, he asserted that the popular agitation for a parliament and for the people's rights movement and the revolts of the last few years were all protests against the despotic methods and arbitrary ways of the Sat-Chō (Satsuma-Chōshū coalition) government. Because of these circumstances the creation of a popular assembly was inevitable, and it would be wisest to convoke one before being compelled to do so by public opinion. He also urged the emperor to take steps at once toward the granting of a constitution. Two years later he made the same point with even greater urgency: "If we put these matters aside today and defer until later, the mad outpourings of mistaken Western ideas, growing worse daily, will finally become uncontrollable, and the harm to the Imperial Household will be incalculable. This is why I consider it essential to establish a constitution today."[51]

In the debate between radicalism and gradualism Motoda could be considered a radical in that he advocated the immediate establishment of a constitution and assembly. However, the constitution had to be based on the unchanged *kokutai*. In this he sided with the most conservative member of the ruling group, Ōki Takatō. By *kokutai* he meant direct rule by the imperial line, descended from the Sun Goddess Amaterasu, and ruling the nation as a family. Changes in the form of government (*seitai*) to meet the special needs of the times could be recommended, provided they were designed to preserve the *kokutai*. Indeed, Motoda pointed out, there had already been many changes in the past, such as Shōtoku Taishi's Seventeen-Article Constitution, the Taika Reform, and the Taihō Code.[52] But concessions on the matter of sovereignty could never be allowed. Sovereignty could not be divided between the emperor and parliament, for to do so would mean an imitation of Western ways that would violate the *kokutai*. A constitution proper for Japan should be granted by the emperor out of his benevolence to the people, constitution based on "the correct way of heaven and earth, founded in the correct way of the ancestors and the national polity, and appropriate to the custom and conditions of the people, high and low, in the past and in the present."[53]

In 1880 Motoda prepared a document entitled "Kokken taikō" (General principles of the constitution), which consisted of seven fundamental points:

1. The Japanese nation is ruled by one divinely descended Imperial line unbroken for ages eternal.

2. The people of Japan revere their Emperor of one line unbroken for ages eternal. Whatever disturbances may occur, they cannot oppose the Emperor.

3. The national teaching takes as its principle benevolence, duty, propriety, deference, loyalty, filial piety, uprightness, and honesty. Sovereign and people, high and low, constitution and laws, none can depart from these principles.

4. The Emperor is sacred and inviolable. Whatever disturbances may occur, his person is not affected.

5. The Emperor wields the power of government and education for the entire nation.

6. The Emperor wields the power of reward and punishment, promotion and demotion and life and death over the people of the entire nation. He disposes in accordance with the Constitution and laws.

7. The people possess the right of freedom of person, residence, and property. These rights may not be circumscribed arbitrarily without reference to the law.[54]

It is immediately clear that the first and second articles were derived from the Shintoistic tradition, common also to the draft constitution of the Genrōin and, in general, to the proposals of the government leaders. The third and fifth articles are exclusively derived from Motoda's Confucianism: the emperor is at the same time the ruler and the teacher.

When all the opinions on the constitution had been presented to the emperor, Motoda was asked to comment in writing on these proposals. He read them very carefully, and in June 1881 presented his views on the different opinions. He did not write much on Yamagata's, Yamada's, or Kuroda's proposals. He accepted Inoue's view that the laws should be based on the customs of the nation, but he rejected Inoue's proposal that the Genrōin be abolished to be replaced by a two-chamber system. He also criticized Inoue's plan for an upper house half appointed and half popularly elected.[55] Motoda rejected Ōkuma's division between party officials and permanent civil servants, and the theory that constitutional government consisted in a contest of political principles between political parties. He accepted Ōkuma's principle that the government should be held by leaders of merit and ability, but he did not agree with the idea of having the cabinet chosen according to the majority in parliament, as it was in the British system. He liked Itō's plan for strengthening the Genrōin and for establishing a Board of Audit, but he did not favor the idea of having the members of this board elected directly by the people. Motoda liked Ōki's proposals best, for he adhered strongly to the ideals of the unique Japanese national polity, the sovereignty of the emperor, and the immutability of these concepts.[56]

After giving his criticism on the proposals of the councilors, Motoda presented his own views. His plan dealt principally with the problem of strengthening the imperial prerogatives against any encroachment by a popularly elected parliament. He proposed to strengthen the upper house, making it a bulwark in defense of the emperor's supreme power. All the members of the upper house should be appointed directly by the emperor. The deliberative assembly, too, was conceived as a means of strengthening the throne, for it not only curbed the arbitrary power of the cabinet ministers, but also provided the emperor with a sounding board for useful opinions from the people.

Motoda did not accept the principle of majority rule. He made a distinction between *shūron* (mass opinion) and *kōron* (correct public opinion). *Kōron* is interpreted in the classical meaning of impartial opinion which is in the public interest, as opposed to private or self-interested opinion. *Shūron*, though held by many people, is not necessarily correct public opinion. Motoda attacked those who advocated popular rights as blindly imitating Western ways and as failing to differentiate between the *kokutai* and the *seitai* on the one hand and *shūron* and *kōron* on the other.[57]

It is clear, then, that the Meiji leaders had, first and above all, a deep and abiding loyalty to their nation and considered the throne a necessary institution for the preservation of the country. However, the depth of this loyalty was matched by their commitment to the development in Japan of a progressive society based on Western methods. A proper recognition of this dual commitment will lead to a better understanding of the ambiguous and ambivalent political thought of many of the official leaders of Meiji Japan.

IV

THE DEBATE ON SOVEREIGNTY
AND NATURAL RIGHTS

While the "ins" were presenting their opinions on the constitution and preparing their plans for a reorganization of the political system, the "outs" were also busy in drawing up private draft constitutions. These drafts can be roughly sorted into three groups: those connected with government circles, those having something in common with the drafts of the Tosa school of constitutional thought, and, finally, those related to the Kōjunsha, a political club.[1]

One of the first private drafts to appear was that of the newspaper *Nichi nichi*.[2] It was probably written by Fukuchi Gen'-ichirō, a close friend of Itō Hirobumi and Inoue Kaoru. The *Nichi nichi* draft was closely connected with government circles; and yet even this semiofficial organ, despite its adherence to the principle that sovereign power lay only with the monarch, stated the propriety of a constitution by social contract. The constitution, according to the *Nichi nichi* draft, was a compact between the emperor, the government, and the people. It established the rights and obligations both of those at the top and those at the bottom and determined the rules for a just government. The first chapter of the draft dealt with the powers of the emperor, stating that the emperor was of divine descent. In the second chapter we read that "all Japanese citizens regardless of birth or position are equal before the law. All citizens according to their wealth are obliged to pay taxes. Equality of opportunity is guaranteed for all by law, and individual liberties are protected in the same way for all." Civil liberties were specified as freedom of worship, opinion, and speech and the protection of private property. Citizens were obliged by law to render military service in defense of their country.

Nichi nichi advocated a system of limited monarchy with clearly defined obligations and checks on the power of the emperor. The government envisioned was very close to a parliamentary cabinet system, responsible to the popularly elected assembly. The division of power between parliament and the emperor followed the English pattern.

Only the first chapter in this draft can be called conservative in tendency, in that it affirmed the special origin of the emperor and his inviolability. The other chapters were relatively liberal in their inspiration and proposals. The government was to be a parliamentary one, but was not to be totally independent of the emperor. The emperor would still have some powers, unchecked and uncontrolled by the popularly elected assembly. Suffrage was not to be universal, but at the same time it was not too narrowly restricted. Rights of citizens were recognized, but the proviso "under the limits of law" could restrict and even cancel them. Provisions about the judiciary were among the most liberal. The freedom of the judiciary from administrative pressure was strongly defended. Although the source of judicial power was recognized to be the emperor, the *Nichi nichi* draft upheld the complete independence of the courts.

After *Nichi nichi* published its draft, the newspaper *Tōkyō Yokohama mainichi* published a few editorials commenting on it.[3] One of the strongest criticisms was that civil rights were restricted by the proviso "according to the limits established by the law." *Mainichi* presented a revised draft of the articles on civil rights. All of them were changed into a negative formulation— for instance, "Parliament cannot limit the freedom of speech or press." As for the conscription law, *Mainichi* objected to such a compulsory system and advocated a method of voluntary military service. But even in *Mainichi's* revisions there appeared a moderate tendency, in not giving all the legislative and executive power to parliament; the emperor was still endowed with considerable power of control.

It is interesting that *Mainichi* and another newspaper, *Chōya shimbun,* strongly attacked the first article of the *Nichi nichi* draft, in which it was stated that the emperor is divine. The reasoning of this attack was that if the emperor were designated as a different kind of human being, then he would be under no obligation to follow the constitution; the divinity of the emperor would therefore be an expedient tool for defending absolutism and despotism. This criticism was well directed, and it was the tragedy of the Japanese liberals that they did not press this fundamental point constantly and strongly enough.[4]

The second group of private drafts belongs to the Tosa school. The drafts in the Tosa tradition are especially distinguishable for their French civil rights orientation. They are identified with the name of Tosa since this was the home of the Risshisha political party, which influenced most of them. The draft constitution representing the Risshisha, known as the "Nihon kempō mikomi-an" (Constitution of Japan: a prospective draft),[5] was prepared by Sakamoto Namio, Ueki Emori, and others. In this draft it was stated that the essential role of a constitution was to limit political power and to guarantee the rights and the liberties of the people. The constitution, therefore, could not be changed without the people's participation. It was clearly stated that the central government was to be limited by the local autonomy of the prefectures. Perhaps for local reasons the Risshisha supported a federal basis for the Japanese government.

In this draft there were no distinctions made between persons in superior and inferior positions before the law. Civil liberties were to be guaranteed: habeas corpus, freedom of opinion, speech, and press, and property rights. Citizens were to pay only those taxes which had been assessed by the national assembly, and they were to be subjected only to those laws which had been approved by parliament. Freedom of association, the right to choose one's residence and job, and freedom of education and of literature—all these rights were stated and defended.

The chapter on civil rights was based on the French constitutions of 1791 and of 1793, and on the Dutch constitution of 1815. Herbert Spencer's *Social Statics* (London, 1850) was also consulted. The Risshisha draft was a strong democratic document. There was no declaration of rights as a preamble, but the fundamental civil liberties of a democratic regime were all there. The legislative power was to belong to the national assembly, and the emperor could veto legislative measures only once. The assembly would have, moreover, the right to conclude treaties with foreign countries, to declare war, and to make peace. The inviolability of the emperor was not recognized; he could be removed from office either for residing abroad or for treason. The sovereignty of the people was stated without reservation. The parliament was to be composed of one chamber, and practically all the decisions of the emperor were subject to the approval of the diet. The resulting system of government was to be one of constitutional monarchy in which the final power of decision rested with the diet alone.

This draft was very progressive, but even more liberal was the draft prepared by Ueki Emori in 1881, entitled "Nihonkoku kokken-an" (Draft constitution of the Japanese nation).[6] On August 18, 1881, Ueki wrote an editorial in the newspaper *Kōchi shimbun*. The constitutions of England, America, and other Western countries, he wrote, could not be considered as ideal and perfect. They had been drafted under special circumstances, often preserving a great number of bad feudal customs. It would be fatal for Japan to praise such charters unconditionally and to try to copy them. Japan should take advantage of a superior ideology to defend the characteristic rights of the Japanese citizens and to preserve the happiness of the country. It should build an ideal constitution based upon reason, democracy, freedom, and equality. In this editorial Ueki criticized all the previous drafts because they were not radical enough.[7]

Ueki's draft constitution, in words reminiscent of the declaration of rights of the French constitution of 1793, stated that the "supreme power of the Japanese nation resides in the whole Japanese people, and is one and indivisible, inviolable, and inalienable."[8] It advocated a federal form of government based on the Swiss constitution of 1848. Under the draft the various prefectures would have very broad autonomous powers, only being deprived of sovereign power in matters of foreign policy; in matters of police, economic problems, and local laws they were independent.

The most important part of this draft was the fourth chapter, which defined the rights and liberties of the citizens. All citizens were to be equal before the law, and there were to be no restrictions on the freedom of individuals but those established by law. All the civil rights were to be recognized and guaranteed: habeas corpus; bearing of arms; freedom of opinion, speech, press, assembly, education, occupation; guarantee of life and health; freedom of religion and worship; rewards and punishments only according to law and established rules; and, finally, the right of open resistance against oppressive governments.

The powers of the emperor were to be limited. He would have the right to ask the legislature for a re-examination of bills approved by the assembly. Only the legislature could make treaties, but the emperor could declare war and make peace. He would also have the power of amnesty, but only after the approval of parliament. The ruler would have no power in matters affecting the rights of the people, the disbursement of funds or changes in state territory.

The sixth chapter of the draft was dedicated to the legislature. Legislative power was to reside in the whole nation and be vested in a unicameral assembly. The legislature was to decide matters of customs duties and internal tariffs, regulate military and judicial laws, control the postal service and the currency, and determine laws concerning foreigners. It could not, however, interfere in the internal affairs of the autonomous prefectures.

The tendency of this draft was to strengthen the rights of prefectures and individuals against the central government. The rights of the individual were to be made inviolable, although, following the Prussian constitution, some civil rights could be revoked in case of war. This document contained probably the most advanced statement of civil liberties. The principles of popular sovereignty, responsible government, separation of powers, federal government, and limited monarchy were also strongly defended. A third draft, drawn up in northern Kyushu by the Chikuzen kyōaikai,[9] belonged also to the Tosa group, although it provided for a bicameral system.

The third category of constitutional drafts, associated with the thought of the Kōjunsha club, was conspicuous because it adopted English constitutional practices. The "Shigi kempō-an" (Private draft constitution)[10] framed by the Kōjunsha was the most characteristic. This document followed closely the description of the British system in Alphaeus Todd's *Parliamentary Government in England,* but constitutions of other countries were also consulted.[11] The emperor, according to this draft, was to rule the country through the cabinet and through the two houses of parliament. He was to be sacred and inviolable, and to exercise his executive power through the cabinet. The annual budget was to be decided by parliament, and with the sanction of the emperor it would become law. The Kōjunsha draft provided for a bicameral system and for a qualified franchise, and the rights of the people were restricted by certain conditions.

Yūbin hōchi shimbun published a draft constitution in 1881 entitled "Shikō kempō sōan" (Private constitutional draft).[12] Its contents are almost identical with the Kōjunsha draft, differing only in formulation and order. Other drafts, too, were greatly influenced by the British constitutional system.

The draft prepared by the Kōjunsha was strongly criticized by Iwakura Tomomi in his opinion on the constitution. He wrote:

The first suggestion that the emperor appoint and dismiss ministers and the second that we seek to avoid collective responsibility are opposed to the opinions of those persons who advocate the establishment of a constitution now. Article 9 of the private draft constitution presented by the Kōjunsha states: "Cabinet ministers shall be of one mind, carry out foreign and domestic affairs, and be collectively responsible." Article 12 states: "The prime minister shall be selected by the emperor according to the will of the people. The other ministers shall be appointed on the recommendation of the prime minister." Article 13 declares: "Cabinet ministers shall be members of the Genrōin or the House of Representatives." Article 17 determines: "When the opinion of the cabinet and the opinion of parliament do not agree, the cabinet ministers shall resign or by special power of the emperor they shall dissolve the lower house." The basic intent of these articles is to establish a "collectively responsible cabinet form of government." Moreover, when the cabinet does not agree with parliament, it will thereupon resign from office and be replaced by one that has the support of parliament. This so-called concept of the alternation of party cabinets is something based on the model of England.[13]

Iwakura opposed these ideas of the Kōjunsha as radical and extreme, leading necessarily to the destruction of the national polity.

The imperial announcement on October 12, 1881, that a

national assembly would be convoked in 1890 marked the beginning of an intensified debate on constitutional problems. Now that the government had committed itself to the convocation of a national assembly and to the establishment of a constitutional form of government, new controversies emerged. Among the crucial problems to be decided none was more important than the fundamental question of sovereignty.[14] The issue was essentially that of the site of sovereign power, whether it reposed in the people, in the monarch, or in both. The "ins" did not take part in this debate directly, but they were well represented by people very close to the official position.

The debate on sovereignty had already begun even before the imperial announcement of October 1881. In September of that year, the Shimeikai, a political club, was founded. Its members were for the most part conservative leaders of the Kumamoto area.[15] In its program the Shimeikai stated with great alarm that the theory of popular sovereignty, invented in Europe a century before, had spread like a violent fire over the world, causing great disaster. It had been propagated also in Japan and there was the imminent danger that it would destroy the traditional structure of the Japanese *kokutai* by advocating a republican form of government. According to Inada Masatsugu, this program was drafted by Inoue Kowashi.[16]

Kōchi shimbun answered immediately with an editorial of October 7, 1881. It said, "In the words of Rousseau, society is built upon a social contract. This is not completely according to historical data, and, therefore, we cannot easily agree with him. However, we firmly believe that society should not exist without a social contract. Thus, we are convinced that sovereignty must reside in the people. Since the people is the nucleus of the state, without the people the state cannot exist. If there is the people, even without a king, society can exist."[17]

On November 9, *Mainichi* published an editorial entitled

"Shuken no shozai ikan" (On the location of the sovereign power).[18] It argued that there were three theories of sovereignty. The first claimed that one person, the monarch, was the locus of sovereignty. Sovereignty thus would become the privilege of the monarch and his will would be law. The second theory located sovereignty in the people, following the traditional reasoning of the Chinese, "Since the Emperor Sun is a man, we too are men." The third theory stated that sovereignty resided neither in one person nor in the people, but in justice. *Mainichi* rejected the first view because, it said, all men were equal; the second because the will of the people was subject to continuous change, and being unstable therefore could not be the source of law. The third view, making justice the repository of sovereignty, was accepted by *Mainichi* as the best and most suitable. Since the representative of justice was the popular assembly, sovereignty resided in parliament. Underlying the *Mainichi* theory was Blackstone's concept that sovereignty is that force which enacts law.

On December 3, 1881, the newspaper *Tōkyō yoron shinshi* countered this editorial by publishing an article "Shuken gairon" (Introduction to sovereignty).[19] This article denied the validity of all three theories presented by *Mainichi,* saying that the first was irrational, that the social contract theory was against historical evidence, and that the third theory was impossible to define, being too vague and utopian. The editorial concerned itself mainly with the second theory, that of the social contract. It was not likely that society had arisen as the result of a contract since there was no historical fact that would support this hypothesis. Moreover, if society were a consequence of a contract, it would be possible to dissolve society by public design, but from the outset this was a patent impossibility. Individual men were born into society, and thus they could not claim that they had built society by a social contract.

Therefore they could not have the right to destroy society.[20] Sovereignty was supposed to repose both in individual men and in society.

The year 1882 saw the great debate on sovereignty being carried on by two great newspapers representing the two main trends of the time: *Nichi nichi,* identified closely with the official position of the government, and *Mainichi,* the organ of the parties opposing the government. On January 14, 16, and 17, 1882, *Nichi nichi* published a serialized editorial entitled "Shukenron" (The theory of sovereignty). It said: "Sovereignty is the greatest power of the nation. It represents the highest and supreme independent power of the country. In relation to foreign countries sovereignty manifests the national independence and defends the honor of the nation. In domestic politics sovereignty means the center of supreme legislative, executive, and judiciary power."[21] On the problem of the repository of this supreme power *Nichi nichi* explained that it was impossible to give a general answer that would be valid for all countries. Different national characteristics, the people's national spirit, and national customs had to be taken into account before defining where sovereignty ought to reside in the various countries. There could be despotic governments, absolute monarchies, or republics. In the special case of Japan, "given the incomparable, unique, and characteristic national polity," sovereignty resided in the emperor. As there had not been any change for 2,500 years in the imperial line, so also there could not be any change in the *kokutai,* and the sovereign power ought to reside solely in the person of the emperor.

Mainichi answered *Nichi nichi's* arguments in a series of editorials published on January 18-22 and 24, 1882. The general title of the series was "Doku Nippō kisha shukenron" (On reading *Nichi nichi's* theory of sovereignty.[22] Starting from the principle that sovereignty is that force which enacts law, *Mainichi* argued that in a despotic monarchy only the king is the source of law, and in a republic sovereignty resides in the whole people. In the case of a constitutional monarchy, sovereignty resides neither in the king alone nor in the people alone, but in the king and in the people. In fact, "The assembly discusses and agrees upon the bills, the king approves. By this cooperation of powers laws are enacted, and society is kept in order."[23]

Mainichi cited the English system of joint rule of the king and the people (*kummin dōchi*) as the best example of a constitutional monarchy. The English legislative power was entrusted to three independent powers: the king, the House of Lords, and the Commons. Hence England could be called not only a monarchy or a demoracy, but also a system of joint rule of the king and the people. *Mainichi* also made a distinction between sovereignty (*shuken*) and privilege (*kunken*). While the king of England might have some prerogatives (*kunken*), such as the privilege of declaring war and making peace, of dissolving parliament, and of veto, he did not have free and independent legislative power, which alone constituted sovereignty. In fact, the king was subject to the constitution and could not change it at his pleasure.[24]

Nichi nichi in turn attacked *Mainichi*'s position in a series of five article published on January 24, 25, 26, 27, and 28, 1882, entitled "Shuken bemmō" (Vindication of sovereignty).[25] First of all it denied that sovereignty could be equated with legislative power. *Nichi nichi* took the view that sovereignty comprised legislative, executive, and judicial power. The English political system was a constitutional or limited monarchy, which was joint rule by the king and the people. However, though it was called "limited" or "constitutional," this system of government had in common with unlimited or absolute monarchy the fact that sovereignty resided in the king and not in the people. *Nichi nichi* said it was a mistake to call the power of declaring war and making peace, the power of dissolving parliament, and the power of veto, privileges; these were sovereign powers, not privileges. The powers of parliament were granted by the king and must be called privileges, not sovereign powers. To call the king's powers privileges granted by the constitution was to follow the false ideas of the social contract.

Nichi nichi also distinguished between a constitution granted by the king and a constitution formed by a sovereign constituent assembly. In the first case, the king freely delimited his own sovereign power and declared these limits in the constitution. This limitation of power was not imposed on the emperor by an outside power, but was based only on the imperial good will. Thus *Nichi nichi* defended the principle that sovereignty in a monarchy—whether despotic or constitutional—always reposed in the monarch. The principle of imperial sovereignty was even clearer in the case of Japan due to the uniqueness of the Japanese *kokutai*. From the beginning of history in Japan the emperor alone had been the repository of sovereign power, and this tradition could not be changed without a deep revolution in the national structure.

In a new series of articles published on January 21 and February 1-5 and 7, 1882, entitled "Byakujaron" (On a false doctrine), *Mainichi* argued that sovereignty in a constitutional state reposed in the national assembly and the king taken together, the king being but a member of the sovereign body. It was not only his good will that bound the king to observe the constitutional law. If the monarch did not observe the constitution, disobedience on the part of the governed to the king's unconstitutional commands would not be illegal. *Mainichi* was fundamentally in favor of the British system of monarchic government; *Nichi nichi,* on the contrary, based its arguments on the Prussian interpretation of constitutional monarchy. *Nichi nichi* maintained also that the state was organic: "When we declare that the state functions organically, we are comparing the political community to a great body which must have a head to govern it. Sovereignty is the head and brains of the organic state." *Nichi nichi* rejected Rousseau's theory as being "not an aspiration for amelioration but a hope for revolutionary change."[26]

Other newspapers, too, participated in this debate on the problem of sovereignty. *Chōya* took sides with *Mainichi* and defended the principle of joint sovereignty of the king and parliament. However, *Chōya* gave a different definition of sovereignty, not limiting it to the legislative power. *Chōya* defined sovereignty as the supreme and unlimited power of the nation. *Hōchi,* too, sided with the camp advocating a constitutional monarchy according to the English pattern.[27]

To understand the atmosphere in which this debate was carried on, it is useful to quote Fukuchi Gen'ichirō, the editor of *Nichi nichi* at the time:

In past times I discussed current problems following the principle of gradualism. Among these problems the most vexatious was the problem of sovereignty. I always upheld the view that in a monarchic form of government—whether an absolute monarchy or a constitutional monarchy—sovereignty always resides in the king. Whenever the problem of sovereignty emerged I published such views, and I thought that public opinion could not disagree with my position. The Tokyo newspapers let their pens run on, piling article upon article, and I attacked their views. Before long I felt that everybody was my enemy. Hitherto I have often had the experience of being surrounded by my adversaries, and I always kept my presence of spirit. But this time, when the number of enemies refuting my views increased and became more violent and arrogant in their attacks on my theory of sovereignty, it was quite frightening . . . I attacked dissenting views and sought support in foreign scholars, but to my regret I could find none. While I usually felt great respect in my attitude toward the English and American authors, I found that my theory was different from theirs. Their works were useless as a defense against the weapons of my enemies.[28]

It was during this great debate that Nakae Chōmin started the publication of his translation of Rousseau's *Social Contract*. This book, despite the fact that it was translated into an extremely difficult *kambun*, or Chinese, style, was highly influential among the intellectuals.[29] With it Nakae Chōmin contributed most of the ideas for the development of the theory of popular sovereignty. Ueki Emori himself took many of his arguments from the *Social Contract*.

The translation of Rousseau's *Social Contract* was published in installments in the semimonthly *Ōbei seiri sōdan*.[30] Nakae added his own notes to the translation, in which he applied Rousseau's theories to the Japanese situation. Stressing Rousseau's theory of popular sovereignty, Nakae declared that the emperor was but a mere official of the people. He defined sovereignty as the expression of the general will of the people, and the government was but an organ of this supreme will. In this world, according to Nakae, there were only two forms of government: one right and the other wrong. The right one was based on the general will of the people and protected the interests and the welfare of the people. This was the only good system of government because the right to govern belonged to the people alone. Despotic government, based on violence and force, was the wrong system. Sovereignty could not be confused with the prerogatives of the monarch because sovereignty was indivisible and belonged only to the people.

In the *Tōyō jiyū shimbun* of March 24, 1881, Nakae wrote an article "Kummin kyōchi no setsu" (Theory of joint rule), in which he defended a "republican" form of government. "Republican" meant for him a system of government in which the executive and legislative powers resided in the people, that is, a system in which power was public, not the private personal property of an individual or a group. Thus the English system of government was a "republican" regime. Any system based on laws made by the people was a republic. In such a system the monarch was but an administrative officer or a civil servant. Nakae upheld the principle that the government—the emperor and the administration—had a clear mandate to obey the will of the people: they had received in trust the welfare of the nation; they were not the repository of sovereignty.[31]

Ueki Emori published a series of editorials in *Kōchi shimbun*. The common title of these editorials was "Kokka shukenron" (On the sovereignty of the state).[32] For Ueki, sovereignty of the state meant popular sovereignty. He first recapitualated the various theories presented by other newspapers on the problem of sovereignty and then went on to criticize each one as wrong or only partially true. Against *Mainichi,* which made sovereignty the power of making laws, Ueki argued that sovereignty was the highest power, and decided all affairs of state. Legislative power was but one element of this supreme power of the nation.

Ueki attacked *Chōya*'s description of sovereignty as supreme unlimited power, not restricted by anybody and capable of determining everything. Ueki argued that there were clear limits on the power of the state; for example, the state could not destroy or annex other nations; it could not limit the freedom of religion or thought; it could not deprive its citizens of the right of private property. Ueki also rejected the theory of *Nichi nichi,* which made the state an organism and compared sovereignty to the head of this organic body. He also denounced *Hōchi*'s theory making sovereignty the combination of legislative and executive power as insufficient. After this criticism, Ueki attempted his own definition of sovereignty as the supreme, legitimate, and most essential power of the state. He said that sovereignty was supreme within the aims of the state and the means necessary to reach such aims. The state had as its goal the protection of the civil liberties of each citizen, and the sovereignty of the state was thereby limited.

Having defined sovereignty, Ueki examined the repository

of this supreme power of the state. The biggest mistake of *Nichi nichi*'s theory on the location of sovereignty was, according to Ueki, to confuse the actual holder with the legitimate one and the exerciser of this power with the basic repository of sovereignty. The problem of the repository of sovereignty, Ueki said, was not a question of who had it, but a problem of who ought to have it.

Ueki stated that the theory of *Mainichi* making the legislative sovereign (the theory of the king in parliament), was incomplete. In this world there were not only constitutional monarchies, but also republics and absolute monarchies. Yet this did not mean that in republics and absolute states there was no sovereignty. With the exception of the regimes of direct democracy, in the other systems sovereignty was exercised by representatives who operated in the name of the people. In the English parliament there was a total delegation of power; the American congress, on the contary, had clearly defined limits. Ueki argued that the opinions of *Mainichi* and *Chōya* making the king in parliament the repository of sovereignty stemmed from the fact that they did not understand the fundamental truth that the only root of sovereignty was the state and the government was but the executor of this supreme power. Ueki accepted with some reserve *Hōchi*'s theory that in a perfect constitutional monarchy sovereignty resided both in the king and in parliament. But, he concluded, it is much better to hold that sovereignty resides in the state, that is, in the people.[33]

Fukuzawa Yukichi, too, took part in the dispute on sovereeignty. His ideas were developed especially in *Teishitsuron* (Imperial House theory), which was published in May 1882.[34] Fukuzawa stated as the fundamental principle of his *Teishitsuron* that the imperial system was outside and above politics and political power. The Imperial House should not be troubled with political strife, since it belonged to the whole of the Japanese nation and took sides with no one. Politicians should not abuse the sacredness and dignity of the emperor either to defend their theories or to attack their adversaries. Fukuzawa added that the emperor must not lean toward the new nor cling to the old; he must be identified neither with the conservative parties nor with the progressive ones. He must always represent the will of the whole nation.

Fukuzawa's view of the sovereignty of the emperor was that the emperor ought not to exercise political power and control over the affairs of state. Fukuzawa strongly advocated for Japan the British system of constitutional government as the most appropriate to the traditions and feelings of the Japanese nation. As in England, so also in Japan the king must reign but not rule. Through long centuries and trials the British had learned the evils of the king's exercising direct political control and the benefits of his presence as the reigning head of the state.

To the opponents who claimed that such a position for the emperor would destroy the dignity and the sacredness of the imperial system and make it an empty shell, Fukuzawa answered that such a view depended on the false idea which made politics the all-embracing aspect of national life. According to Fukuzawa, politics was only one aspect— and an unpleasant and violent one at that—of national life. It was essentially based on strife, one party fighting the other in order to keep or achieve power. And political power was an extreme thing, like fire and water, like the heat of summer and the cold of winter. The emperor alone was like an eternal spring, which soothes everyone who basks in it. It was fortunate for a nation to possess such a moderating and harmonizing force. Republics did not know the benefits of such a system.

Fukuzawa felt that the emperor must not interfere in the detailed direction of state affairs. The emperor was the symbol of the unity of the nation, and his foremost duty was to encourage goodness, reward virtue, and promote the cultural and spiritual aspects of the nation. Should the emperor meddle in political affairs he would cease to be the center of union and would become the leader of a faction that represented only one part of the nation. The emperor must sign all the bills which had been passed by the diet without having the power of veto. Only in this way would it be possible to preserve the dignity of the emperor. The deliberations, though signed by the emperor, would remain the decisions of the majority in the diet, and should they lead to failure the responsibility would rest with the majority, not with the emperor. The emperor would not become the target of criticism and opposition.

A perfect constitutional system, according to Fukuzawa, involved the principle of the rotation of power. The opposition was always ready to take over the reins of government if the majority failed in its trust, and if the people, through elections, decided that the time had come for a change. In such a perfect political system there was always an alternative available. This situation demanded elements of fluidity, tension, and plurality in the body politic, though at the same time the elements of continuity and union would be preserved by the people's accepting the rules of the game.

According to Fukuzawa, in Japan the parties represented the plurality principle, while the emperor was the symbol of unity and continuity. Thus, the citizens would obey the government because it was the government of their beloved and sacred emperor, but at the same time they could criticize it because it was a government formed by political parties. The division and strife among parties must be based upon a fundamental unity. Parties must be part of a unified whole. The emperor alone, above all division and above all factional interests, was the center to which the sentiments of the whole Japanese nation converged. Especially in times of struggle and crisis the citizens must be able to look up to the emperor and find in him the principle of continuity and union.

In consonance with these ideas Fukuzawa saw as a good sign

the emergence of political parties in Japan, both progressive (the Jiyūtō, or Liberal Party, and the Kaishintō, or Progressive Party) and conservative (the Teiseitō, or Imperial Party). Both conservative and progressive movements must coexist in a constitutional form of government, but even they were not enough for the well-being of the nation. The imperial system was also necessary for the welfare of the Japanese nation. It was wrong to attack the imperial institution in order to advocate the civil rights of the people. So also it was wrong to curtail the civil rights and freedoms of the people, adducing as an excuse the defense of the prerogatives of the emperor. The emperor must be left out of this political strife, for he was the only pacifying force. He had authority but not coercive power. While coercive power forces people to obey, authority makes people obey spontaneously, said Fukuzawa. The more obedience was free from constraint, the greater the prestige and authority of the emperor would become.

When Fukuzawa spoke of the Imperial House, he meant not necessarily individual emperors, but the imperial institution in itself. The prestige of the imperial system was not based on the individual qualities of the emperor; it stemmed mainly from the social, historical, and psychological traditions of the Japanese nation, which from the time of the establishment of a unified state reached the consensus that only one person, the descendant of the unbroken line of the imperial family, could express and give final sanction to the general will of the people.

Fukuzawa did not say that the system he advocated—party government together with the imperial institution as the symbol of unity and as the promoter of arts and culture—was the best for every country in the world. Here, too, he upheld the "relative" principle. The way to express the general will of the state was not the same for all nations; it differed according to different places and different traditions. Fukuzawa thought that the British system of constitutional government was the closest to the Japanese mentality, and thus ought to be the model for the new political system of Japan.

For Fukuzawa constitutional government was not a matter which could be solved by mere laws. Laws could deal only with the outward organization of the state; they could not command the emotion of loyalty. Government depended on a way of life and of national feeling. The unity of the people in a constitutional regime did not belong to the realm of mere speculation; it was based on the imponderable world of feeling and sentiment. A constitutional form of government could only survive if it was backed up by national feeling and tradition. National feelings and historical traditions always contain hidden elements that cannot be expressed in clear and distinct laws. To this imponderable realm of emotions and traditions belonged the imperial system. Fukuzawa's suggestion that the emperor should be kept outside and above politics was not accepted by the framers of the Meiji Constitution. It has, however, become a reality in the postwar constitution of Japan.

The debate on sovereignty was closely connected with the controversy on the natural rights theory. Some of the best-known intellectuals of the day—Katō Hiroyuki, Yano Fumio, Baba Tatsui, Ueki Emori, and others—took part in this new battle. The publication of Katō's *Jinken shinsetsu* (New theory of human rights) in October 1882 marked the beginning of the debate. Katō violently attacked the natural rights theory as an illusion and a strange fancy. Yano wrote his *Jinken shinsetsu bakuron* (Refutation of *Jinken shinsetsu*) in November 1882. He also published a series of editorials in *Mainichi* entitled "Criticism of *Jinken shinsetsu*." Two months later, in January 1883, Baba Tatsui published *Tempu jinkenron* (On natural rights), and in the same month Ueki Emori published the famous *Tempu jinkemben* (In defense of natural rights). Katō presented a theory of the state based on positivism, evolutionism, and power. All the others attacked Katō's views and defended a liberal progressive system based on a universal basis of inalienable human rights.[35]

Katō Hiroyuki has given us a vivid description about the change of his political ideals from liberalism to conservatism:

> I, too, once worshipped the doctrine of natural rights. My early writings, the *Shinsei tai-i* and the *Kokutai shinron* among others, greatly evidence this orientation. Later, after I came to believe in the truth of the theory of evolution, I developed serious doubts over the validity of natural rights. When I investigated the writings of various theoreticians, I was not able to find any attacking this theory. It was in November 1879—I have forgotten the day—that I first made a speech attacking the natural rights theory. I also made a similar speech on March 7, 1880. In June of that year I read a book by Carneri, an Austrian, which argued the relation between morality and evolutionism. This book held that Darwin's theory of evolution made possible a proper understanding of mental phenomena. It pointed out that the theory of natural rights had no validity. We are not "endowed" with rights; we *acquire* them. For the first time I saw clearly that our rights are those which we as individuals have been able to acquire . . . I saw clearly that our individually acquired rights are inextricably tied to the fortunes of our country. I felt an indescribable joy at finding views which I had begun to hold earlier expressed in this book. Later, in a work on the history of civilization written by the German Henne am Rhyn, I again found confirmation of my view that the natural rights theory was mistaken. This book held that the strong suppress the weak, the superior dominate the inferior; that this was an unchanging law of nature from ancient times to the present.[36]

Henry Thomas Buckle's classic *History of Civilization in England* (London, 1857, 1861) made Katō realize that "metaphysics was an illusion." The works of Darwin, Spencer, and Haeckel were also influential in changing Katō's cosmologic concepts and his philosophy of life. It was probably his positivistic outlook that made the theory of natural rights unacceptable to him. For Katō, natural rights could not be established as a concrete scientific phenomenon, but were an abstract construct of mind. Using the Darwinian theory of natural selection, he refuted the claim that man is born with the right of liberty, equality, and self-government. He argued that there were variations among men owing to differences in heredity and environment.

Katō attacked Rousseau as a proponent of chimeric ideas without precedent from ancient times to the present. The theory of natural rights could not be established as a historical fact by any proof or test; it was nothing more than a wild fancy. On the other hand, the theory of evolution, which contained the principle of the survival of the fittest, was indeed the manifestation of a universal law. In the face of this great truth, according to Katō, the natural rights theory should vanish like a mirage, for there was nothing more fantastic than the statement that all men are born free and with the natural right to self-government. The proponents of natural rights stated that since these rights were given by nature they could not be violated or alienated. But, Katō said, there was no proof that these rights existed; they were fancies in the mind of utopian scholars.

Evolutionism, however according to Katō, could be proved scientifically. In ancient times, as in the primitive societies of today, the only rule was the survival of the fittest, and there were no natural rights. But as the world progressed in enlightenment, the level of intellectual vigor increased, and the evil aspects of the struggle for existence and the survival of the fittest diminished. In the struggle for survival, competition for power was the most violent. In Japan, as well as in Europe, the military classes and the nobility had obtained political power and the right to determine the general trends of society. In America and in Europe there had been a recent change. The middle classes had reached political power because they had achieved a superior level of spiritual and intellectual power, enough to sway society in accordance with their wishes. Katō said:

According to this theory [evolutionism and the survival of the fittest], the gradations of inferior and superior in plants and animals are a result of the double process of heredity and mutation. Consequently, to accomplish the purpose of the maintenance and growth of life mutual competition is generated, in which the superior always conquers and the inferior is defeated. Only in this way is life carried on. By this means alone, is it possible to transmit one's acquisitions to one's descendants; and this eternal and unchanging principle of nature can be said to be the supreme rule for all. The universe is like one great scene of carnage. In order to preserve their existence and to aggrandize themselves, all things are in constant competition on this battlefield and strive mightily in this battle to the finish. The result of this is always the confirmation of the principle of the survival of the fittest.[37]

This fact, said Katō, had been confirmed by historical evidence from ancient times to the present, and it wiped out any specious proof of the existence of natural rights to liberty, equality, and independence. The only rights which exist are those which have been taken by force from others.[38]

In the second chapter of *Jinken shinsetsu* Katō dealt with the origin and progress of rights.[39] He quoted Carneri to prove that there are no natural human rights, only acquired rights. These rights live or die with one's own country. Rights come into being together with the establishment of the state, through the protection of the ruler, in whose hands resides the supreme power. All sorts of rights originated in progressive stages as acquired rights and were consequent upon the growth and perfection of the state and of a solidly based society.

In the third chapter Katō discussed plans to advance the progress of human rights.[40] He adopted the doctrine of gradualism, stating that political reforms and political institutions had to be adapted to the level of the civilization of the various countries. There were some rights which were suitable for the European situation, but they were unsuited to oriental nations because these nations had a lower level of civilization. Since the emergence of the natural rights theory radical plans had been proposed: an electoral system with universal suffrage, a unicameral parliament, a party-cabinet system, and a popular election of prefectural officials. The people's rights movement was advocating fantastic reforms which had not ever been practiced even in Europe or America. They would lead the country to a republican form of government or even to a socialistic and communistic society.[41]

Katō was astute enough to see that the theory of the survival of the fittest was a two-edged sword. If in the competition between the people's rights movement and the government the former won, Katō, according to his theory, would be forced to admit that the victory was a legitimate one. Accordingly, though he began by using the notion of the survival of the fittest to attack natural rights, he then modified it into a different theory. First, he said, it was not physical prowess that counted among human beings, but rather mental fitness. Then he introduced a distinction between real and false survival. He admitted that sometimes inferior groups attain power, but claimed that this was a temporary phenomenon and could not become permanent. He specifically attacked the people's rights movement, saying that if the people fought the government, they would bring harm to society.

Yano Fumio, in his *Jinken shinsetsu bakuron*, strongly criticized Katō's views.[42] He accused Katō of ignoring the fundamental distinction between human law and the law of nature. If these two laws were the same, then Katō would be right in affirming his rule of the survival of the fittest, and the strong and the fit would have a right to oppress the weak. But, Yano said, these two laws are different. The physical situation (the law of nature) might well change, but human rights based on human law do not change. The rights of human beings, according to Yano, are divided into legal and moral principles, and the legal ones are based on the moral ones. The source of moral principles is, moreover, the fact that heaven endows human beings with reason, which is simply the principle of the greatest happiness for the greatest number. Human rights are based on the unchangeable human nature, whose fundamental aspects include the struggle for survival, social inclinations, and the intellectual power to create the greatest happiness. The struggle for survival resists invasion of individual rights, but at the same time the social nature of man works toward the common welfare, and intellectual power works to create the greatest happiness for the greatest number.

Human rights, wrote Yano, are not like the laws of nature, which inevitably follow their course, but instead are from time to time violated. This violation notwithstanding, it is precisely in the existence of the right to oppose and revolt that man's natural rights are expressed: "A tyrannical government is biased and partial in its attitude toward the people; to one section it affords an irrational happiness, to another irrational hardship. These classes are extremely unequal and greatly unbalanced; one segment of the people thus inflicts humiliations on the other. To prevent this inequality and unevenness, which lead to irrational infliction of humiliation, to escape this by the power of that rationality which is concomitant with equality, is consequent upon the natural right to equality."[43]

Baba Tatsui, too, attempted a refutation of Katō's principles. In his *Tempu jinkenron,* he argued that there is in truth a distinction between tangibles and intangibles. The truth of mankind is made up of abstract principles like liberty, equality, happiness—in other words, spiritual principles—and one of these is the principle of natural rights. In this connection Baba wrote: "Katō Hiroyuki supposes that because men have from ancient times struggled for existence and have often left evidence of having made progress, that this is how progress is accomplished. Katō then presents this as the only way in which progress can be made."[44] According to Baba, Katō was presenting a particular fact of the past as a general principle, elevating a past experience to a universal rule.

Ueki Emori's refutation of Katō's evolutionism was centered especially on the concept of happiness. A human being has the right to devote his life to happiness, and this very right of happiness is naturally endowed and proved by the fact that only human beings have the impulse to seek it. Happiness summarizes all the rights and laws of human beings: "From this word 'happiness' the rights which man is naturally endowed with should be clear. Man's aspiration for happiness is something which comes from nature. And by the fact that man acquires happiness, he demonstrates that he is fit to receive this gift. Therefore, for man to plan on happiness is in accord with reason, which is an attribute of man, and it is moreover proper for man to achieve this. This is a right which concerns man. Can this, then, not be called a natural human right?"[45]

The Japanese liberals had adopted the modern European natural rights theory and blended it with utilitarian theories without stopping to think of the difficulties involved in such theories.[46] And Katō, by applying the theory of the survival of the fittest to defend the status quo was adopting another form of natural rights theory, reserved to the privileged classes, without admitting that only struggle could decide who the fittest were. In this way not stability, but a permanent violent revolution, could be the only form of social organization.

The debates on sovereignty and natural rights were fought chiefly by borrowing liberally from Western authors. Fukuchi Gen'ichirō of *Nichi nichi* was probably unique in using the traditional Japanese *kokutai* in defending his theory of sovereignty. However, even Fukuchi often used Burke and Austin in his arguments. Katō clearly stated that Carneri, Jhering, Schaeffle, and Henne am Rhyn had given him the best arguments in defense of his theories. Rousseau, Mill, Bluntschli, Buckle, Spencer, Darwin, Burke, Hobbes, and many other Western authors were introduced to Japanese circles. While all these authors had formulated their theories in answer to some concrete historical and sociopolitical situation, in Japan their theories were often transplanted to a different milieu and given a universal value.

The early debates on gradualism and radicalism allowed free discussion on the position of the emperor. The ideas expressed in Katō Hiroyuki's *Kokutai shinron* were the common opinion of the Meirokusha and the intellectuals of the day. The ruler and the people were not of a different nature, but both had the same rights. To say that all the land was the private property of the emperor or that all the people were his retainers was despicable nonsense. In the second decade of the Meiji era, however, the theories on the emperor became more complex and confused.

From the second decade on, both the ruling group and the opposition accepted the principle that the emperor occupied a special position in the Japanese nation. The rulers insisted on the principle of political sovereignty of the emperor; the intellectuals outside of the government often had recourse to what could be called the spiritual and cultural transcendence of the imperial system. Motoda Eifu was the most explicit in combining both spiritual and cultural pre-eminence and political sovereignty. It is also interesting to observe that, while in the first decade only one anonymous draft constitution used the term *Tennō* (literally, "heavenly emperor") when referring to the emperor, and all the other drafts used *kōtei* (emperor) or *teiō* (monarch)—terms used when dealing with non-Japanese monarchs—from 1880 on, *Tennō* became the usual term in all constitutional drafts.[47]

This attitude of sentimental attachment to the imperial institution explains many seeming contradictions and ambiguities in the political theories of many leaders in early Meiji Japan. Beyond this agreement on the special place of the emperor, we find a deep gulf between the two opposing camps. There was, first of all, the problem of generations. In the early eighties—and especially in the mid-eighties—the gap brought about a dislocation of unusual magnitude in Meiji Japan. Ueki Emori and his liberal group were all in their twenties or early thirties.[48] The people in the government were in their forties or older.[49] The ruling group had already made a revolution, the intellectuals of the people's rights movement were too young to judge the present with knowledge of the past. The young were eager to push forward with further social and political transformations. For the older leaders, the revolution had already been accomplished, in the main, and they wanted now to stabilize and organize what they had already achieved.

The work of destruction, according to the older generation, could not continue indefinitely, and society had to be oriented toward reconstruction. The young intellectuals wanted a more thorough job done of destruction and revolution; the old, in their desire to strengthen the new social and political order, were looking more and more toward conservative traditions from which society and the state could take their identity.

The attempt to stabilize Japanese society, after the exhilarating era of civilization and enlightenment, forced a re-examination of the historical and social context in which Japan was living. It was here that a deeper sense of national consciousness gradually emerged. The first period was characterized by the desire for national unification and national independence: Westernization, civilization, and enlightenment were essentially means to those goals. Now a new period began, the period of national identification. Constitutionalism was accepted as a necessary element of the new nation, but the tendency became stronger and stronger among the government leaders to have a Japanese form of constitutionalism. The forces brought into play by the far-reaching educational, economic, and social changes decreed by the Meiji leadership prevented a complete return to the past, but at the same time the unchecked spirit of freedom and equality that was the result of the contact with Western thought was now considered dangerous for the survival of the Japanese nation. The natural rights theory, with its implication of equality and freedom, was now attacked as corrosive to the social order. Conservative theories were sought both in traditional Japan and in Western currents of thought.

The second reason for the gulf between the government and the people's rights movement was the fundamental ambivalence of the Western world itself. Though the Western world of the late nineteenth century was not divided into two camps as it is today, Western thought on the state was clearly divided into two different ways of defining the role of the political community and the individual. There was, on the one hand, the liberal way of solving political and social problems. Freedom of the individual and limitation of the power of government were the cardinal points of this liberalism. It was not a "democratic" liberalism as we understand it today, but it strongly defended the theory of a limited government. But there were also other strains of thought in the West. Conservatism, reaction, social evolutionism, extreme nationalism, Hegelian statism, and many other theories stressed the rights of the state over the individual, and denied or considerably weakened the rights of the human person.

It is wrong to identify Western political thought with only the democratic strain. It is true that the Western world was the first to find legal political means to defend the rights of the individual, but it does not follow from this that Japan did not become a real democracy because it did not adopt Western political institutions. The explanation "Western technology,

Eastern ideology" is too simple. In Europe, today as well as in the nineteenth century, there existed different systems of government, stretching all the way from reactionary regimes to democratic or quasi-democratic ones. Nothing expresses better this ambivalence of the Western world than the words of the great promoter of fine arts, Okakura Kakuzō, on his return from a tour of Europe and America in 1887: "Where is the essence of the West in the countries of Europe and America? All these countries have different systems; what is right in one country is wrong in the next; religion, customs, morals—there is no common agreement on any of these. Europe is discussed in a general way; and this sounds splendid. The question remains, however, where in reality does what is called Europe exist?"[50]

A third observation, on the economic development of Japan, leads to a more accurate appraisal of the Meiji system. In the political sphere, the Meiji leaders had closed the channels of upward mobility, as far as the highest posts of command were concerned. At the very top a handful of nobles and ex-samurai bureaucrats, not more than twenty all told, continued to monopolize the highest offices of state. Below this level, however, and in many other fields, modernization created a slowly expanding elite whose elements competed vigorously for status, power, and wealth. The scope of personal opportunities in public and private life became wider and wider. The Meiji leaders were building a political system in which political power could be kept in their hands, but at the same time they were largely abandoning state initiative in industrial enterprise and putting their trust increasingly in private interests. As the structure of national life developed and matured in both public and private sectors, more and more men climbed the newly erected ladders of influence and wealth.

If the Japanese leaders adopted a kind of authoritarian system, this does not necessarily mean that they were following traditional methods of so-called "oriental despotism," Authoritarian systems could be very modern and very Western. The Japanese state in the early eighties was tending to be authoritarian but never monolithic. Political power and economic power were both tightly held, but not in the same hands. Self-oriented goals and motives were very strong in this period. As in all successful organization, the regime stabilized itself partly by the very fact that it gave scope to personal initiative, risk-taking, and self-help in new avenues of national life. In economic affairs, perhaps even more than in politics, it encouraged the rise of new leadership based on achievement. It preserved order because it was not only authoritarian but fostered change. Japan avoided the stagnation which characterizes so many despotic systems, at the same time avoiding the disasters that unrestrained and aggressive totalitarian regimes inflict on their people.[51]

Probably the most characteristic distinction of the Meiji leadership was the division between political and nonpolitical realms of action. In politics the Meiji leaders tended toward an authoritarian regime; in other fields they were much more liberal. There was a deep secularism in their attitudes. They did not want to be involved in any sort of religious or thought control. The only thing they would not tolerate was a challenge to their political power. In the other spheres, they attempted to open channels of social mobility and social status to appease the best among the leaders of the opposition.

A fourth conclusion on the debates of the seventies and early eighties consists in an indictment of this period for its intellectual poverty. Despite the extreme interest and political importance of the controversies on the national assembly, sovereignty, and natural rights, this early period of Meiji Japan had little to offer in the broad sense of an intellectual, philosophical synthesis. Politics became all-pervasive, and foreign theories were often accepted indiscriminately for their political value without being examined for their philosophical premises. It was a shallow period in the cultural history of Japan, if culture is to include not only the political aspect but all the branches of human creation. No real philosophical thought, no real historiography, no independent analysis of Japanese society, appeared in this period. It was not until the mid-eighties that a richer phase began.

V

THE GERMAN INFLUENCE: ROESLER AND THE FRAMING OF THE CONSTITUTION

The Meiji leadership was committed to an authoritarian form of government; at the same time it was also clearly committed to a constitutional system. The middle and late eighties saw the efforts of the most capable leaders directed to the formulation and rationalization of this ambivalent system. Because German sociopolitical ideas played an important role in this process of rationalization it is necessary to examine closely the phenomenon of German influence on the Japanese leaders.

All the standard Western works on Meiji Japan refer in passing to the "deleterious" influence of German, particularly Prussian, political and legal theories. The names of Hermann Roesler, Rudolf von Gneist, and Lorenz von Stein are often mentioned, but it is difficult to find any detailed analysis of their thought. The reactionary, conservative, and absolutist implications of German influence on Meiji Japan are accepted as a postulate which needs neither proof nor explanation. There have been a few detailed works in Japanese dealing with the problem of the German influence. Suzuki Yasuzō,[1] Shimizu Shin,[2] Inada Masatsugu,[3] and recently a German scholar, Johannes Siemes,[4] who has spent many years doing research in Japan, have brought to light the complexity of the problem.

To understand the political and social ideas of the German scholars who influenced the framers of the Meiji Constitution, we first have to examine the political institutions of Germany in the second half of the nineteenth century. These institutions had remained in the stage of representative, not parliamentary, government. A charter had been granted by the crown, creating a system of popular representation limited in function to the approval of laws. Parliament was excluded from any executive power; this administrative power belonged to the crown and was exercised through its ministers, who were responsible to the monarch and independent of the vote of the assembly. The German political system had remained intact and received no influence from parliamentary ideas of French origin. This was due to the consistent efforts of the imperial government, which had the consent of the educated classes. The parliamentary form of government was thought to be a feeble and inefficient system with sham popular sovereignty that paved the way for the influence of amateur politicians.

Many German scholars worked in Japan during the middle Meiji period, and they were responsible for many changes. The names of Paul Mayet, Otto Rudorff, Albert Mosse, Karl Rudolph, and Erwin Baelz are among the most famous.[5] But in political thought, the three men considered to have exercised the most influence on the Japanese leaders are Hermann Roesler, Rudolf von Gneist, and Lorenz von Stein. Only Roesler worked in Japan; the other two scholars were contacted by Japanese leaders in Europe.

Roesler was hired by the Japanese government as adviser on legal affairs in October 1878, and until 1893 he was one of the most trusted and esteemed collaborators of Itō Hirobumi.[6] Rudolf von Gneist's first contact with the Japanese goes back as far as 1872, when Kido Takayoshi, traveling through Europe as a member of the Iwakura Mission, sought his scholarly advice on constitutional problems. But Gneist's contribution to Japanese thought is remembered especially for his talks with Itō in Berlin in 1882.

Stein's connection with the Japanese started also at the time of the Iwakura Mission. In 1873 Vienna was holding the International Exhibition, and Itō and Iwakura traveled to Vienna for the purpose of observing the modern products and inventions presented at the exhibition. Stein was present at a reception in honor of the Japanese mission, the first contact the Japanese had with this famous sociologist.[7] Stein's influence, however, is due particularly to the lectures he gave Itō in Vienna in 1882. Since Stein influenced both Gneist and Roesler, it seems appropriate to begin with his social and political ideas.

Lorenz von Stein (1815-1890) was one of the great German social scientists of the nineteenth century, but he is relatively unknown to the English-speaking world. As Kaethe Mengelberg has aptly written: "From the vantage point of the 20th century his vision in the interpretation of social trends and his merits in analysis deserve to be reconsidered and should secure him a permanent place in the history of sociology."[8] Stein was one the first nonsocialist social scientists to have given a critical analysis of the forces of capitalism and to have predicted the social tensions of future decades. The concepts of "proletariat" and of "class" and the historical role assigned to them in the development of capitalism were originally Stein's contributions. Marx himself was influenced by Stein's works.[9]

According to Stein, the moving force in history is the individual and his destiny. The essential function of both state and society is to further the individual's interest in his self-fulfillment. Any deviations from this purpose lead to contradictions and conflicts. The course of history, then, consists of the triangular struggle of the individual, the state, and society, all of which are highly interdependent. Human existence is unalterably imbedded in society and the fundamental energy in society is the interest of all members in acquiring or strengthening their independence. Hence there arises constant friction between the "haves" and the "have nots," between those who are dependent on others and those who have others dependent on them. The lower classes, said Stein, can improve their lot only at the expense of those with established privileges. Consequently, a constant struggle between the various classes of any society is one of the major factors shaping the sociopolitical process. To this process is added a new element, the state, which greatly varies, complicates, or enriches conditions, as the case may be. The state is the personification of the general will. In principle, the state is beyond class antagonism, its functions being to secure perfect freedom and, thereby, to further the development of all individuals. Within its conceptual framework, all are free and equal. But the state so formulated is merely an abstraction, an ethical ideal. In reality this ideal becomes constantly distorted, because the ruling class uses the state in order to secure its position.

In order to pave the way for a solution to the social question Stein demanded a reform from above carried out by a "social monarchy."[10] He urged the amelioration of the conditions of the lower classes but held that this should be accomplished by the state. His was a conservative socialism which sought to do away with class conflicts and contradictions and looked to the realization of social harmony through the development of a broadly based bourgeoisie in an ideal state of moral persons and ideas. Standing above and outside society, the state is to bring about a reform of society. The ruling interests of society should be subject to the forces of the state; and contradictions and conflicts within society should be solved by the assurance of freedom to every individual through legal equality and the continuous process of acquisition of property and education.

Two kinds of transformation are possible, according to Stein: political reform and revolution. Revolution would, however, establish equal rights only for one part of society, the victorious part. In the case of reform, state power would have to yield to the demands of the dependent class and sanction the fact of social equality by recognizing legal equality. The state must provide for the welfare of all individuals and in this way achieve social harmony among the classes.

Revolution, Stein held, is futile. There would be no more liberty if labor were to dominate than if capital were in power. Reform rather than revolution is the way to solve the modern problem confronting an industrial society. Stein would avoid all such utopian goals as the realization of general equality or the abolition of poverty. There must be a gradual and systematic establishment, by legislation and administrative action, of conditions that open to every possessor of the power to work the opportunity to become the possessor of capital. For an industrial society, capital is the expression and realization of that control over external things which is the essence of liberty. Where liberty in this sense does not exist, the social order stands in opposition to the idea of free personality and, therefore, cannot endure.

Stein believed that reform must come through a social monarchy, which systematically defends the interests of the oppressed classes against their oppressors and, thus, plays the harmonizing role in the perennial conflict of classes against classes. The constitution and the administration of the political system must conform to the economic and social principles of what he called "social democracy," in which the industrial class war and the social revolution are the central issue of serious political theory and action.

Stein's ideas cannot be called reactionary. He conceived as history's ultimate goal the realization of the individual person's freedom and independence. This essentially liberal theme of his social philosophy has been disregarded by many authors who put him indiscriminately among the Prussian authoritarian scholars. If a comparison can be useful, Stein should be compared to Tocqueville. The interest of both was primarily focused on the French Revolution. Both attempted an interpretation of this revolution not so much as a political event but as a manifestation of a great global movement toward social democracy, whose real object was less a new form of government than a new form of society, less the achievement of political rights than the destruction of privileges.[11]

Gneist's theory of the state loses sight of Stein's all-inclusive sociopolitical system and stresses the legal aspect of the state. Gneist was essentially a jurist who wanted to solve the conflicts within society through his theory of the *Rechtsstaat* (legal state), based on self-government.[12] By constitutional government Gneist meant a system in which the administration was duly subjected to laws passed by parliament, with judicial independence being maintained at the same time. He criticized the system of parliamentarianism in central Europe because it was only a representation of party interests. To this kind of parliamentarianism he opposed a system in which the people take part in government and the highest interests of the state are defended. The means to achieve this was self-government, which, for Gneist, meant the old English form of government, under which the business of government was discharged by honorary officials. It was not merely local government because it was integrated in a central administration under the monarch and parliament. The failure to achieve this integration of self-government and parliamentarianism was Gneist's explanation for the failure of constitutional government in continental Europe.

The chapter on France in Gneist's classical work *Der Rechtsstaat* expresses this view with great clarity.[13] For Gneist the French system represented the triumph of politics over the legal sense of the nation, that is, the French people did not have consciousness of acquired rights. He found the cause of this lack of legal feeling in the political work of the French monarchy. The French kings had succeeded in completing the unification of the state, but at the price of reducing the privileged classes to subjection by arbitrary and violent means. This was fatal to the development of public law. Later the revolutions, for all the violence of their opposition to absolutism, carried on the same work of unification and subjection. This lack of a legal sense and the incessant political transformations of the state destroyed all stability of government in France and involved public administration in the fluctuations of party politics and frequent ministerial crises. Gneist contended that the idea of the sovereignty of the people, in the sense of a mere disorganized plurality of individuals, overthrew the legal basis of the constitution, enslaved the exectuive to the legislative assemblies, and made the slave executive a tyrant in its relation to the citizens. The functionary had the rights of the individual at his own mercy; his responsibility, civil and criminal, was practically nonexistent. Thus, Gneist concluded, arose the strange paradox that a sovereign people could not safeguard the most elementary conditions of individual security from the caprice of the executive power. The reason was that this sovereignty of the people was a mere appearance and exhausted itself in the act of voting in the election of political representatives. From the complex organism of English law, France had gleaned only the idea of election. The vote came to be regarded in France not as a right acquired by the exercise of an independent and energetic political activity, but as an innate right.

Gneist's political ideal was to go back to the traditional parliamentary system of England. The English parliament was for Gneist a stable and organic force because it was a combination of forces organized in varying degrees through every stage in the social hierarchy. The French parliament, on the contrary, was an unstable, inconstant, disorganized force because it was an isolated apparition. It was arbitrary in its omnipotence and worked in a social world ruled by a uniform bureaucracy which by its operation prevented the citizens from habituating themselves to the functions of self-government.

The true basis of constitutionalism lies, Gneist believed, in the widespread feeling of the people of their rights, which form a limit to the caprices not only of the government but also of political parties. Liberalism, according to Gneist, consists not in an empty show of political forms, but in a firm consciousness of rights, which, without identifying government and governed, the state and the people, determines their relations in such a way that no political encroachment, whether from above or below, can disturb them.

The state, according to Gneist, is a civil juridical association, in the sense that the achievements of its ends must take place within the forms and limits of law. The foundation of the state based on law, the *Rechtsstaat,* is self-government, understood not as the mere participation of the people in the legislative assembly, but also as the possession of governmental functions by local bodies. The mere extension of suffrage to the whole population seemed to Gneist a danger to social order and in no way essential to public law. To take part in the government is not an innate right but must be acquired, like any other right, by the personal discharge of duties.

Gneist's fundamental defect, which was strongly pointed out by Roesler, was that he did not realize that his *Rechtsstaat* might in fact be a legalized system of oppression.[14] A governing class might practice self-government to the detriment of other classes. Then what would become of guaranteed rights? Roesler rightly pointed out that the mistake of Gneist was that "the state based on rights" could become a mere abstraction, something unreal. The *Rechtsstaat* acquired solidity only when Gneist treated it as an aspect of the development of the English political system; taken by itself, it is only an empty form, equally capable of justifying the status quo and feudal reactionary claims.

Hermann Roesler, following Stein's tradition, attempted to build his political system on a social basis. In 1871 he published his first major work, *Ueber die Grundlehren der von Adam Smith begründeten Volkswirtschaftstheorie* (On the basic principle of the economic theory of Adam Smith).[15] In it Roesler criticized Smith for misinterpreting the foundation of economic life. Economic laws, he said are not solely a result of a struggle for profit; they are based also on historical and communal ideas of law and right. This law and right, as the essence and inner core of communal life, Roesler called *soziale Recht*. This was the central idea of his sociopolitical thought.

Roesler's emphasis on social law led to open conflict with the diehards of classic economic liberalism. He strongly criticized the abuses of unchecked capitalism in his second work, *Das soziale Verwaltungsrecht* (Social administrative law).[16] This work upheld a new conception of administrative and social law. Roesler saw the individual involved in a social context: the individual develops his personality only in a web of communication with other personalities. The state becomes the central connecting organ of all activities in the web of communal civilized life. Human individuals live in a chain of small social bodies, with their specific goals and their inherent rights and laws. These rights and laws do not depend on the state's decision: they are prior to the state. The state exists not to define the laws and the rights of the social bodies, but to protect them and to integrate all the different intermediary societies into a social whole. Thus, the essential function of the state can be summarized as a threefold mission: protection of the rights of the individual; management of foreign affairs, especially the defense of the nation's own independence and interests; and coordination of social bodies, integrating them into a social whole.

When Roesler spoke of social law (*soziale Recht*) he meant all the rights and obligations involved in a communal organization whose purpose was a civilized life. Social law was the harmonizing law of the activities of the various organizations and social bodies. Roesler's fundamental principle was that all civilization was social, and that to lead a civilized life cooperation was necessary. Thus the sphere of rights of the individual and the group was defined and measured by the task to be fulfilled. A university, for instance, was autonomous and possessed inherent rights and obligations in the fulfillment of its mission of scientific research.

In the introduction to *Das soziale Verwaltungsrecht* Roesler explained on what principle the modern state must be founded:

The essence of the modern state cannot be grasped without a deep understanding of modern society. Today society is a separate entity, not in the sense that it is outside of the state or that it is stateless, but in the sense that it is independent from the state and leading a life of its own through its own organs. An old form of administrative system cannot be imposed on the organization of modern society. Present cultural life demands a new political and legal organization. New tasks, new obligations, and new functions of the state structure cannot find their solution in the old system. Many political discussions and many political ills could be avoided if this truth were known and followed.[17]

In the nineteenth century the state could not stay aloof from the social realities of the nation: it had clear responsibilities in the newly emerging industrial society. Roesler was an advocate of political and social monarchy. He wanted a strong monarchic system in which the political action of the ruler would be synonymous with the will of the nation. He advocated a strong central power that could really lead the people. In the independence of parliament he saw the social law endangered rather than assured. A parliament, with its various and conflicting political parties, he felt, must necessarily play class against class and interest against interest, with the danger that a tyranny of the majority might arise. To prevent the pressure of classes and interests and to safeguard the welfare of the people, there must be an established institution above parties, and such an institu-iion must have its authority based not only in the written constitution but especially in the living tradition of service to the whole people. For Roesler this institution was constitutional monarchy.[18] He was totally opposed to state absolutism, but at the same time he was opposed to mass democracy and simple rule of the majority. He thought that only a "social monarchy," being above class interests and class divisions, could see to it that all members of society had equal freedom and equal opportunity of development, a freedom and an opportunity which could not be sufficiently ensured by universal suffrage and political parties alone. Roesler's error was in overstating the power of the monarch to lead competently in a political sense and to serve as a means of harmony and compromise for the welfare of all.

These were the theories of the German scholars who advised the Japanese "founding fathers" or who, as in the case of Roesler, took an active part in the framing of the constitution. Their social ideas were different, but they had in common the principle that broad powers should be given to the monarch and that a system of party cabinets was divisive and against the general interests of the country. Though socially or legally speaking they might be called liberal and progressive, in politics they tended to defend conservatism and the rights of the monarch. It was this consensus in the political sphere that made their influence felt in Japanese circles.

As we have seen, Itō Hirobumi headed a group which went to Europe in the spring of 1882 with the purpose of studying the various systems of constitutional monarchy.[19] Itō consulted Gneist from May to July 1882, and later from November of the same year till February of the following year. Albert Mosse, at the time a young assistant professor under Gneist, also gave a series of lectures to Itō's group.[20]

Gneist centered his remarks on difficult points which had emerged in the constitutional practices of various countries. We can deduce the content of the talks from letters Itō sent home from Germany and from notes taken by Itō Miyoji.[21] Gneist often stressed the point that a constitution must be rooted firmly in the history of the country and in the national character of the people. It must not be an abstract document or an imitation of other constitutional charters. Itō Miyoji summarized Gneist's talks in a few points:

1. In the case of the establishment of a diet in Japan, questions of diplomacy, military organization, and financial matters should not be subject to the decisions of the diet. Otherwise no real monarchy could be established. Military and financial power and diplomatic relations belong to the powers of the monarch. Military and economic powers are of especially decisive importance.

2. The constitution must be built upon a solid basis. As in the case of Germany, the constitution must be strengthened by the social organization. Up to fifty years ago the British constitution was very strong because it was based on this social system, but lately it has degenerated a little. This social system of self-government was the most suitable in the German regime. Those who have more duties have more rights; thus those who pay more taxes have greater electoral rights and at the same time receive greater honors.

3. In the United States the powers of the cabinet ministers are very weak; in England the ministers are controlled by parliament. Japan should not follow these examples. The Prussian ministers are the foundation for preserving the power of the central government. Parliament should have the power of correcting the eventual mistakes of the ministers, but on political matters of the common good the ministers should not be controlled by the assembly, so that they may freely pursue the welfare of the people. The emperor may preside over the cabinet meetings.

4. It is desirable to organize a deliberative council on legislative and executive matters composed of present and former ministers, high-ranking civil servants, and nobles.

5. The upper house should be composed of nobles and high officials. The number of hereditary members should be below one third of the total membership. The other two thirds should be ap-

pointed, not popularly elected. One hundred and fifty would be ideal for the total membership.

6. The lower house is composed of the people's representatives. It should number from three to four hundred. The upper house and lower house control each other mutually. In order to prevent universal suffrage and the eventual dangers of a democratic system, electoral rights should be distributed according to economic power and the number of duties performed.

7. If one gives parliament discretionary powers on financial matters, then the cabinet becomes subservient to the assembly, and the ministers are appointed by the majority in parliament. This must be avoided by all means. If approval is needed from the assembly for any monetary disposal and if the budget has to be passed by a law of parliament, it is impossible to run an efficient administration. Law is above the budget and it is permanent. To implement these laws it is necessary to spend money. Thus sometimes the administration will have to spend money that it is not allowed by the budget.

8. It is not convenient to allow the diet to discuss all legislative matters. Economic matters, family legislation, and the penal code should be handled by the diet. All other problems should be resolved by the administration. Since Japan is still in a revolutionary period in which many reforms are necessary and have to be carried through, it is better not to give all legislative power to the diet, but to reserve broad decree powers to the emperor. Otherwise, if the consent of the diet should be required for all reforms, the great task of the revolution would come to a standstill.

9. The British for a long time considered the cabinet and the members of parliament as advisers. That is, the king, being the ruler, had to govern the whole country and conduct all the state affairs. But today it is not longer so; the British system has become a regime or political factions, and the British king does not conduct state affairs. This is the misfortune of the British Empire and the beginning of the decline of the British nation.

10. In the case of Japan, the constitution should, of course, be granted by the emperor. For the revision of the constitution it is not advisable to convoke a constituent assembly, because it might pro-

voke social upheaval. Rather, the revision should be handled in the diet like any other legislative matter.

11. The monarch has to protect the poor classes; he has to honor the upper classes by appointing their members to the upper house and other councils and by naming them to the highest ranks of the bureaucracy. By establishing good relations with these upper classes, the monarch builds out of them a bulwark in defense of the throne.

12. To strengthen the country, the establishment of religion is necessary. Buddhism, as the traditional religion of Japan, should be declared the religion of state. The other religions should be recognized as private. It is a good policy to introduce Protestantism, but one must be careful in not allowing Catholicism to become too powerful. Moreover, monogamy should be established.[22]

In general, Gneist's observations defended a strong political conservatism. Itō himself, in a letter to Matsukata Masayoshi, the minister of finance, said that Gneist's political ideas were too conservative and too authoritarian for the Japanese situation.[23] Mosse's lectures were held from May 25 to July 29, 1882, and from November 14, 1882, to February 19, 1883. They followed the fundamental principles of Gneist's thought and constituted a systematic course on constitutional government.[24]

During the summer of 1882 Itō traveled to Vienna to meet Stein. In the letter he sent to Iwakura on August 11, 1882, three days after the first meeting with Stein, Itō wrote:

By studying under two famous German scholars, Gneist and Stein, I have been able to reach a general understanding of the structure of the state. Later I shall discuss the way to achieve the great objective of strengthening the foundations of the imperial sovereignty. Indeed, the trends in our country today erroneously lead to a belief in the works of the extreme liberal radicals of England, America, and France and to considering these theories as the supreme norm. In such a way they lead virtually to the overthrow of the state. In having found principles and means of reversing these trends, I believe I have rendered an important service to my country, and I feel that I can die a happy man.[25]

In the same letter, noting that Stein classified nations as constitutional monarchies or republics, Itō went on to outline the characteristics of a true monarchy. The monarch, first of all, was superior to the legislative and executive branches; he suffered neither the restrictions of law nor punishment. The monarch alone could sanction laws and ordinances. Under a monarchy a clash between the assembly's legislation and government ordinances was to be avoided by allowing the cabinet to originate all legislative enactments, and any enactments of the assembly would have to have cabinet approval before receiving the monarch's sanction. Finally, Itō observed that when the power of a constitutional monarch was abridged in any way, the form of government tended to republicanism and to the practice of selecting prime ministers from the majority party. Thus, though nominally monarchic governments, some European countries were closer to the republican system than to the monarchic one.[26]

Through Gneist's and Stein's doctrines Itō became even more convinced of the need for a strong sovereign and a weak assembly, and he was strengthened in his idea that the party cabinet system was a threat to monarchic power. The influence of Gneist and Stein, however, has often been overstressed. It was a good weapon for Itō to be able to quote the opinions of the two great German scholars, but actually Itō's idea were already well formed before he went to Europe. A sign that Gneist and Stein did not, after all, play a leading role is the fact that the lectures given by the German scholars were not found in the documentary material used in the drafting of the Meiji Constitution.

The influence of Roesler, on the other hand, was of vital importance. As Suzuki Yasuzō has pointed out: "Roesler's contribution to the framing of the Japanese constitution extended over a long period of time and was extraordinarily vital. From the initial works of formulation of the constitution to the final conclusive discussions, Roesler played a decisive role. Not only among the foreign advisers but even among the Japanese leaders, with the exception of Itō Hirobumi and Inoue Kowashi, nobody played such an important role."[27]

As we have seen, in 1881 the fundamental principles on which to base the future constitution had alredy been decided and determined in Iwakura's documents.[28] These documents had been prepared by Inoue Kowashi, as is clear from Iwakura's and Inoue's letters and from the manuscript found among Itō Hirobumi's papers.[29] Inoue based his arguments and principles on the answers Roesler had submitted in July 1881 in answer to Inoue's question on the executive power of the monarch. Roesler explained:

The sentence "The king's government only means the custody of the royal seal" must have been uttered by the former French president Thiers when he was prime minister under the Orleans monarch.

In my opinion, parliamentary government involves the principle that the king is the head of the state, but he does not exercise any real power himself. The prime minister exercises the administrative power and is responsible to parliament, not to the king. This is the meaning of the above-mentioned sentence. England follows such a system of parliamentary government.

In Prussia, however, the king is the real head of government, and Thiers' slogan does not apply there. In England the cabinet is constituted by the union of the ministers. In Prussia the king settles on his own the issues submitted to him by the ministers; there is no cabinet which can discuss the supreme powers of the king, both civil and military. Administrative power resides only in the king. Accordingly, we must say that in Prussia the king actually administers the affairs of state.[30]

In this document Roesler accepted the German tradition of constitutionalism which allowed participation of the people only in the legislative process but not in the executive power. Roesler wanted a representative form of government but not a parliamentary system. Inoue Kowashi submitted the following question: "In Prussia there is no such a thing as a collective responsibility of the cabinet in handling state affairs. Moreover, the king can keep in power a cabinet which has lost the majority in parliament. Could you explain the pros and cons of such a system?" Roesler sent a lengthy answer, which was almost literally reproduced in Iwakura's opinion on the constitution.

As you have pointed out, in Prussia the ministers are not held collectively responsible for the actions of each separate member of the cabinet. Protected by the king, they can stand against a majority in parliament without having to resign their posts. On the other hand, according to the customary law of England the English ministers lose their administrative power if they do not get the majority in parliament. Consequently, in Prussia there is no parliamentary government, that is, government by the majority in parliament and subject to the control of political parties; in England we can see such a parliamentary government. In order to build a representative government it is not necessary to have a parliamentary cabinet.

We have to look further to see where sovereignty resides in a constitutional monarchy. In a constitutional monarchy sovereignty resides in the monarch; in a republic it resides in the people. But it can happen that in countries having a monarchic system name and reality may be conflicting. Although, according to English customary law, it is clearly stated that sovereignty is shared by the king and parliament, in reality this clause remains in the realm of nominal definitions. The king is a figurehead with mere honorary powers and privileges, without any real political power. Even though the king's power might at times become stronger than usual, he remains essentially *a mere ornament in the structure of the state.*

In Prussia things are quite different. Sovereignty lies squarely with the monarch. The article of the constitution which requires the approval of parliament [for the enactment of laws] limits the monarch's sovereignty only in order to prevent deficiencies in the exercise of the sovereign power.

In Prussia it was the army, instituted to protect the monarchy, that laid down the fundamental principles of a constitutional monarchy. In earlier times in Prussia the king was not only the commander-in-chief of the army, but also the real ruler who decided state policy. More recently, about thirty years ago, the Prussian king granted a constitution. This constitution, however, did not strip the king of his sovereignty, but only limited it. Since the constitution was made to guarantee in a practical way the rights and prerogatives of the king and not those of parliament, the authority of the king remains intact to this day.

If we compare the constitutional development of these two countries [England and Prussia], the following points become evident.

1. In Prussia the constitution explicitly states that the king himself can appoint and dismiss cabinet ministers. Ostensibly, at least, the English constitution states this same principle, but in fact in England this clause is a dead letter, since in practice appointments and dismissals of ministers depend on the majority in parliament. In England the ministers are thus representatives of the majority party, and it is natural that they should be responsible to this party. In Prussia, however, ministers are directly appointed by the king and the law recognizes them as representatives of the king. Therefore, the ministers are responsible only to the king; they are not in any way responsible to parliament. They are not representatives of parliament, nor have they been chosen from among the members of parliament. Even when the ministers are opposed by the majority and supported in turn only by a parliamentary minority, they can still function freely in their office. The king protects the ministers by his own responsibility. Since according to the constitution the king is not responsible to the people, so also the ministers cannot even indirectly be held responsible to parliament.

2. In England annual taxes may be levied only by parliament. Even taxes necessary for the maintenance of the army may be levied only after the approval of parliament. If the government levies taxes without such approval, the Supreme Court must protect the people against such action. Thus the court decrees that these taxes are un-

constitutional and invalid. That is why the ministers cannot levy taxes without previous approval of parliament.

In contrast to this, things in Prussia are different. Although in article 5 of the constitution it is stated that taxes cannot be levied without the approval of parliament according to article 109, if the cabinet and parliament cannot agree on the annual budget the budget of the previous year remains in force. Thus in Prussia taxes may be levied even without the approval of the people. The courts must recognize as valid the budget of the previous year and are not expected to protect the people from such unauthorized taxes.

In this way the ministers in Prussia are not bound by the majority in parliament; they can publicly take an independent stand. It is always possible for the ministers to meet state expenses and to fulfill their obligations competently without any regard for a parliamentary majority.[31]

There must have been hundreds of questions and answers like these. More than 160 have been preserved in the Japanese translation. Most of the originals (in English, French, and German) were lost in the destruction of the Imperial Archives, in Toranomon, during the great earthquake of 1923. All of these opinions were carefully worked out, often with supplementary material in order to present a historical and systematic treatment of the topic in question.[32]

The central problem in the framing of the constitution was the sovereignty of the emperor: in what way should his independent sovereign powers be defined and by what constitutional means should they be protected? These were the fundamental questions that the founding fathers were confronted with. In 1887 and 1888 many drafts were prepared, and the differences among them were always concerned with the articles on the emperor. Among the most important drafts was one prepared by Roesler.[33] The Meiji Constitution bears a very close resemblance to Roesler's draft, with one very important exception; it concerns article 1 of the constitution.

Article 1 of the Meiji Constitution in its final formulation reads: "The Empire of Japan shall be reigned over and governed by a line of Emperors unbroken for ages eternal." Roesler was opposed to the mythological implications of this article. His proposed article reads: "The Japanese Empire is one indivisible constitutional monarchy." It went against his scientific convictions to accept the myth of an eternal progenitor as the founder of the imperial family as the fundamental article of the constitution.

After the final draft had been prepared, Roesler was asked by Itō to write a commentary on the constitution. He was requested to explain its meaning to official bodies and to make them understand its significance. Roesler's commentary gives a summary of his political theories. It is useful to examine it in detail in order to understand the ideas which formed the background for many political decisions made by the Meiji leaders.[34]

In his introductory remarks, Roesler defined the nature and the essential elements of a constitutional government. The constitution was for him "the fundamental law by which subjects are admitted to the enjoyment of certain rights in respect of the government." Through the constitution governmental powers were to be controlled by or brought under the influence of the people. Constitutional government was opposed to absolute government, under which the people have no political rights, that is, no legal powers of controlling and influencing the acts of government. Because the people at large cannot directly take part in the administration of the affairs of state, a representative assembly is essential for controlling and examining the acts of government. A constitutional government can be either simply representative or parliamentary. In a parliamentary government the balance of political power rests in the national assembly, while in a representative government the balance rests in the chief of state, who in the case of a monarchy is the king. In Japan, under the proposed constitution, a representative, not parliamentary, form of government was to be established. This did not mean that in the long run Japan could not have a parliamentary government. It appeared wiser, Roesler said, to let the constitutional system gradually develop, following the necessary steps of progress and avoiding rash and radical changes in pursuance of lofty theories. He felt this to be especially true in the case of the parliamentary system, in those countries where it had come into practice; it had proved to be by no means an entirely satisfactory experience, and had been found more and more wanting. Roesler felt that the most essential political right to be defended by a constitution was the right of voting on laws and taxes. The constitution should be a constitution by charter, and not by compact. Once in force, it should become the law of the land and not be changed without the vote of the national representation.[35]

Commenting on article 1 of the Meiji Constitution, Roesler explained that there were two fundamental principles involved in this clause:

1. The Japanese Empire shall remain an Imperial Monarchy so that any other form of government and especially the republican governments can never be made the law of Japan . . .
2. The Empire of Japan shall be reigned over and governed by the Emperor. This confirms not only the abolition of any divisional power of government, as it had been exercised in old Japan by the territorial princes (Daimyo) or by a military commander (Shogun). It confirms also the entire unity and concentration of the monarchical power in the hands of the Emperor.[36]

In his commentary on article 1, Roesler avoided all reference to the mythological implications of the "unbroken line for ages eternal." He said only that the system of monarchic government was the one which was exclusively suitable to the country and congenial to the national character.[37]

Probably the most enlightening pages on the nature of the

state as envisioned by the new constitution are contained in the commentary on articles 4, 5, and 6.[38] They are the clearest expression of the uneasy compromise the Meiji leaders were attempting to reach between an absolute form of government and a parliamentary regime in which parliament represented the supreme power of the nation. Article 1 and the first paragraph of article 4 would seem to define the Japanese state as an absolute monarchy, the emperor being the sovereign who combined in himself all supreme powers. The second paragraph of article 4 and all of article 5, however, defined the powers of the emperor as limited. Roesler's commentary runs as follows:

The Emperor exercises the governmental power according to the provisions of the constitution. The governmental power is not of private, but of a public, nature: it should not be exercised licentiously, but for the welfare of the people. This nature and object is inherent to every system of government; it must produce certain limits to the exercise of the governmental powers to prevent rashness and deviation of judgment. In an absolute government, such limits are found in religious and moral precepts, in traditions, in education, in a certain organization of government, and the like; in a constitutional government they are determined by law and become so more effectual. The general constitutional limit is a certain concurrence of the people, and a proper legal foundation of the government. Thus, laws require the consent of the national assembly; all governmental acts require the signature of the ministers; justice is administered by independent judges according to law. Other special limits are expressed in the constitution with regard to particular affairs, as for financial affairs, and so on. Such limits are not contrary to the nature of the sovereign power, insofar as they do not unreasonably check and weaken it; for the sovereign power must not be absolute in all respects and to all extent. On the other side such limits are essential to the nature of constitutional government, which is destined to establish certain political rights and lawful liberty of the subjects with regard to the government, as has been shown in the introductory remarks above.[39]

The first and most important limit which the constitution imposed on the powers of the emperor, Roesler said, was the necessary consent of the diet for all exercise of legislative power. This represented "the most important limit because the law is the highest and most general form of rule for human conduct in a state."[40] In a constitutional government, rules of law could not be imposed, altered, or abolished without the national consent.[41]

On article 6, which read, "The Emperor gives sanction to laws and orders them to be promulgated and executed," Roesler distinguished four stages in the legislative process: initiative, deliberation, sanction, and promulgation. Initiative was the prerogative not only of the emperor but also of the diet. Deliberation was the act that especially limited the legislative power of the emperor. This right of deliberation resolved upon and settled the subject matter or the content of law; it was to be exercised through declaring consent to or dissent from a bill and by making amendments. The diet, through this right of deliberation, could decide on the usefulness of laws and their conformity to the true principles of justice and the actual interests of the country. Without this right of deliberation, reserved to the diet, Japan would have an absolute government: "There could, indeed, be no true and effectful constitutional government if the parliamentary votes upon laws could be put aside according to the pleasure of the monarch, whose legislative power would then be unlimited in every respect."[42]

Roesler was thinking of an absolute king who spontaneously wanted to limit his own power by granting a constitution. This limitation would not imply, however, that there was any sovereign power in the diet or in the people. The king's sovereignty would be derived from the old conception of monarchy in which the "divine" rights of the king are supposed to come directly from God without any intervention of the people. The actual power of the emperor would be made "natural" by such arguments as: "The Emperor holds his power from Heaven through the medium of His glorious ancestors, but not from any human authorization; consequently He cannot be held responsible to His subjects, but to Heaven alone."[43]

While accepting this principle of political irresponsibility, Roesler at the same time saw that real limits would be imposed on the emperor's exercise of his sovereign power through the right of initiative and particularly the right of deliberation of the diet. Roesler was too much of a monarchist not to uphold the sovereign powers of the emperor; but he was also too much of a liberal not to affirm the indispensable need for checks and limits on this sovereign power.

Besides the legislative functions of the diet, Roesler upheld the independence of the courts as a bulwark against administrative absolutism: "The security of individual rights and of personal liberty is immediately and entirely based on the independent dispensation of laws in all civil and penal cases."[44] As the emperor could not alter the law, so also he could not influence the courts' decisions. The judges could not be removed at will by the emperor; only the courts could pass judgment on the judges. Roesler worked also for the establishment of a Court of Administrative Litigation as a constitutional guarantee that the existing laws and the rights of the individual would be respected by the administrative authorities.[45]

Roesler defined the rights guaranteed by the constitution as positive rights. According to him, the state had no power to define what the natural rights were. The definition of natural rights would disrupt the peaceful relation between ruler and ruled and would instigate social discord and revolutionary upheaval. But Roesler added:

No doubt the natural law, that is to say, the sense of natural justice, necessity and utility, underlies the positive law, but its formation as such must be governed by the considerations of the actual condition and wants of each nation. For Japan the constitutional declaration of rights and duties of the subjects has this particular historical significance, that the people at large are now forever relieved from the burdens of the absolute and feudal government and can without difference of unequal classes or orders, freely and safely enjoy their rights, personal or of property, and discharge their duties under the protection of the law. Thus the declaration of rights is a conspicuous mark of progress to a true constitutional government.[46]

The rights defended in the constitution were all conditional and might suffer exceptions in cases of extraordinary necessity. For superior to every law is the supreme law of self-preservation and safety of the state: *salus publica suprema lex esto*. Whenever the existence and the highest interests of the state and the maintenance of a lawful government are at stake, the carrying out of extraordinary measures for such ends cannot be hindered or opposed "upon mere titles of rights of private individuals."[47]

Roesler's thought has been examined here at some length because his influence was very important in the period of the final formulation of the constitution and of the political system of Meiji Japan. The essentials of the constitution had already appeared in 1881 in the constitutional outlines put forward by Iwakura. These had been prepared by Inoue Kowashi, who, in turn, had based his documents on Roesler's answers. Following Iwakura's death, the Roesler-Inoue-Iwakura chain of constitutional thought simply became the thought of Roesler being refracted through Inoue to Itō Hirobumi. By virtue of the unbroken existence of the Roesler-Inoue combination it is clear that their line of thought was basic in the formulation of the Meiji charter. Roesler's ideas were the mainstream of constitutional thought, owing to Inoue's great personal respect for Roesler and to the fact that Roesler's statements on politics, not greatly different from those of Gneist and Stein, were not overshadowed by the doctrines of these two scholars despite the appeal that they held for Itō Hirobumi.

It was unfortunate that Roesler did not understand the real position of the emperor in the long political tradition of Japan. Roesler built his system of imperial sovereignty on the assumption that the emperor would play a very active role in the actual direction of politics. He wanted, for instance, the cabinet meetings to be presided over by the emperor. In fact, however, the emperor had never been, at least in the last few centuries of Japanese history, an actual ruler. Although the emperor had always remained implicitly or explicitly the primary source of legitimacy, he was, as far as the active decision-making process was concerned, a political nonentity, a mere ornament in the political structure. The mythological implications which Roesler did not accept but which were clearly expressed in article 1 of the constitution were the basis for denying in practice to the emperor all political power and all active involvement in the decision-making process of government.

Roesler wanted the emperor to be above political divisions of parties and to represent the undivided interests of the state. But if the emperor was not supposed to soil his hands in politics, who was going to decide what the undivided interests of the state were? A majority party at least would represent the partial interests of the majority, but what solution could Roesler give if a small group of persons decided independently what the national interests were and then used the name of the emperor to impose on the nation their uncontrolled authority?

Roesler asked himself this question, and his answer was that a small group of dedicated "aristocrats" were always better qualified to govern the country than the leaders of political parties supported by the changeable masses. The intimate and prolonged contact with the Meiji leaders had convinced Roesler that these leaders were the best people available to solve the difficult problems of modern Japan. Roesler thought that Japan had in these leaders a real aristocracy, based on a long tradition of service and sound moral principles and capable of perpetuating itself. He was convinced that, for the time being, there was no other concrete alternative. The French system appeared to him as a continuous revolution; and the British system, he thought, was premature for Japan.

As a general conclusion on the problem of the German influence it can be said that the Japanese leaders were mainly interested in the *political* theories of the German scholars. Though in the system of Stein, Gneist, and Roesler many of the legal and social aspects might be liberal, their political conclusions, dissected from the whole, were extremely conservative. The political conclusions of the three German scholars were very similar: they were based on the monarchic principle as defended by the German conservative school of monarchic constitutional law. The monarchic principle, as understood by this school, meant that all state power, legislative, executive, and judicial, was united in the monarch. The sovereignty of the monarch was the original and highest power, encompassing all public power in the state. The monarch determined all operations of the state and gave validity and authority to them. Stein, Gneist, and Roesler coincided in upholding this monarchic principle, which could so easily be turned into a system of administrative transcendentalism and cabinet irresponsibility.

VI

THE NEW THEORY OF THE STATE:
INOUE KOWASHI, ITŌ HIROBUMI,
AND THE CONSTITUTION

Itō Hirobumi returned from his mission to Europe on August 3, 1883. In an address to the throne on September 19, Itō summed up constitutional government as being based on two principles. The first principle was that there could be no taxation without the consent of the persons taxed. This notion, according to Itō, was only applied in England. The second and more recent principle was that of the separation of the three powers, with the legislature having the sole right to originate legislation. Yet regardless of the existence of these concepts, Itō informed the throne that Japan's unique national polity, in which one line of emperors had reigned from time immemorial, should serve as the basic orientation of a constitution for Japan.[1]

In an article written in 1909 entitled "Some Reminiscences of the Grant of the New Constitution,"[2] Itō described some of the difficulties the Japanese leaders confronted when they were framing the constitution. Mere imitation of foreign models would not suffice, "for there were historical peculiarities of our country which had to be taken into consideration."[3] The central point of discussion was how to resolve the fundamental problem of the relation between the principles of imperial sovereignty and restrictions upon the government: "In formulating the restrictions on its [the Crown's] prerogatives in the new Constitution, we had to take care to safeguard the future realness or vitality of these prerogatives, and not to let the institution degenerate into an ornamental crowning piece of the edifice. At the same time, it was also evident that any form of constitutional *regime* was impossible without full and extended protection of honour, liberty, property, and personal security of citizens, entailing necessarily many important restrictions of the powers of the Crown."[4]

Itō went on to tell of another difficulty in the formulation of the fundamental law of the nation. In the Japan of the eighties there was a deep division of opinions on the state:

We were just then in an age of transition. The opinions prevailing in the country were extremely heterogeneous, and often diametrically opposed to each other. We had survivors of other generations who were still full of theocratic ideas, and who believed that any attempt to restrict an imperial prerogative amounted to something like high treason. On the other hand, there was a large and powerful body of the younger generation educated at the time when the Manchester theory was in vogue, and who in consequence were ultra-radical in their ideas of freedom. Members of the bureaucracy were prone to lend willing ears to the German doctrinaires of the reactionary period, while, on the other hand, the educated politicians, having not yet tasted the bitter significance of administrative responsibility, were liable to be more influenced by the dazzling words and lucid theories of Montesquieu, Rousseau, and other similar French writers.[5]

Such was the background when Itō returned to Japan in 1883. Before we discuss the actual framing of the constitution it is of special interest to examine two important changes in the governmental structure which paved the way to the enactment of the constitution and the opening of the diet. These two changes were the establishment of a new peerage and the creation of the cabinet system.

As far back as 1876 there had been proposals for a peerage system. In that year the Justice Department had already drafted a plan for a system of three ranks: prince, count, and baron. The rank of baron was reserved for the ex-samurai. In 1878 another draft proposed five ranks, whose members were to be selected from the old court nobility and from people who had rendered meritorious service to the state. In this new plan there was no formal mention of the ex-samurai class. In 1881 Itō Hirobumi submitted a plan for a system of five ranks composed not only of old court nobles but also of ex-samurai and commoners of special merit. No rank was reserved to a particular class. The new aristocracy was expected to serve as a bulwark to defend the imperial institution.

Iwakura Tomomi opposed Itō's plan because it did not take into account the fundamental distinction of stations in life. Iwakura accused the han-based government of having destroyed the proper relations between ruler and subject and the traditional relations between high and low. Iwakura adduced three reasons for this state of affairs: the administration had become prey to han factionalism; the land had been distributed to the people; and finally, the finances of the Imperial House were under the control of the Finance Department. To change the situation, Iwakura suggested that the state-owned land should become the property of the emperor, and that the land under private ownership should be commuted into land held under long-term tenancy.

Iwakura intended to strengthen the imperial powers not only in relation to the rights of the people, but also in relation to the rights of the han coalition, which was running the government. In this desire of complete imperial independence from all restrictions Iwakura's ideas were in some respects close to those of Fukuzawa Yukichi. Iwakura wanted the emperor to be above the administration. Inoue Kowashi and Itō Hirobumi wanted the administration to be identified with the emperor: government and imperial system had to be one.

From this difference of opinions on the independence of the imperial institution emerged also the contrast of opinions on the peerage system. Iwakura, too, wanted five ranks, but these were to be distributed according to traditional stations in life. The old court nobility should be restored to its original privileges and political powers and should have a pre-eminent role in the defense of the imperial institution. Inoue Kowashi and Itō opposed such a system, for they were concerned with winning the best ex-samurai over to the government side. They rejected a close peerage system based on blood, and accepted an open system based mainly on achievement.

Because of Iwakura's opposition, Itō's plan of 1881 could not be carried out immediately. As soon as Itō returned from Europe the peerage system was enacted without great difficulties, especially because in the meantime Iwakura had died in July 1883. The Peerage Ordinance, promulgated on July 7, 1884, created five ranks: prince, marquis, count, viscount, and baron. The establishment of the peerage was an advance move to provide the national assembly, once it was opened, with a majority of peers in the upper house who would serve as a check against the lower house.[6]

The next step toward the reorganization of the governmental structure came in December 1885, when the Dajōkan was superseded by a modern cabinet system. Under the Dajōkan mode of government there had existed an inner council composed of junior councilors responsible for the various departments. Yet the officials who advised the emperor and exercised control over the departments were the chancellor and the ministers of the Left and Right. It often happened that these three chief ministers were not always in accord with the junior councilors or in agreement among themselves. Moreover, as long as this traditional form of government continued to function it would be difficult to open the three top places to people outside the court nobility. There was also the problem of superfluous expenditure through the unnecessary increase of officials and the duplication of work.[7]

The New Theory of the State

The actual plans for the reorganization of the central government started in May 1885, after Itō had returned from his mission to China to sign the Tientsin Convention, also known as the Li-Itō Convention. After many discussions and proposals Sanjō Sanetomi turned in his resignation as chancellor of the Dajōkan. This memorial of resignation was prepared by Inoue Kowashi, who also had drafted the plan for the new cabinet system. In this document Sanjō gave the reasons why he thought that the Dajōkan should be abolished and replaced by a cabinet:

> When in the second year of Meiji [1869] a new system of government was introduced, under which six departments were created, these departments were placed under the direct authority of the Dajōkan according to the Taihō Code and became subordinate branches of the administration. From this time on the government has been conducted in such a way that the departments were to receive their instructions from the Dajōkan. It was necessary for all the memorials to the throne to pass through the Dajōkan. This system, although suited as a temporary expedient to the exigencies of the time, is not only against the principle of personal government by the emperor but also tends to lessen unduly the responsibilities of the various ministers of departments and cause obstruction of public business.[8]

Sanjō, following Itō's plans, proposed that the cabinet should be made a supreme council of ministers having direct approach to the emperor. The various ministers should, in the cabinet, take part in the general administration of the country, and outside the cabinet be responsible for the administration of their departments. Sanjō also specified that a prime minister should be given control over all ministers and all state affairs, so that the whole administration might be run with uniformity and expedition.

On December 22, 1885, the regulations known as "Naikaku shokken" (Official powers of the cabinet) were issued. This document is divided into seven articles. Article 1 gave the prime minister control over all executive departments and declared that the prime minister, as the head of the other ministers, should report on state affairs to the emperor and, upon receiving his orders, give instructions on the course of administrative policy. Article 2 authorized the prime minister to demand explanations and investigate the activities of the various departments. Article 3 empowered him to suspend decisions of the executive departments when it was deemed necessary and to wait in the meantime for the imperial decision. Article 4 gave the prime minister supervisory control over the legislation-drafting committees within the departments. Article 5 required the prime minister and any minister whose jurisdiction was concerned to countersign laws and ordinances. Article 6 specified that each cabinet minister should make occasional reports to the premier, though in military matters the minister of the Army was to report to the prime minister what the General Staff Office reported directly to the throne. The last article declared that the affairs of a disabled minister could be administered by another cabinet minister.[9]

Itō Hirobumi became the first prime minister under the new cabinet system. After completing the administrative reorganization the time came for the drafting of the constitution. The leaders participating directly in the project were Itō Hirobumi, Inoue Kowashi, Itō Miyoji, and Kaneko Kentarō. In addition, Roesler and Mosse were taking part as legal advisers. Each of the Japanese drafters had more or less specific legislative objectives assigned to him. Itō Miyoji was responsible for the Law of the Houses, Kaneko was in charge of the Law of Election of the Members of the House of Representatives and the Ordinance Concerning the House of Peers, and Inoue Kowashi was entrusted with the Constitution and the Imperial House Law.[10] Inoue's legislative assignment was, of course, the most important. If any one man can be pointed out as the outstanding contributor to the formulation of the Meiji Constitution in particular and of the Meiji political system in general, Inoue Kowashi is that man. His ideas represented not only his personal beliefs, but they also constituted the fundamental guidelines in the framing of the constitution. Since he very seldom appeared in the limelight of Meiji politics, his contribution is somewhat obscured.[11]

National unity and national strength were, as we have seen, the main problems of the Meiji leaders. How should these goals be achieved? There was the moral and religious approach of the Imperial Household bureaucrats; there was the military and authoritarian approach of those advocating the invasion of Korea; and there was the liberal constitutional approach. Inoue attempted a synthesis of these conflicting approaches, trying to avoid all extreme positions. He dedicated all his energies to building the modern Japanese state in a period when, though the sway of traditional customs and values was still powerful, the influence of Western culture had become irresistible.

Inoue was from Kumamoto, and therefore he did not belong to the Satsuma-Chōshū coalition. That he was able to work closely with the "ins" of the court party and with the Satsuma and Chōshū leaders is in itself a proof of his diplomatic and adaptable spirit. While all the other bureaucrats under the order of the great Meiji leaders lost their individuality or their jobs, Inoue was able to keep both until his death.[12]

Inoue joined the government about the same time that another Kumamoto man, Motoda Eifu, was called to render service as the emperor's tutor. Motoda belonged to the conservative group. Inoue, in comparison, could be called rather progressive and liberal. Motoda worked closely with the members of the Imperial Household, while Inoue was at the service of the people immediately responsible for the political decisions.

Inoue started his government service in 1871 as a secretary in the Department of Justice. In 1872 and 1873 he traveled to

Europe to investigate the legal systems of the West. From September 1874 he worked under Ōkubo Toshimichi, and, at Ōkubo's death, under Iwakura Tomomi and later under Itō Hirobumi. We have already pointed out that Iwakura's opinion on the constitution in 1881 was written by Inoue, who was under the influence of Roesler. In a letter to Itō in July 1881, Inoue expressed the same fundamental ideas on what the constitution should be:

> To put into effect a Prussian-style constitution is an extremely difficult task under existing circumstances; but at the present time it is possible to carry it out and win over the majority and thus succeed. This is because the English-style constitution has not become firmly fixed in the minds of the people. Among the samurai in the country-side more than one half, no doubt, have a lingering desire to uphold the imperial house.
>
> But if we let pass by this opportunity and vacillate, within two or three years the people will become confident that they can succeed, and no matter how much oratory we may use, it will be difficult to win them back. Most of the political parties will be on the other side, public opinion will cast aside the draft of a constitution presented by the government, and the private drafts of the constitution will win out in the end.[13]

These ideas of Inoue's were not formed on the spur of the moment, nor were they solely due to Roesler's influence. Inoue had visited Europe in 1872 for a full year and had studied the legal systems of various countries.[14] He noticed that France was always in turmoil, though it prided itself of a constitution based on a social contract. Prussia, on the contrary, was peaceful, and the relations between monarch and people were well defined and stable. The Prussian constitution was not derived from a social contract, but was granted by the monarch. Inoue's preference for the Prussian system goes back to his first-hand experience in Europe. Roesler helped Inoue find the ideological framework on which to base a political system.

The New Theory of the State

It is hard to present a systematic analysis of Inoue Kowashi's thought. His published books and writings are very few.[15] Many of his manuscripts political or legal opinions were generally answers to particular questions from Iwakura or Itō which emerged from concrete, well-defined situations. Although these documents may not express the whole range of his thought, they at least give us the outline of his political system. One of these important documents was "Kyōiku-gi" (Opinion on education),[16] which Inoue wrote for Itō. It was an answer and criticism of "Kyōgaku taishi" (The great principles of education),[17] a document written by Motoda, which purported to express the emperor's own sentiments on education. Motoda severely criticized Western-style texts on ethics as responsible for the decline in public morals. The Japanese family system and loyalty to the state were being destroyed; students were being taught high-sounding academic theories and empty arguments. Motoda advocated a return to the teaching of the Chinese classics and the Confucian virtues. Inoue accepted the description of the evil customs of the day, but he stated that the evils in the educational system were more apparent than real. Educational methods stressing scientific and technical education were not invalid, he said; and vaunted educational abuses were simply a reflection of the rapid changes stemming from the restoration itself. The changes had been too rapid, and the sphere of liberty in speech and action had been greatly increased. The former samurai found their new status not to their liking and were criticizing the new regime. To this discontent was added the new, extreme ideological movement that was coming from Europe and spreading itself all over the nation. It was too early to critizice the new system, said Inoue. This system had been established for the welfare of the country, and it would be tragic if it were changed without trial and were replaced by the old educational system. Inoue warned that if radical methods were used to try to extirpate these fleeting ills, the country might easily fall into the errors that had plagued Tokugawa Japan. Accordingly, political moralizing and speeches were certainly not the need of the day.[18]

Motoda had advocated the establishment of *kokkyō,* or national doctrine.[19] Inoue answered that it was not the role of the state to establish a national religion or to decide the way of thinking of the country. The imposition of ethical principles was outside the province of politics. However, history, literature, language, and good manners must be protected, because they were constitutive elements of the nation. Practical sciences especially should be taught more thoroughly so that the students would not involve themselves in idle political discussions. Thus the first and fundamental principle for Inoue was that of separation of state and religion. This concept holds that there are some spheres in which the state cannot interfere because they are not political matters. He was against any indoctrination program; he stressed the necessity of a good technical education, not only to prepare the students for the new tasks of modernization and industrialization, but also to keep them free of dangerous political ideologies. This principle of the separation of state and religion was later often upheld by Itō Hirobumi and Inoue in the discussions on the constitution and in the formulation of the "Kyōiku chokugo" (Imperial rescript on education).[20]

The second basic principle of Inoue's political thought was also formulated in opposition to Motoda's ideas. In 1879 Motoda had presented a memorial to the throne on the establishment of constitutional government,[21] urging the issuing of a constitution. This constitution, however, was supposed to be like the Seventeen-Article Constitution of Shōtoku Taishi, defining the general rules of administration without any concessions to the principles of joint rule or of limited government. Such joint rule would mean an imitation of Western ways, which would violate the national polity. Itō showed Motoda's documents to Inoue. Inoue pointed out that despite its title the Seventeen-Article Constitution of Shōtoku Taishi did not represent a real constitutional government but merely set up public service regulations. Real constitutionalism, said Inoue, involved the fundamental principle of joint rule by the king and the people and joint decision by the people and the king. Without legislative participation of the representatives of the people, there could not be constitutionalism. A constitutional form of government demanded clear limits on the powers of the monarch and a sharing of the legislative power with the people.[22] This principle of participation in the legislative process was basic in Inoue's thought, and he never wavered in its defense.

The third principle of Inoue's system was transcendentalism, that is, the conviction that the cabinet should be above political parties and free from the interference of the diet in exectuive matters. This principle was stated openly in Iwakura's opinion on the constitution, which Inoue prepared, and in the letters he wrote to Itō and Iwakura during the political crisis of 1881. In these documents Inoue strongly attacked the English form of constitutional government as it was advocated by Ōkuma Shigenobu.[23] Also, because he was under the influence of Roesler, Inoue defended the Prussian-style constitution and, therefore, the principle of transcendentalism. The administration had to be above all political division and struggle. The cabinet could not be a party cabinet, because by definition a party cabinet would represent only the interests of one part of the state. Behind this theory of political transcendentalism was the Hegelian ideology of the role of the state. This ideology had influenced Stein and through Stein had been accepted by Roesler and Inoue. Society was essentially class society, and class struggle was the true content of society. The general and inalterable condition of society was the struggle between a dominant and a dependent class. The social order was necessarily a class order; its prime feature was self-seeking, that is, the general inclination of each to acquire the means for his own independence and the means for making others dependent. In contrast to the principle of society, the principle of the state was the development, progress, wealth, power, and intelligence of all individuals without distinction, positing all individuals as free and equal. The state preserved the common interests, impartiality, and freedom from the conflicting private interests of society. Only the state could give a superior spiritual and moral sense.

Inoue's opposition to the party-cabinet principle is found in this ideology. He asked Roelser what the basis of a true form of constitutional government had to be. Roesler sent him a long and detailed description of his sociopolitical system. Roesler saw that the development of society would lead necessarily to a democratic form of government. He predicted that the bourgeoisie would become the dominant class in Japan. It should be checked so as not to undermine the security of other classes, both that of the landowners and that of the proletariat. Roesler said that the state's most urgent task was to maintain impartially the welfare of the whole and a harmonious social balance through social legislation and an active administrative policy that worked for the physical and cultural welfare of the lower classes. To overcome class conflict and to maintain an ethical political attitude that placed the welfare of the whole above class interest, the institution of hereditary monarchy was necessary. This monarchy, possessing the loyalty of the people, would care for the common welfare and would become the custodian of the weak.[24]

The final principle of Inoue's system was the *kokutai*. He was opposed, as we have seen, to any imposition of a state religion or state ethical code. Yet he and Itō strongly felt that there was the urgent need for a rallying point of the loyalty of all citizens. In Europe and in America religion and a long tradition of limited government were the "pivot" of the constitution. Japan had neither a religion nor a political tradition which could become the central point of the new constitutional government. It was for this reason that Inoue and Itō had recourse to what Roesler criticized as mythological principles. The reign of an unbroken line of emperors for ages eternal thus became the first principle of the Japanese political system.[25]

The preparatory work of the constitution started officially with Itō's mission to Europe in 1882. Actually, however, Itō and his collaborators were engaged in the drafting of the constitution only from 1886 to the spring of 1888. As soon as the work of drafting the constitution began, Itō Hirobumi presented to Inoue, Itō Miyoji, and Kaneko an outline of instructions to follow in the formulation of the charter:

1. The general principles relating to the Imperial House should be separated from the constitution by enactment of an Imperial House Law.

2. Consideration of the national polity and the history of Japan should be the fundamental principles that guide the drafting of the constitution.

3. The constitution should be only a general outline concerning the administration of the empire; and it should be written in such a way that it may respond flexibly to the development of the national destiny.

4. The law of the houses and the election law for members of the House of Representatives should be determined by statute law.

5. The organization of the House of Peers should be determined by imperial ordinance, and any amendments of this ordinance should require the consent of the same house.

6. The territorial boundaries of the Japanese empire should not be included in the constitution but fixed by statute.

7. Impeachment of state ministers should be excluded. Both houses should have the right to address the throne.[26]

These seven points, together with Iwakura's fundamental principles, formed the basis and the distinguishing features of the Meiji Constitution. Before reaching the final draft, known as the Imperial Draft Constitution (Goshijun-an), over ten drafts had been prepared. Among them the most important ones were Drafts A and B by Inoue Kowashi.[27] In Draft A the comments of Roesler and Mosse were appended, and in Draft B the pertinent clauses of foreign constitutions were appended to each article. These drafts were prepared and presented to Itō around May 1887. These two drafts were very close to the final Meiji Constitution; there were, however, a few important differences. Inoue's drafts did not have any special article on the sacredness and inviolability of the emperor. The consent of the diet was made necessary not only in legislative matters, but also for the ratification of special treaties. The people were designated as citizens, not as subjects. The equality of all before the law, regardless of birth and status, was clearly expressed. Free enterprise and freedom of education were recognized and defended. However, the right of the diet to initiate legislation was not included in Inoue's drafts. In general it can be said that Inoue's documents were much more liberal than the Meiji Constitution and, for that matter, Roesler's draft.[28]

In June 1887 Itō Hirobumi and his most trusted collaborators withdrew to the little island of Natsushima, between Yokohama and Yokosuka. There Itō Hirobumi, Inoue Kowashi, Itō Miyoji, Kaneko Kentarō, and Roesler discussed in great secrecy the constitutional problems. Because the drafting activities were kept closely hidden from public view, rumors began to circulate as to the philosophical tenets of the constitution, some claiming that the draft followed the English line of constitutional government, and others describing the draft as conservative and Bismarckian.

Itō Hirobumi, using Inoue's Draft A as a basis, wrote a revised draft known as the "Natsushima sōan" (Natsushima draft), the name being taken from the place where it was prepared.[29] This draft represented a combination of Roesler's and Inoue's drafts; its general tendency, however, was more conservative than the documents on which it was based. The people became Japanese subjects; the emperor's person was declared sacred and inviolable. The rights to initiate legislation, to petition the throne, and to question the ministers disappeared.

As soon as the Natsushima Draft was completed, Inoue Kowashi appended his "Chikujō iken" (Article-by-article opinion)[30] and proposed some revisions. Roesler, too, suggested some changes in his "Kempō sōan shūsei iken" (Opinion on the revision of the draft constitution).[31] Inoue, in his suggestions, for instance, opposed the insertion of the sacredness and inviolability of the emperor's person. He argued that the concept of sacredness (*shinsei*) did not belong to constitutional law. Moreover, he said, the word "inviolable" was very difficult to translate into Japanese. Inoue preferred that those concepts be expressed in the preamble of the constitution, not in the body of the document.

Once again Itō Hirobumi, Inoue, Itō Miyoji, and Kaneko examined the Natsushima Draft, together with Inoue's and Roesler's comments, and by the middle of October 1887 a revised plan was completed. Inada Masatsugu calls it the "October Draft."[32] This draft accepted many of Inoue's suggestions. If the Natsushima Draft was closer to Roesler's ideas, the October Draft corrected the ultraconservative tendencies of Roesler's transcendentalism and reflected Inoue's desire to give a greater role to the diet.

After the completion of the October Draft, Itō Hirobumi and Itō Miyoji departed for a tour of inspection of the defense fortifications in Kyushu and Okinawa. They were absent from November 8 to December 17, 1887. During this period Inoue Kowashi continued his research on the constitution and submitted a long series of questions to Roesler and Mosse. These questions dealt with a broad range of constitutional problems, especially with the power of the emperor and the diet. Roesler again and again repeated his arguments in favor of a strong monarchic system. The diet, according to Roesler, was not a parallel organ to the king, nor was it an organ having sovereign powers. The diet was completely subordinate to the monarch, and, within the limits determined by the constitution, it had the right to help the king in the exercise of his sovereign powers. The emperor was the only independent repository of sovereign power, but through the constitution he was to determine freely the limitations on the exercise of this sovereignty. The constitution did not involve any separation or division of powers as did the English or French models, but only a limitation in the exercise of these powers.[33] Roesler always tended to enlarge the independent power of the executive, and he interpreted the emergency powers in a very illiberal way.

Following these discussions Inoue prepared his "Shūsei iken" (Revision opinion).[34] On his return Itō Hirobumi examined Inoue's opinion, and in January he called together his collaborators and they prepared the "February Draft."[35] This draft is very similar to the October Draft, the only difference being a somewhat more precise and appropriate formulation. The February Draft was revised in a few places and commentary was appended to each article. After this revision, it became the final draft, entitled "Dai Nihon teikoku kempō" (Imperial Constitution of Japan)[36].

This summary description of the numerous drafts and revisions, of the prolonged discussions and investigations, more than anything else speaks of the seriousness and dedication of the Japanese founding fathers. They were forming a new constitution, and at the same time they were laying down the foundations of a new legal and political terminology where there had been none before. It is too simple to describe these men as bent on framing an absolutist document concentrating all power in the hands of the emperor, or rather in the hands of the "oligarchy." To say that Itō and Inoue agreed with the reactionary views of German scholars wholeheartedly and without any hesitation[37] seems to be an oversimplication of the constitutional history of early Meiji Japan. Here too one has to take into account the ambivalent commitments of the Meiji leaders. They were trying to build a strongly centralized government. They were not ready to yield power to the opposition. Yet they were not simply power-hungry; they were not willing to accept any solution, even if it favored a more authoritarian form of government, if they did not see how it could be combined with a true form of constitutionalism.

After being completed, the final draft was presented to the emperor in April 1888. But now the problem arose of what to do next. What procedure should be used in ratifying the draft? One proposal was to submit the draft to the Genrōin for deliberation; Itō rejected this proposal because he was afraid of the liberal ideas of the Genrōin. Another plan recommended that it be discussed by a constitutional council composed both of government leaders and private citizens. It had already been decided that the constitution should be one granted by the emperor; thus the idea of a constituent assembly was discarded. Itō, however, rejected also the conservative suggestion that approval by the emperor alone would be sufficient. The proposal of discussing the draft only in the cabinet meetings was rejected by Itō, because in case of divisions of opinion the emperor himself would have to be called upon to resolve the stalemate. This direct involvement would cause trouble to the emperor, forcing him to take sides. Finally, Itō decided that the draft should be discussed and ratified by an *ad hoc* council, the newly established Sūmitsuin, or Privy Council.[38] On April 30, Itō resigned from his post as prime minister and became president of the Privy Council so that he could closely control the discussions and eventual revisions.

The Privy Council was formally opened on May 8, and the discussions began on the Imperial House Law, the Imperial Constitution, the Law of the Houses of the Diet, the Election

Law, and the Imperial Ordinance concerning the House of Peers. These discussions continued until January 1889. During that time the Privy Council met in forty-one regular sessions and three special meetings, all but one of which were held in the presence of the emperor.

On the first day of the meetings a summary of Roesler's opinion on the draft constitution was distributed for the benefit of the participants. The discussions were very lively and very outspoken. Shimizu Shin, in his book *Teikoku kempō seitei kaigi* (The council for the enactment of the Imperial Constitution),[39] gives a detailed description of the meetings and discussions. This book was published in 1940 when chauvinistic nationalism was rampant. It was immediately banned because its contents called into question some of the tenets of official ideology, which made the constitution a direct manifestation of the Emperor Meiji's benevolence. It is difficult to understand why Western authors writing after 1945 about the making of the Meiji Constitution have failed to consult this valuable work.[40] Inada Masatsugu also gives a lengthy survey of the series of discussions and changes in the draft constitution.[41]

More than a month was spent in the examination of the Imperial House Law. On June 18, 1888, the Privy Council began the discussions on the draft constitution.[42] On this occasion Itō Hirobumi spoke about the principles that had guided the framers of the constitution. This speech is of vital importance to an understanding of Itō's constitutional ideas. It reveals in Itō a deep understanding of the working of a constitutional government. Here Itō spoke about one of the most crucial problems in political life: every system of government, especially a constitutional form of government, requires the rationalization of a system of fundamental beliefs of religious or quasi-religious character into a political way of life. It was Japan's tragedy that the only set of beliefs around which the new system was being built was the myth of the *kokutai*, capable of totalitarian, reactionary interpretations. In this respect, Motoda Eifu and Itō Hirobumi, though differing in their premises, were upholding the same political rationalization. Itō said:

Up to this day in oriental countries, there has been no example of constitutional government. Japan is the first country to try such a system. We are attempting a new creation, and we cannot predict now whether this step will serve the interests of the nation or not. Twenty years ago we abolished the feudal system and opened relations with foreign countries. We chose this path for the progress of the nation, and we cannot change it now. The result will be seen in the future if we now start with caution. As you all know, during this century all over Europe constitutionalism has been adopted, but this is not a sudden creation. European constitutionalism is rooted in a long history and its beginnings go back to the ancient past. In our country, however, constitutional government is a completely new phenomenon. Therefore, in establishing this new constitution we must first discover what is the "pivot" which sustains our country. What is the cornerstone of our country? This is the problem we have to solve. If there is no cornerstone, politics will fall into the hands of the uncontrollable masses; and then the government will become powerless; and the country will be ruined. To preserve its existence and to govern the people, the state must not lose the use of the administrative power. Constitutionalism in Europe has more than a thousand years of life. The people have been nurtured in this system. Moreover, religion has been the foundation of this form of government and has penetrated deeply into the hearts of the people. The people thus have a fundamental consensus.

In Japan, however, religion does not play such an important role and cannot become the foundation of constitutional government. Though Buddhism once flourished and was the bond of union between all classes, high and low, today its influence has declined. Though Shintoism is based on the traditions of our ancestors, as a religion it is not powerful enough to become the center of union of the country. Thus in our country the one institution which can become the cornerstone of our constitution is the Imperial House.

For this reason the first principle of our constitution is the respect for the sovereign rights of the emperor. But at the same time, in order to prevent the danger of abuse in the exercise of these sovereign powers, clear checks and limits have been established. The ministers are thus held responsible, so that power may not be abused.

Because the imperial sovereignty is the cornerstone of our constitution, our system is not based on the European ideas of separation of powers or on the principle in force in some European countries of joint rule of the king and the people. This is the fundamental principle of this draft constitution, and it will become evident in every article.[43]

Briefly stated, Itō recognized that constitutional government was a difficult political system. Written law was not enough. Itō understood clearly that in Europe and in America religion and long traditions of individual freedom formed the basis of constitutionalism. But in Japan religion was weak, and there was no tradition of responsible participation of the people in the affairs of state. Only the Imperial House could become the foundation of the new constitutional system. This speech defended clearly the idea of the *kokutai,* which built the nation around the emperor, who was the center of authority and the holder of all sovereign power. But Itō recognized also that there must be some limits and some checks so that the sovereign power of the emperor would not be abused. This fundamental idea of a limited political system, that is, of a real constitutional government, was even more strongly upheld by Itō during the discussions on article 5, which reads: "The emperor exercises the legislative power with the consent of the imperial diet." There was lively discussion on the propriety of the word "consent" (*shōnin*). Some members of the Privy Council wanted the word changed, for they held that the consent of the diet would destroy the sovereign power of the emperor.

Mori Arinori, then the minister of education, fought vigorously to have the word "consent" deleted from the draft. He argued that to accept the right to consent would change the traditional Japanese *kokutai* fundamentally and would introduce into Japan the principle of joint rule by the emperor and the people. The principle of consent would reduce the emperor to the position of the English monarch, who was a superfluous and useless ornament: "By giving the right of decision to the majority in the diet the sovereign power of the emperor is being given away to the diet as has happened in England."[44]

Mori and other members of the Privy Council advocated a system in which the diet would serve only as a sounding board. The diet was supposed to reflect public opinion and thus help the government to reach a sound judgment on pending legislation, but in no way was it to decide legislation. The power of decision remained intact in the hands of the emperor; this supreme power was indivisible and could not be shared with the diet. According to this opinion, article 5 would have to be revised to read: "The emperor exercises the legislative power after having consulted the imperial diet." The emperor accordingly was left free to follow whatever course he deemed best, even if the parliamentary majority had decided against such a law.

This was a clear rejection of constitutionalism as Itō and Inoue understood it. Itō forcibly defended the principle that without diet control of legislative matters there could not be real constitutional government:

There can be different interpretations of the word "consent"; but the fact remains that if we want to establish a constitutional government we have to give the right of decision to the diet. Without the consent of the diet, budgets or laws cannot be determined. This is the essence of constitutional government. In Europe there are different constitutional systems: there is the English one and the German one; there are also different interpretations on the limitations of power, but on the fundamental principle they are all agreed. Once they establish a constitutional government, the cabinet has a double responsibility, to the king and to the diet . . . In this sense there is a limitation also on the executive power. Moreover, in the legislative power, without the consent of the diet no laws can be enacted. These two limits constitute the real meaning of constitutional government. Without these two points there cannot be real constitutionalism. To disguise the two principles in the constitution would also mean the negation of the true meaning of a constitutional system.[45]

On February 15, 1889, a few days after the proclamation of the constitution, in his address on the constitution to the Conference of Presidents of Prefectural Assemblies, Itō again had the chance to express his views on the constitutional rights of the diet:

It may be asked why is it necessary to establish a diet to deliberate on the pros and cons of government? In the first place, the enactment of law requires consultation with representatives of the subjects. Secondly, the fixing of the state budget, i.e., the annual income and expenditure, requires the discussion of the many. The annual revenue of the state treasury consists of taxes levied on the people, and as the annual revenues are used to meet the expenditure necessary for the existence of the state, the consultation and decision of the diet should in all fairness be asked. This, in short, is the most valid reason for the establishment of a diet to deliberate on the pros and cons of government. One may say that in our constitution these two elements are provided for systematically.[46]

These few passages show Itō as a middle-of-the-roader. He resisted the pressure of the progressives on the constitutional question. He also showed himself capable of taking a firm stand against the more reactionary elements in government. The discussion on article 5 gave him one occasion to show his moderate tendencies; another occasion came in the discussion of the title of chapter II of the draft. The proposed title read "Shimmin kenri gimu" (Rights and duties of subjects). Mori Arinori objected to this and contended that the title should be changed to read "Shimmin no bunsai" (The status of subjects).[47] The word "rights" was inappropriate, Mori said, because in regard to the emperor, the Japanese subjects had nothing but a definite station in life and obligations. Itō replied by pointing out that Mori's contention was tantamount to repudiating the concept of constitutional law itself. Itō explained what the purpose of a constitution was:

> We must confess that [Mori's] theory is against all constitutional or legal thought. The spirit behind the establishment of a constitutional form of government is first to impose restrictions on the powers of the monarch and second to secure the rights of the subjects. Thus if the constitution does not express the rights of the subjects but lists only their obligations, the drafting of a constitution is pointless. In whatever country, when you do not protect the rights of the subjects and do not limit the power of the monarch, you have a despotic government, in which the rights of the ruler become as unlimited as the duties of the subjects. The main purpose of a constitution is to establish limits on the powers of the monarch and to define clearly the rights and duties of the subjects . . . [Mori's] revision is thus against constitutional law. If you take away from the constitution rights and duties, then the constitution loses its role of protecting the people.[48]

This was a clear profession of constitutionalism: the constitution was established to set up a system of well-defined limits on the power of the monarch and to protect the rights of the people. If this principle had been kept in mind in the years following the promulgation of the Meiji Constitution, the accusation of absolutism and totalitarianism would not have been made. Whatever the later development of Japanese politics and political thought might be, it remains true that Itō, in the presence of the emperor, had defended with strong words the real meaning of a limited constitutional government.

In 1899, ten years after the promulgation of the constitution, Itō Hirobumi made a speech in his native town of Hagi. He explained in plain language the final goal of the reforms undertaken since the Meiji Restoration: to have the people take an active role in the decision-making process of the nation:

> They [the Japanese people] now have the right to share in legislative rights, which come from the Emperor's sovereign powers, and to elect and send representatives. Having the right to send representatives they can, indirectly, voice their opinions on the advisability and the faults of their country's administration. Thus, every member of the nation—be he a farmer, craftsman, or merchant—must become familiar beforehand with the merits and demerits of questions of government . . . To resolve a situation in which the opinions of the people are so diverse as to seem impossible of reaching a decision we have established a parliament to make the decisions on the basis of majority rule of its members. If you do not send representatives who are well informed on matters of government, the rights which you have earned by great effort will prove ineffective in practice.[49]

As in Inoue Kowashi's thought, so also in Itō's we do not find any identification of religion and state which later, in the Showa period, was presented as an original characteristic of the *kokutai*. The explanation of article 28, which reads, "Japanese subjects shall, within limits not prejudicial to peace and order and not antagonistic to their duties as subjects, enjoy freedom of religious belief," has no reference whatsoever to a special position reserved to Shintoism or to a state religion. Itō was very far from defending the theory of *saisei itchi* (union of state and religion) as an element of the new political structure. Institutionally speaking, Shinto was not accepted in the formulation of the new system. However, Shintoist assumptions—the divinity of the emperor and the imperial line— remained part of the basis of the extraconstitutional rationalization of the Meiji political system.

Itō opposed the idea of *kokkyō,* or national doctrine, for he was afraid that such a doctrine might become the vehicle for suppressing religious freedom, hindering the progress of education, and unnecessarily narrowing the activity of the intellectual world. Itō also feared an intermingling of religion and philosophy in government because it was not in keeping with the practice of modern states and reflectd the weak and ineffectual policies of the nineteenth century Tokugawa regime.

The explanation attached to article 28 was later published in Itō's *Kempō gikai* (Commentaries on the constitution) published in 1889. In order to understand the modern tendencies of the framers of the constitution it is useful to quote at length this commentary:

In Western Europe, during the middle ages, when religion exercised an ascendent influence, it was mixed up with politics, internal as well as external, and was very often the cause of bloodshed; while in the countries of the East, strict laws and severe penalties were provided in order to suppress religion. But the doctrine of freedom of religious belief, which dates back four centuries, first received practical recognition at the time of the French Revolution and of the independence of the United States of America, when public declaration was made on the subject. Since then, the doctrine has gradually won approval everywhere, until at present every country, although maintaining in some cases a state religion, and in others favoring a particular creed in the organization of society or in the system of its public education, nevertheless grants to its people by law entire freedom of religious beliefs . . .

Freedom of conscience concerns the inner part of man and lies beyond the sphere of interference by the laws of the State. To force upon a nation a particular form of belief by the establishment of a state religion is very injurious to the natural intellectual development of the people, and is prejudicial to the progress of science by free competition. No country, therefore, possesses by reason of its political authority, the right or the capacity to an oppressive measure touching abstract questions of religious faith. By the present Article, a great path of progress has been opened up for the individual rights of conscience, consistent with the direction in which the Government has steered its course since the restoration.[50]

It is true that the exterior forms of worship, the ways of propagating a religion, and the formation of religious associations and meetings were made subject to general legal or police restrictions, but these restrictions were also applied in other countries to prevent the disruption of public order.

The principle of freedom of religion and of separation of state and church was upheld also in the preparation of the Imperial Rescript on Education. Blatant statements in the original draft which attempted to impose moral and religious ideologies were altered, in order to make the rescript as universal as possible. In a letter to Yamagata Aritomo, prime minister at the time, Inoue remarked that "according to principles of constitutional government, the sovereign does not interfere with the freedom of conscience of his subjects."[51] Motoda Eifu, in contrast, believed that the sovereign was obliged to lead his subjects in the way of virtue and must therefore direct their moral lives.[52] In the same letter to Yamagata already quoted, Inoue spoke of the fundamental principle of freedom of philosophical and intellectual investigation: "In this rescript, philosophical reasoning must be avoided, for philosophical reasoning always somehow arouses opposite ideas. The basic idea of the 'Way' should be entrusted to the investigation of philosophers. It is something that should never be fixed by the ruler's decree."[53]

Inoue's main contribution in the formulation of the Imperial Rescript on Education was in bringing into the final draft the constitutional principle which was not understood by Motoda Eifu. Motoda tried to criticize openly Western ideas and to expunge from the rescript all passages which he felt reflected Western utilitarianism. However, his attempt to remove the phrase inserted by Inoue, "respect the constitution and observe the laws," on the ground that it detracted from the concentration of all allegiance in the person of the emperor, was rejected by the emperor himself after several days' contemplation.[54] The final draft of the rescript was compiled by Inoue, and it was so worded that it could please everybody, without drawing either on Chinese learning or on Western ways. While Motoda tried to formulate a code based on feudal Confucianism, Inoue attempted a combination of different principles; the principle of the *kokutai* with its mythological and ultranationalistic implications was blended with the principle of modern constitutionalism.

This modern aspect was always present in Itō Hirobumi's mind, too. He felt that Japan had to be modernized and that the governmental structure should be patterned along constitutional lines. Strength and influence as a world power would be forthcoming to a Japan that absorbed the knowledge of Western science and modified its legal and administrative forms to fit in better with those of modern states.[55]

Itō's political thought would be completely vindicated of the accusation of reactionary authoritarianism and absolutism if one were to stop here. But to Itō's thought, as often happens in the case of practical politicians, there was also another side. Itō, like Roesler and Inoue, strongly believed in transcendentalism. The cabinet was above political divisions and out of the reach of the political parties' control. Itō often spoke about the cabinet's responsibility, but never did he come out openly stating that this responsibility was *to* the diet or *to* the people. He stated that irresponsible government had to be prevented, and thus he made the cabinet ministers responsible for all decisions made. But to whom were these ministers responsible? According to Itō, they were responsible only to the emperor. We have here a classic example of the vicious circle: to prevent the abuse of the sovereign power of the emperor, the ministers are held responsible; but this responsibility is to the emperor. The emperor is thus left out of control; he is by definition, in the strict legal sense of the word, irresponsible. Itō did not foresee the possibility of any emperor being not only legally but also mentally irresponsible, in which case the cabinet would be left without any possible means of control: "If Ministers of State were not responsible, the executive power could easily overstep the limits of law, which would thus become a mere collection of nominal enactments. The responsibility of Ministers is, as it were, a pillar supporting the Constitution and the law."[56] So far, this statement could be applied to any form of real constitutionalism, even democratic constitutionalism. But Itō continues in the same document: "When a Minister of State errs in the discharge of his functions, the power of deciding upon his responsibility belongs to the Sovereign of the State. He alone can dismiss a Minister, who has appointed him. Who then is it, except the Sovereign, that can appoint, dismiss and punish a Minister of State? The appointment and dismissal of them having been included by the Constitution in the sovereign power of the Emperor, it is only a legitimate consequence, that the power of deciding as to the responsibility of Minister, is withheld from the Diet."[57]

Itō, however, allowed some kind of indirect control to the diet insofar as the diet could put questions to the ministers and demand open answers from them before the public, and could petition the emperor presenting its views. This Itō called "an indirect method of controlling the responsibility of the ministers."[58]

Behind this idea of mitigated transcendentalism were the social ideas of the conflict and harmony Itō had learned from Roesler and Stein:

Administrative affairs ought to advance hand in hand with the march of social improvement. Since the Restoration the condition of society has been greatly changed with the downfall of the feudal system, and the mode of living and all sorts of undertakings have assumed an entirely new phase and are now in a career of striking progress. Now in this transition from the old to the new order of things, we inevitably find many forces in a stationary and unprogressive state, while other elements and antagonistic tendencies may be found perpetually conflicting with each other and thereby preventing a happy harmonization of social life. It is the Government's purpose to superintend these social forces, to protect deserving ones, and to point out the direction in which they ought to be conducted so as to secure the gradual and complete results of progress. It is owing to these circumstances that embarrassments and difficulties of an extraordinary nature are encountered in the field of administrative affairs.[59]

According to Itō, only an institution above the perpetual conflicts which were being fought in society between reactionary and radical forces could promise a steady advance in the way of progress and modernization. This institution was the imperial system, whose executive power was exercised by the cabinet. This was also the rationalization of Yamagata Aritomo *chōzen naikaku shugi* (the principle of a transcendental cabinet).[60] The crucial problem of political science which deals with consensus and conflict in society was solved by the Japanese leaders' acceptance of Stein's, Gneist's, and Roesler's notion of the state as the synthesis and the harmonizing principle among conflicting forces in society.

The theory of the state emerging from the rationalization of the leading figures who framed the Meiji Constitution is not easy to define. Perhaps the characteristics we have observed in Inoue Kowashi and Itō Hirobumi might serve as the guideline. These essential elements were the notion of the *kokutai,* based on the imperial line unbroken for ages eternal, the theory of transcendentalism, and the conviction that a modern form of government implied constitutionalism, that is, real limitations of the imperial powers, participation of the diet in the decision-making process, and the defense of the rights of the citizens.

The notion of the *kokutai* was forced into the constitution because of the absence in Japan of a tradition based on religion and long experience of constitutional rights. The Japanese leaders thought that the *kokutai* was the only possible principle which could give union and continuity to the Japanese nation. The *kokutai* myth was reinterpreted to involve the principle of absolute sovereignty of the emperor. Thus Itō's and Inoue's desire to build a modern state founded on modern thought had no application in the first article of the constitution. The emperor was made the repository of sovereign power. Apparently this sovereign power came from the divine ancestors. Because of the divine nature traditionally accorded to the Sun Goddess Amaterasu, her command to her descendants to come down to earth and rule forever over the Japanese islands, and hence also the source of the emperor's sovereignty were regarded as divine. This idea is clearly expressed in the Imperial Oath, made in the sanctuary of the Imperial Palace upon promulgation of the constitution. This oath was prepared by Inoue Kowashi.

In accordance with the Grand Design [Amaterasu's commandment], *coeval as it is with heaven and earth, and in accordance with this design alone, We have succeeded to the Divine Throne* . . . In view of the progressive tendency of human affairs and the advance of civilization, it has been incumbent upon us, for the sake of clarifying the instructions bequeathed by the Imperial founder Amaterasu of Our House and by Our other Ancestors, to establish fundamental laws and clearly explain their provisions so that they may serve on the one hand as a guide for Our Imperial posterity and may on the other amplify the means by which Our subjects shall assist the Imperial rule. Not only that but these laws have been created so that the teachings of Our Ancestors may be faithfully observed forever and eternally; and through their observance, the foundation of the state shall be increasingly strengthened and the welfare of the Japanese shall constantly advance. Hence we now establish the Imperial House Law and the Constitution which we solemnly regard as merely *a reiteration in Our own day of the grand precepts of government*

that have been handed down by the Imperial Founder of Our House and by
Our other Imperial Ancestors to their descendants.[61]

This oath clearly suggests that the emperor's occupation of
the throne, his sovereignty, and the constitution itself derived
solely from his divine ancestors, which would seem to give him
unbridled authority. But on the other hand, the emperor's
power under the constitution was not unlimited, and his judgments or even his commands had no legal force in themselves.
To be effective as state law, his judgments and commands had
to be countersigned by a state minister. This meant essentially
that the government was conducted by the emperor upon the
advice of his ministers. Yet to establish as the government an
emperor who was surrounded by his ministerial advisers
meant in practice the implementation of the theory of a transcendental cabinet. The emperor's prerogative became the unchecked authority of the cabinet. In substance, this was in accordance with the constitution because, in spite of the theory
that sovereignty was vested in the emperor, the government
was actually operated according to the views of the cabinet; and
any matter submitted by the cabinet to the emperor was always
approved. In no case was there any instance of the emperor's
withholding approval from a cabinet proposal.

What is more, the cabinet in any of its arbitrary decisions
could benefit from the protection afforded by the mystic
prestige of an aloof emperor since the cabinet's conduct was
regarded in a legal sense as the exercise of an imperial prerogative legitimately based on the advice of imperial ministers. This
was one of the possible alternatives if the *kokutai* and transcendentalism were stressed; the result was an irresponsible
transcendental government. That this type of government was
very conspicuous in Japan after the Manchurian Incident needs
no comment here.

In accordance with the idea of the *kokutai* and transcendentalism, the constitution put the greatest stress on the prerogatives of the emperor and, consequently, of the cabinet. Article 1 embraced the principle of direct personal rule by the emperor. The relation between the diet and the emperor was characterized by a division of power that left the diet overshadowed by the emperor. The emperor sanctioned laws and ordered them to be promulgated and executed; he convoked the diet, opened, closed, and prorogued it; he dissolved the House of Representatives; he could issue imperial ordinances in the place of laws, when the diet was not sitting, if the public safety demanded such action; he determined the organization of the different branches of administration and he fixed the salaries of all civil and military officers, whom he appointed and dismissed; he had supreme command of the army and navy; he declared war, made peace, and concluded treaties; and he conferred titles of nobility, rank, order, and other marks of honor. All of these things he was entitled to do without seeking prior approval of the diet.

Nevertheless, these so-called arbitrary actions of the emperor did require the countersignature of a state minister, which made the emperor less autocratic than an absolute monarch. But the restraining influence of a minister of state did not apply equally to each of the powers reserved to the emperor. The supreme command of the military and the conferring of titles and marks of honor were regarded as special prerogatives that depended solely upon the emperor's personal sanction. In particular, the emperor's command over the army and navy was beyond all advice-giving authority of the ministers. The special position of the military was not explicitly stated in the constitution; it was handed down by custom and by certain laws enacted prior to the constitution. As in the case of the ministerial decisions, the decisions of the military—even the most disastrous decisions of the 1930's—could be sanctioned as expressions of the emperor's direct will. The provisions of the constitution stressing over and over again the prerogatives of the emperor could have worked to the promotion of the common good of the Japanese people only if there had been some way of guaranteeing that all the emperors would be outstanding leaders and all the cabinet ministers and military chiefs would be dedicated solely to the interests of the nation and not susceptible to error and internal division and strife.

Roesler's thought on transcendentalism was based on his assumption that only an aristocratic form of government could resolve the class struggle and the other social problems emerging from modern society. He did not realize that the Japanese leaders did not constitute a real aristocracy which could transmit its values and characteristics to the following generations, and that even among the leaders themselves there existed profound divisions and factionalism.

But in the political system emerging from the Meiji Constitution there was also another side, the side of constitutionalism and liberalism. Notwithstanding the emperor's right to rule directly, his exercise of the rights of sovereignty was limited. The limitation of power differed according to whether the particular sphere of government concerned was the judicial, the executive, or the legislative branch. The judicial power, for example, had to be exercised by the courts of law according to law, independently of all interference from the executive even though this was done in the name of the emperor. The legislative power, which was to be exercised in principle by the emperor himself, still required the consent of the diet. No law could take effect without such consent. The diet thus was not a mere administrative office of the central government. Against Torio Koyota a member of the Privy Council, who tried to interpret the diet as an "office for administering the emperor's government," Itō had replied in the discussions of the Privy Council that such an interpretation was in conflict with the purpose of establishing a constitutional government.[62]

Next to its legislative authority of giving consent and initiating legislation the second most important function of the diet was its right to make representations to the government with regard to the law or to any other subject, to make addresses to the emperor, and to receive petitions from the people. And third in order of importance was the diet's right of self-government, which entitled both houses to establish, apart from what was provided for in the constitution and in the Law of the Houses, the rules necessary for the management of their internal affairs.

In addition to these rights, the diet had the power to question and to receive reports from the government as provided by the Law of the Houses. The government, however, was under no responsibility to the diet: this was, as we have seen, the principle of transcendentalism. Thus the idea of having cabinets formed from members of the diet and having cabinets subject to votes of no confidence was not expressed in the constitution. Yet it was impossible for the cabinet to remain completely independend of the diet, and votes of no confidence were indeed taken. When they were taken, the government chose in parliamentary fashion between resigning en bloc or dissolving the lower house and calling for a general election.

It is the independence of the judiciary power that especially reveals the liberal side of the Meiji political system. Article 57 of the constitution reads: "The Judicature shall be exercised by the Courts of Law according to law." This provision of the constitution made it explicit that the law would be the basis for judicial decisions and that the judicature would be absolutely independent of all authority, particularly the executive. So that this independence could be not even indirectly violated it was established that the judges should hold their positions for life. Except when a judge happened to be in compulsory retirement or except when placed on the waiting list, he could not be transferred to another official position, or to another court, nor could he be suspended, dismissed, or have his salary reduced unless he received a criminal sentence or disciplinary punishment by the court itself. Ishii Ryōsuke points out an interesting incident to show the tradition of judicial independence in Japan:

> The big test for this declared independence of the courts was not long in coming. On May 11, 1891, only a few months after the *Constitution* has gone into effect, the Crown Prince of Russia, later to become Nicholas II, was attacked and cut on the head with a saber by Tsuda Sanzō, a member of the Russian Prince's police guard. In view of the delicate relations between Japan and Russia at this time, the government wanted the attack treated as though it were an offence against the Japanese Imperial family so that the attacker would suffer the extreme penalty of death. The government's position on this case was also shared by a majority of the Supreme Court justices. Having the attack treated as an offence against the Imperial Family was the only way the death penalty could be imposed; for the *Old Criminal Code* (1882) did not permit capital punishment for attempted murder. In spite of the pressure for a death sentence, however, Chief Justice Kojima Iken was able to persuade his fellow justices through sheer reason alone to accept a different view, and eventually on May 27 the Supreme Court only sentenced the police guard to a life term of hard labor. While the Chief Justice's act of persuasion was in itself a violation of judicial independence, the outcome of the case was nevertheless a shining example of the judiciary's independence of the executive and was tremendously significant for having put just such an impression in the minds of the Japanese.[63]

Itō Hirobumi clearly accepted this principle of judicial independence. Although he tried hard to show that the judicial power belongs to the emperor alone, and that no theory of the separation of the three powers can be applied to the Japanese case, Itō openly stated that "trials must be conducted according to law; the law is the sole standard for conducting trials, which must always be conducted in a court of law."[64] Itō pointed to the difference between the administrative and the judicial power, both of which were necessary for the welfare of the nation:

> In the judiciary, law is everything, and the question of convenience is left out of consideration. In the administrative, however, measures are taken to meet the ever changing requirements demanded for the convenience and necessities of society; and law simply shows the limits beyond which they are not permitted to obtrude. Such being the distinction between the nature of the administrative and that of the judiciary, were there only administrative officials and no judicial functionaries, the rights of individuals would be in danger of being made subservient to the ends of social convenience and would ultimately be encroached upon by power.[65]

The final basic element of the new theory of the state was the idea that the Japanese people had rights and were not mere subjects at the mercy of the government. The traditional view of the Japanese social and political system held that the retainer and subject could not appeal against his lord because the retainer owned his lord absolute obedience. Chapter II of the constitution, therefore, represented a break with the past, and guarantees against the executive power were clearly stated and determined. However, these rights were not recognized as natural rights, but as gifts from the emperor. Moreover, these rights and liberties could be altered and limited by legislative power. Because there existed no specific constitutional provisions to determine what degree of legal restriction would be suitable in case of emergency, the way was open to serious infringements of individual liberties through legislative acts, as was the case after the middle 1920's.

Though limited, the rights guaranteed by the constitution were of great value. These were the liberty of abode; freedom from illegal arrest, detention, trial, or punishment; right of trial by a lawful judge; the inviolability of the individual's home; the right to the secrecy of the mail; the inviolable right of property; freedom of religious belief; the liberty of speech, writing, publication, public meetings, and associations; and the right of petition. Among these rights, as we have already pointed out, one of the most notable was the freedom of religious belief, understood as a principle of noninterference on the part of the state in religious and intellectual matters. At the same time, however, we cannot say that the later rationalization which made of Shinto some kind of national religion, compelling each Japanese regardless of his faith to accept it, was completely unrelated to the constitution.

CONCLUSION

What was the idea of the state which was the basis of Meiji political thought and institutions? Do we have to accept the assumption of the 1930's that the Meiji Constitution and the Meiji leaders built an absolute state based on the unchanged and unchangeable *kokutai?* These are the questions that have confronted us in the course of this study.

The Meiji leaders first and foremost wanted to build a strong national state. This meant, in other words, antifeudalism and centralization. The drive for power of the Meiji leaders was motivated not only by personal and factional ambitions but also by the conviction that a strong nation required a single center of authority. More than anybody else among the early Meiji leaders, Kido Takayoshi embodied this antifeudal drive toward unification. Unification and centralization meant the suppression of the han system and the establishment of the prefectures and also revolution in the social hierarchy. A long series of decrees abolished the privileges of the upper classes; and new social strata were brought into the highest levels of political responsibility. Education and the conscription laws were very powerful instruments for leveling off class distinctions and for instituting the beginnings of a merit system.

In the process of building the nation the Japanese leaders had in mind the Western pattern of modern government. The most powerful countries in the West were based in one way or another on constitutional governments. Constitutionalism appeared to the Japanese leaders as a necessary element for a strong modernized country. They were convinced that Western ideas of popular participation in government could not be suppressed altogether. They accepted as a necessary goal the sharing of power—the principle of *kummin dōchi*—or at least the principle that the imperial powers must be limited by the participation of the representative assembly in the legislative process.

The Western example was one reason for the acceptance of some form of constitutional government. Another powerful factor was the people's rights movement. Although the followers of this movement could be accused of unenlightened sectionalism and selfishness, they must be given credit for their battle for a more liberal form of government. Even in their inconsistency and in their selfishness the "outs" were a constant reminder to the "ins" that something had to be done to create a real constitutional system.

The third and probably the most important factor leading to constitutionalism was the division and factionalism among the "ins" themselves. To prevent arbitrariness and dissension in the administration it seemed expedient to promulgate a constitution in order to check factionalism, define responsibilities, and create a balance of power among conflicting personalities and groups.

A new theory of the state emerged from the framing of the Meiji Constitution: it was based essentially on an uneasy marriage of absolutist ideas with modern constitutional principles bound together by mythical traditions. The commitment to constitutional principles cannot be discarded simply as a useful means to appease the popular movement. The statements of Itō and Inoue are too frequent and too clear to be explained away as hypocrisy or sham constitutionalism. The Meiji Constitution was not as illiberal and absolutist as some interpretations assume. It contained provisions for its own amendment and was framed in such a way as to allow for further development in the direction of democratic government.

Notwithstanding the commitment to constitutional government, there were, however, in the political ideas of the Meiji leaders and in the Meiji Constitution strong authoritarian and reactionary implications: these can be summed up in the principles of the *kokutai* and transcendentalism. The Meiji leaders often sought to rationalize modern Western ideas and institutions through recourse to Japanese history and Japanese traditions. Itō's *Commentaries on the Constitution* displays a constant effort to refer all dispositions of the Meiji Constitution to past experiences and to prove that the new system was but an organic outgrowth of genuine Japanese traditions. While the Itō Mission was abroad studying various constitutional systems, particularly the Prussian one, Inoue Kowashi was left in Japan to delve deeply into Japanese history and mythology. By putting the emperor on a mythological throne out of the reach of popular control, the Japanese leaders were building a myth that later could be used to deny the fundamental element of constitutional government, the active participation of the people in political life, and the clear and effective limits imposed on the government powers. This transcendence of the imperial system was defended not only by the leaders in the government but also by leaders in the people's rights movement.

The mythological and quasi-religious formulation of the *kokutai* was not called into being for the first time by the constitution, nor was it carried out to its logical conclusions by the political leaders of early Meiji Japan. This formulation came later and it took more than twenty years after the promulgation of the Meiji Constitution for its final and comprehensive definition. This work was done by legal theorists like Hozumi Yatsuka and Uesugi Shinkichi and by nationalist philosophers like Inoue Tetsujirō and Kihira Masami. The roots, however, were all there in the Meiji Constitution and in some aspects of the political philosophy of the Meiji leaders.

The final answer to the central question of this study is that the Meiji leaders actually thought they had achieved a synthesis of disparate elements. In reality they had committed themselves to an ambiguous and ambivalent system in which limited government and transcendentalism, modern ideology and *kokutai,* and freedom of thought and imposition of a national myth were mixed but never assimilated. There was never a clear adjustment between the *kokutai* and constitutional monarchy; there was only an uneasy compromise by which constitutionalism and parliamentary government came into force in the twenties, but which also allowed the downfall of constitutionalism and the establishment of an authoritarian militarist dictatorship in the late thirties. The Meiji political rationalization allowed either a liberal interpretation or an absolutist reactionary one. The resolution was left to future generations.

The same kind of contradiction appeared in the power structure which emerged from the implementation of the constitution. The Meiji Constitution had built a pluralistic system in which the cabinet, the bicameral diet, the Privy Council, and other organs were supposed to be parts of the same body. The coordinating power was in theory the emperor. But Itō Hirobumi and Inoue Kowashi had rejected Roesler's proposal for a personal role of leadership by the emperor. In Itō's plan there was no place for the emperor to lead and control the various organs of government. This pluralistic system was conceived as a bulwark against the people's rights movement and at the same time as a compromise against a despotic monarchic system. Actually the extraconstitutional institution of the *genrō* (elder statesmen) replaced the emperor in his role of coordinating power. The *genrō* were the men behind the scenes maneuvering and pulling wires, especially in times of crisis and clashes among the multiple organs. Roesler had thought of the Meiji leaders as

Conclusion

an aristocracy and had expected them to form an aristocracy above division and petty interests. One doubts whether the identification of the *genrō* and the emperor can be said to represent what Roesler called "social monarchy." The resolution of pluralism in the power structure was placed in an extraconstitutional body with the inevitable result of irresponsibility and irrationality.

As far as the relations between cabinet and diet were concerned, though the Meiji Constitution stressed the idea of transcendental cabinets, in fact, the cabinet had neither the power nor the authority to disregard the diet or the political parties. Furthermore, in spite of the *hambatsu* (han clique) bureaucratic tendencies, the Meiji Constitution demanded a power structure including both diet and political parties. The tragedy of Japanese politics did not have its only origin in the Meiji Constitution or in the theories of the leaders of the Meiji political system. It was also the failure of the diet and the political parties to understand and take advantage of the rights and powers given them by the constitution that prevented the emergence of a genuine democratic system. As long as the diet and the parties existed there could be no pure absolutism or pure bureaucratic transcendentalism. The Meiji political system both in theory and practice was a mixture of authoritarianism and constitutionalism, a hybrid "absolute constitutional monarchy."

BIBLIOGRAPHY

NOTES

GLOSSARY

INDEX

BIBLIOGRAPHY

Akita, George. "Development of Parliamentary Government in Meiji Japan." Ph.D. thesis; Harvard, 1960.

——"The Meiji Constitution in Practice: The First Diet," *Journal of Asian Studies,* 22:31-46 (November 1962).

Allen, G. C. *A Short Economic History of Modern Japan, 1867-1937.* London, 1946.

Anderson, Ronald S. *Japan: Three Epochs of Modern Education.* Washington, D.C., 1959.

Asai Kiyoshi 浅井清. *Meiji rikken shisōshi ni okeru Eikoku gikai seido no eikyō* 明治立憲思想史に於ける英国議會製度の影響 (The influence of the English parliamentary system upon Meiji constitutional thought). Tokyo, 1935.

——*Genrōin no kempō hensan temmatsu* 元老院の憲法編纂顛末 (An account of the draft constitutions by the Genrōin). Tokyo, 1946.

Bailey, Jackson H. "Prince Saionji and the Popular Rights Movement of the 1880's," *Journal of Asian Studies,* 21:49-63 (November 1961).

Beckmann, George M. *The Making of the Meiji Constitution.* Lawrence, Kansas, 1957.

Bellah, Robert N. "Values and Social Change in Modern Japan," *Asian Cultural Studies,* 3:13-56 (1962). Tokyo: International Christian University.

Brown, Sidney D. "Kido Takayoshi and the Meiji Restoration: A Political Biography, 1833-1877." Ph.D. thesis; University of Wisconsin, 1952.

Bibliography

———"Kido Takayoshi (1833-1877): Meiji Japan's Cautious Revolutionary," *Pacific Historical Review*, 25:151-162 (1956).

———"Ōkubo Toshimichi: His Political and Economic Policies in Early Meiji Japan," *Journal of Asian Studies*, 21:183-197 (February 1962).

Clement, Ernest W. *A Short History of Japan.* Tokyo, 1936.

Conroy, Hilary. *The Japanese Seizure of Korea, 1868-1910.* Philadelphia, 1960.

Craig, Albert M. *Chōshū in the Meiji Restoration.* Cambridge, Mass., 1961.

Dore, R. P. *City Life in Japan.* Berkeley and Los Angeles, 1958.

Emerson, Rupert. *From Empire to Nation.* Cambridge, Mass., 1960.

Feldman, Horace Z. "The Meiji Political Novel: A Brief Survey," *Far Eastern Quarterly*, 9:245-255 (May 1950).

Friedrich, Carl J. *Constitutional Democracy.* Rev. ed.; Boston, 1950.

Fujita Tsuguo 藤田嗣雄. *Meiji kempōron* 明治憲法論 (On the Meiji Constitution). Tokyo, 1948.

Fukuzawa Yukichi. *Autobiography,* tr. Eiichi Kiyooka. Tokyo, 1960.

Fukuzawa Yukichi zenshū 福沢諭吉全集 (Collected works of Fukuzawa Yukichi). 21 vols.; Tokyo: Keiō Gijuku hensan 慶応義塾編纂, 1958-1963.

Gneist, Rudolf von. *Der Rechtsstaat und die Verwaltungsgerichte in Deutschland.* 2nd ed.; Berlin, 1879.

———*The English Constitution,* tr. Philip A. Ashworth. 2 vols.; New York, 1886.

———*The English Parliament,* tr. R. Jewery Shee. Boston, 1886.

Hackett, Roger F. "Yamagata Aritomo: A Political Biography." Ph. D. thesis; Harvard, 1955.

———"Nishi Amane: A Tokugawa-Meiji Bureaucrat," *Journal of Asian Studies*, 18:213-225 (February 1959).

Hall, Robert K. *Education for a New Japan.* New Haven, 1949.

Bibliography

———ed. *Kokutai no hongi: Cardinal Principles of the National Entity of Japan*, tr. John Owen Gauntlett. Cambridge, Mass., 1949.

Hamada Keiji. *Prince Itō*. Tokyo, 1936.

Harootunian, Harry D. "The Progress of Japan and the Samurai Class, 1868-1882," *Pacific Historical Review*, 28:255-266 (August 1959).

Hattori Shisō 服部之総. *Meiji no seijikatachi* 明治の政治家たち (Political leaders of Meiji Japan). 2 vols.; Tokyo, 1950, 1954.

Hijikata Kazuo 土方和雄. *Nakae Chōmin* 中江兆民. Tokyo, 1958.

Horie Eiichi 堀江英一 and Tōyama Shigeki 遠山茂樹, eds. *Jiyū minkenki no kenkyū* 自由民権期の研究 (Studies on the era of the people's rights movement). 2 vols.; Tokyo, 1959.

Hozumi Yatsuka 穂積八束. *Kensei taii* 憲政大意 (Essentials of constitutional government). Tokyo, 1917.

———*Kempō teiyō* 憲法提要 (Manual of constitutional law). 7th ed.; Tokyo, 1940.

Idditti Smimasa. *The Life of Marquis Ōkuma: A Maker of Japan*. Tokyo, 1940.

Ienaga Saburō 家永三郎. "Kyōiku chokugo seiritsu no shisō shiteki kōsatsu" 教育勅語成立の思想史的考察 (An ideological historical consideration of the making of the Imperial Rescript on Education); *Shigaku zasshi* 史学雑誌, 56:1173-91 (December 1946).

———*Kindai seishin to sono genkai* 近代精神とその限界 (The modern mind and its limitations). Tokyo, 1950.

———*Nihon kindai shisō shi kenkyū* 日本近代思想史研究 (Studies in the history of modern Japanese thought). Tokyo, 1953.

———"Nihon ni okeru kyōwashugi no dentō" 日本に於ける共和主義の伝統 (The tradition of republicanism in Japan); *Shisō* 思想, No. 410:1109-25 (August 1958).

Ike Nobutaka. *The Beginnings of Political Democracy in Japan*. Baltimore, 1950.

Inada Masatsugu 稲田正次. *Meiji kempō seiritsu shi* 明治憲法成立史 (History of the framing of the Meiji Constitution). 2 vols.; Tokyo, 1960, 1962.

Ishida Takeshi 石田雄. *Meiji seiji shisō shi kenkyū* 明治政治思想史研究 (Studies in the history of Meiji political thought). Tokyo, 1954.

Bibliography

————*Kindai Nihon seiji kōzō no kenkyū* 近代日本政治構造の研究 (Studies in the political structure of modern Japan). Tokyo, 1956

Ishii Ryōsuke 石井良助. *Tennō: Tennō tōji no shiteki kaimei* 天皇— 天皇統治の史的解明 (The Tennō: Historical studies on the imperial rule). Tokyo, 1952.

————*Meiji bunkashi: Hōseihen* 明治文化史—法制編 (History of Meiji culture: The legal system), vol. 2. Tokyo: Kaikoku hyakunen kinen bunka jigyō kai 開国百年記念文化事業会, 1954.

————ed. *Japanese Legislation in the Meiji Era,* tr. and adapted by William J. Chambliss (Centenary Culture Council Series, vol. 10). Tokyo, 1958.

Itō Hirobumi. *Commentaries on the Constitution of the Empire of Japan,* tr. Itō Miyoji. 2nd ed.; Tokyo, 1906.

Itō Hirobumi den 伊藤博文伝 (The life of Itō Hirobumi). Tokyo: Shumpo-kō tsuishō kai 春畝公追頌会, 1943).

Iwanami kōza: Nihon rekishi 岩波講座—日本歴史 (Iwanami lectures: Japanese history). 21 vols.; Tokyo, 1962-1964.

Jansen, Marius B. "Ōi Kentarō: Radicalism and Chauvinism," *Far Eastern Quarterly,* 11:305-316 (May 1952).

————*Sakamoto Ryōma and the Meiji Restoration.* Princeton, 1961.

Kamishima Jirō 神島二郎. "Inoue Kowashi: Kokka kikō no seisaku" 井上毅: 国家機構の制作 (Inoue Kowashi: The formation of the state structure); in *Nihon no shisōka,* I, 153-172.

Kawabe Kisaburō. *The Press and Politics in Japan.* Chicago, 1921.

Kido Takayoshi nikki 木戸孝允日記 (Diary of Kido Takayoshi). 2 vols.; Tokyo, 1932.

Kikuchi Dairoku. *Japanese Education.* London, 1909.

Kōsaka Masaaki 高坂正顕. *Meiji bunkashi: Shisō genronhen* 明治文化史 —思想言論編 (History of Meiji culture: Thought and speech). Tokyo: Kaikoku hyakunen kinen bunka jigyō kai, 1955.

————ed. *Japanese Thought in the Meiji Era,* tr. and adapted by David Abosh (Centenary Culture Council Series, vol. 9). Tokyo, 1958.

Lebra, Joyce C. "Ōkuma Shigenobu and the 1881 Political Crisis," *Journal of Asian Studies,* 18:475-487 (August 1959).

Bibliography

Lockwood, William W. *The Economic Development of Japan*. Princeton, 1954.

Lorenz, Reinhold. *Japan und Mitteleuropa*. Brünn, 1944.

McLaren, Walter W., ed. *Japanese Government Documents, 1867-1889* (Transactions of the Asiatic Society of Japan, vol. 42), Pt. 1. Tokyo, 1914.

Maruyama Masao 丸山真男. "Fukuzawa ni okeru 'jitsugaku' no tenkai" 福沢における実学の転回 (The conception of realism in Fukuzawa); *Tōyō bunka kenkyū* 東洋文化研究, 3:1-20 (March 1947).

——"Fukuzawa Yukichi no tetsugaku" 福沢諭吉の哲学 (The philosophy of Fukuzawa Yukichi); *Kokka gakkai zasshi* 国家学会雑誌, 61:129-163 (September 1947).

——*Nihon no shisō* 日本の思想 (Japanese thought). Tokyo, 1961.

Matsumoto Sannosuke 松本三之介. "Tennōsei hō shisō" 天皇制法思想 (Legal theory of the imperial system); in Ukai Nobushige et al., eds., *Nihon kindai hō hattatsu shi*, X, 15-32.

Mayo, Marlene June. "The Iwakura Mission to the United States and Europe, 1871-1873," *Researches in the Social Sciences on Japan*, 6:28-47. Columbia University, East Asian Institute Studies, 1959.

MBZ: Meiji bunka zenshū 明治文化全集 (Collected works of Meiji culture), comp. Yoshino Sakuzō 吉野作造. 2nd ed., 16 vols.; Tokyo, 1955-1959.

Meiji bunka zenshū, see *MBZ*.

Meiji shiryō kenkyū renrakukai 明治史料研究連絡会, ed. *Kindai shisō no keisei* 近代思想の形成 (The formation of modern thought). 6 vols.; Tokyo, 1959.

Mengelberg, Kaethe. "Lorenz von Stein and His Contribution to Historical Sociology," *Journal of the History of Ideas*, 22:267-276 (1961).

Minobe Tatsukichi 美濃部達吉. *Kempō oyobi kempōshi kenkyū* 憲法及び憲法史研究 (Studies in constitutional law and constitutional history). Tokyo, 1908.

——*Kempō satsuyō* 憲法撮要 (Manual of constitutional law). 5th ed.; Tokyo, 1935.

Bibliography

Mombushō ishinshiryō hensankai 文部省維新史料編纂会編, ed. *Ishinshi* 維新史 (History of the Restoration). 5 vols. and supplement; Tokyo, 1934-1941.

Murakami Shunsuke 村上俊亮 and Sakata Yoshio 坂田吉雄, eds. *Meiji bunkashi: Kyōiku dōtokuhen* 明治文化史—教育道徳編 (History of Meiji culture: Education and morals), vol. 3. Tokyo: Kaikoku hyakunen kinen bunka jigyō kai, 1955.

Nagai Hideo 永井秀雄. "Meiji kempō no seitei" (The establishment of the Meiji Constitution); in *Iwanami kōza: Nihon rekishi,* XVI, 187-224.

Nagai Michio 永井道雄. "Mori Arinori: Meiji kyōiku no kensetsusha" 森有礼—明治教育の建設者 (Mori Arinori: The builder of Meiji education); in *Nihon no shisōka,* I, 137-152.

Nihon no shisōka 日本の思想家 (Japanese thinkers), ed. Asahi Jānaru 朝日ジャーナル. 3 vols.; Tokyo, 1962-1963.

Norman, E. H. *Japan's Emergence as a Modern State.* New York, 1940.

Ōe Shinobu 大江志乃夫. *Meiji kokka no seiritsu* 明治国家の成立 (The formation of the Meiji state). Tokyo, 1959.

Oka Yoshitake 岡義武. *Kindai Nihon no keisei* 近代日本の形成 (The making of modern Japan). Tokyo, 1947.

Okazaki Yoshie, ed. *Japanese Literature in the Meiji Era,* tr. and adapted by V. H. Viglielmo (Centenary Culture Council Series, vol. 1). Tokyo, 1958.

Ōkubo Toshiaki 大久保利謙. *Meiji kempō no dekiru made* 明治憲法の出来るまで (The drafting of the Meiji Constitution). Tokyo, 1956.

———ed. *Ōkubo Toshimichi bunsho* 大久保利通文書 (Documents of Ōkubo Toshimichi). 10 vols.; Tokyo, 1927-1931.

Ōkuma Shigenobu, ed. *Fifty Years of New Japan.* 2 vols.; London, 1910.

Osatake Takeki 尾佐竹猛. *Ishin zengo ni okeru rikken shisō* 維新前後に於ける立憲思想 (Constitutional thought before and after the restoration). Tokyo, 1929.

———*Nihon kenseishi* 日本憲政史 (History of constitutional government in Japan). Tokyo, 1930.

Bibliography

———*Nihon kenseishi taikō* 日本憲政史大綱 (An outline of Japanese constitutional history). 2 vols.; Tokyo, 1938, 1939.

Ōtsu Jun'ichirō 大津淳一郎. *Dai Nihon kenseishi* 大日本憲政史 (History of Japanese constitutionalism). 10 vols.; Tokyo, 1927-1928.

Ōtsuka Minao 大塚三七雄. *Meiji ishin to Doitsu shisō* 明治維新独逸思想 (The Meiji Restoration and German thought). Tokyo, 1943.

Piovesana, Gino K., S. J. "The Beginnings of Western Philosophy in Japan: Nishi Amane, 1829-1897," *International Philosophical Quarterly*, 2:295-306 (May 1962).
———*Recent Japanese Philosophical Thought, 1862-1962: A Survey*. Tokyo, 1963.

Reischauer, Edwin O. *Japan: Past and Present*. Rev. ed.; Cambridge, Mass., 1953.
———*The United States and Japan*. Rev. ed.; Cambridge, Mass., 1957.

Roesler, Hermann. *Ueber die Grundlehren der von Adam Smith begründeten Volkswirtschaftstheorie*. Erlangen, 1871.
———*Das soziale Verwaltungsrecht*. 2 vols.; Erlangen, 1872, 1873.
———*Gedanken über den konstitutionellen Wert der deutschen Reichsverfassung*. Rostock, 1877.
———"Commentaries on the Constitution of the Empire of Japan." MS in the National Diet Library, Tokyo; 1889.

Rosovsky, Henry. *Capital Formation in Japan*. Glencoe, Ill., 1961.

Rōyama Masamichi 蠟山政道. *Nihon ni okeru kindai seijigaku no hattatsu* 日本に於ける近代政治学の発達 (The development of modern political science in Japan). Tokyo, 1949.

Russell, John R. "The Development of a Modern Army in Nineteenth-Century Japan," *Researches in the Social Sciences on Japan*, 6:48-54. Columbia University, East Asian Institute Studies, 1959.

Sakata Yoshio 坂田吉雄. *Meiji ishinshi* 明治維新史 (History of the Meiji Restoration). Tokyo, 1960.

———ed. *Meiji zempanki no nashonarizumu* 明治前半期のナショナリズム (Nationalism in the early Meiji period). Tokyo, 1958.

Sakisaka Itsurō 向坂逸郎 ed. *Kindai Nihon no shisōka* 近代日本の思想家 (Thinkers of modern Japan). Tokyo, 1954.

Sansom, George B. *The Western World and Japan.* Rev. ed.; New York, 1958.

Satow, Ernest. *A Diplomat in Japan.* London, 1921.

Scalapino, Robert A. *Democracy and the Party Movement in Prewar Japan.* Berkeley and Los Angeles, 1953.

Shimizu Shin 清水伸. *Dokuō ni okeru Itō Hirobumi no kempō torishirabe to Nihon kempō* 独墺に於ける伊藤博文の憲法取調と日本憲法 (Itō Hirobumi's constitutional investigation in Germany and Austria and the Japanese constitution). Tokyo, 1939.

———*Teikoku kempō seitei kaigi* 帝国憲法制定会議 (The council for the enactment of the imperial constitution). Tokyo, 1940.

Shively, Donald H. "Motoda Eifu: Confucian Lecturer to the Meiji Emperor," in David S. Nivison and Arthur F. Wright, eds., *Confucianism in Action* (Stanford, 1959), pp. 302-333.

Shōgiku Kido-kō den 松菊木戸公伝 (The life of Prince Kido Takayoshi). 2 vols.; Tokyo: Kido-kō denki hensan kai 木戸公伝記編纂会, 1927.

Siemes, Johannes. "H. Roesler no kempō riron ni okeru shakai hatten to rikkenshugi no kankei" H. ロエスラーの憲法理論に於ける社会発展と立憲主義の関係 (Social progress and constitutionalism in Roesler's constitutional theory); *Kokka gakkai zasshi,* 75:1-41, 181-202, 306-330, 418-424 (1962).

———"Hermann Roesler und die Einführung des deutschen Staatsrechts in Japan," *Der Staat,* 2:181-196 (1963).

Smith, Thomas C. *Political Change and Industrial Development in Japan.* Stanford, 1955.

Smith, Warren W. *Confucianism in Modern Japan.* Tokyo, 1959.

Soviak, Eugene. "Baba Tatsui: A Study of Intellectual Acculturation in the Early Meiji Period." Ph. D. thesis; University of Michigan, 1962.

———"The Case of Baba Tatsui: Western Enlightenment, Social Change, and the Early Meiji Intellectual," *Monumenta Nipponica,* 18:191-235 (1963).

Bibliography

Stead, Alfred, ed. *Japan by the Japanese*. London, 1904.

Stein, Lorenz von. *Geschichte der sozialen Bewegung in Frankreich von 1789 bis auf unsere Tage*. 3 vols.; Hildesheim, 1959.

Suzuki Yasuzō 鈴木安蔵. *Kempō no rekishiteki kenkyū* 憲法の歴史的研究 (Historical studies in the constitution). Tokyo, 1934.

————*Meiji shonen no rikken shisō* 明治初年の立憲思想 (Constitutional thought in the early Meiji period). Tokyo, 1938.

————"Hermann Roesler und die japanische Verfassung," *Monumenta Nipponica*, 4:53-87, 428-453 (1941); 5:61-114 (1942).

————*Kempō seitei to Roesler* 憲法制定とロエスレル (Roesler and the framing of the constitution). Tokyo, 1942.

Tabata Shinobu 田畑忍. *Katō Hiroyuki no kokka shisō* 加藤弘之の国家思想 (Katō Hiroyuki's theory of the state). Tokyo, 1939.

————*Katō Hiroyuki* 加藤弘之. Tokyo, 1959.

Tanaka Sōgorō 田中惣五郎. "Inoue Kowashi" 井上毅; in Konishi Shirō 小西四郎, ed., *Nihon jimbutsushi taikei* 日本人物史大系 (Biographies of Japanese personalities; Tokyo, 1959-1960), V, 224-251.

Tokutomi Iichirō 徳富猪一郎. *Kōshaku Yamagata Aritomo den* 公爵山県有朋伝 (The life of Prince Yamagata Aritomo). 3 vols.; Tokyo, 1933.

Tōyama Shigeki 遠山茂樹. *Meiji ishin* 明治維新 (The Meiji Restoration). Tokyo, 1951.

Tsuji Kiyoaki 辻清明. "Lorenz Stein no gyōseigakusetsu" ロレンツシュタインの行政学説 (Lorenz Stein's theory of public administration); *Kokka gakkai zasshi*, 57:1113-53, 1406-36 (1943).

Tsunoda Ryusaku, William Theodore de Bary, and Donald Keene, eds. *Sources of Japanese Tradition*. New York, 1958.

Ukai Nobushige 鵜飼信成 et al., eds. *Nihon kindai hō hattatsu shi* 日本近代法発達史 (History of the development of modern Japanese law). 14 vols. and supplement; Tokyo, 1958-1962.

Umetani Noboru 梅溪昇. *Meiji zenki seijishi no kenkyū* 明治前期政治史の研究 (Studies in the political history of early Meiji Japan). Tokyo, 1963.

Bibliography

Uyehara, George Etsujirō. *The Political Development of Japan, 1867–1909.* London, 1910.

Van Straelen, Henricus. *Yoshida Shōin: Forerunner of the Meiji Restoration.* Leiden, 1952.

Watanabe Ikujirō 渡辺幾治郎. *Nihon kempō seitei shikō* 日本憲法制定史講 (History of the making of the Japanese constitution). Tokyo, 1937.

――――*Nihon kinsei gaikōshi* 日本近世外交史 (Diplomatic history of modern Japan). Tokyo, 1938.

――――comp. *Nihon kensei kiso shiryō* 日本憲政基礎資料 (Basic historical materials on Japanese constitutional government). Tokyo, 1939.

Webb, Herschel F. "The Mito Theory of the State," *Researches in the Social Sciences on Japan,* 4:33-52. Columbia University, East Asian Institute Studies, 1957.

Wilson, Robert. *Genesis of the Meiji Government in Japan, 1868-1871.* Berkeley and Los Angeles, 1957.

Yamashita Tokuji. *Education in Japan.* Tokyo, 1938.

NOTES

INTRODUCTION

1. *Kokutai* was originally a Chinese term used to mean "organ of the state" or "organization of the state." In Japan this term was used first by Kitabatake Chikafusa (1293-1354), the author of *Jinnō shōtōki* (Record of the legitimate succession of the divine emperors). Kitabatake had as his aim giving as much support as possible to the claims of the Southern Court. He wanted not only to show that the Southern Court had legitimate claims to the throne, but also to emphasize the uniqueness and the divinity of the imperial line, so that the people might feel impelled to give loyal and unselfish service to the rightful emperor. Kitabatake claimed that the uniqueness of the imperial institution made Japan superior not only to China but also to India. He placed special emphasis on the idea that a very close relation existed between the emperor and the people; this relation he called *kokutai*.

2. For an English translation of *Kokutai no hongi* see Robert K. Hall, ed., *Kokutai no hongi: Cardinal Principles of the National Entity of Japan*, tr. John Owen Gauntlett (Cambridge, Mass., 1949).

3. *Ibid.*, p. 80.

4. *Ibid.*, pp. 80-81.

5. *Ibid.*, pp. 89-90.

6. *Ibid.*, p. 91.

7. The emergence of the concept of *kazoku kokka* (family-nation or family-state) has been thoroughly examined in Ishida Takeshi, *Meiji seiji shisō shi kenkyū* (Studies in the history of Meiji political thought; Tokyo, 1954), pp. 3-149. Ishida traces the origin and implications of the family-state conception and attempts to steer a middle course between two extreme views: the one that the family-state theory was an opportunistic invention of the Meiji leaders in order to secure the subjection of the people, the other that the continuity of this notion from ancient times is beyond dispute.

8. *Ibid.*, pp. 105-114.

9. Hozumi Yatsuka, *Kempō teiyō* (Manual of constitutional law), 7th ed. (Tokyo, 1940), p. 493. Hozumi's work was the definitive statement of the conservative school of constitutional law in prewar Japan. According to Hozumi, the semimystical concept of the *kokutai* implied full sovereignty only in the emperor; the diet, cabinet, Privy Council, and courts were but organs

of the imperial sovereignty. The *kokutai* became in Hozumi's interpretation a supreme political and legal postulate.

10. George Etsujirō Uyehara, *The Political Development of Japan, 1867-1909* (London, 1910), pp. 106-107.

11. See the editorial in the newspaper *Chōya shimbun* (Feb. 11, 1889). The editorial concluded by saying that the great task confronting the Japanese after the promulgation of the constitution was not vocal criticism but active work to see to it that the constitution was accepted in the political life of the nation.

12. Fukuzawa compared the making of the Meiji Constitution with the way in which the constitutions of other countries were promulgated and found it a matter for the highest congratulation that in Japan the constitution was not the result of popular pressure and popular discontent but was granted by the emperor. Fukuzawa dismissed the various agitations of the political parties and other associations for a constitutional form of government as "simply the handiwork of idle *shizoku* [ex-samurai] who desire to annoy the government because they cannot obtain office." See Fukuzawa Yukichi, "The History of the Japanese Parliament," in Walter W. McLaren, ed., *Japanese Government Documents, 1867-1889* (*Transactions of the Asiatic Society of Japan,* Vol. 42, Tokyo, 1914), Pt. 1, pp. 577-580.

13. Takada Sanae, a member of the first diet and later Minister of Education, in an article in the journal *Kempō zasshi* (Feb. 15, 1889), stated that the Meiji Constitution upheld the fundamental principles of every enlightened charter of foreign countries and marked the beginning of a new system of government in which the people take active part in the affairs of state. But he also stressed the point that in the constitution there was a grave ambiguity: the constitution did not determine in clear terms to whom the cabinet ministers were responsible. The newspaper *Ōsaka mainichi shimbun* (Feb. 14, 1889) stated that the new constitution upheld the principle of joint rule by the monarch and the people and defended the rights of the individual. At the same time the *Ōsaka mainichi* expressed its doubts on the nobility and on the upper house. It stated that the way of selecting the upper house members was absurd because Japan had neither an aristocracy of blood nor a select group of capable men. The same paper reserved its sharpest criticism for the system of ministerial irresponsibility. Many other opinions of newspapers and magazines are reported in Inada Masatsugu, *Meiji kempō seiritsu shi* (History of the framing of the Meiji Constitution), 2 vols. (Tokyo, 1960, 1962), II, 912-957. Inada's volumes seem to be the definitive work on the framing of the Meiji Constitution. A monument of scholarly research, Inada's contribution has been my main source. The two volumes consist of two thousand pages of documents, many of them published for the first time, and an accurate and brief commentary.

14. *Meiji bunka zenshū* (Collected works of Meiji culture), comp. Yoshino Sakuzō, 2nd ed., 16 vols. (Tokyo, 1955-1959), X, 47. The first edition of *MBZ* was published in 24 volumes from 1928 to 1930. This is a monumental compilation of materials on all aspects of Meiji culture assembled by a research staff

Antifeudal National Unification

under the general editorship of Yoshino Sakuzō, who was aided by Osatake Takeki. It consists in part of reprints of important documentary materials, books, essays, and articles, and in part of specialized introductions by acknowledged Japanese authorities.

15. Quoted in Nagai Hideo, "Meiji kempō no seitei" (The establishment of the Meiji Constitution), in *Iwanami kōza: Nihon rekishi* (Iwanami lectures: Japanese history), 21 vols. (Tokyo, 1962-1964), XVI, 192.

I. ANTIFEUDAL NATIONAL UNIFICATION

1. For the history of the restoration and all documents related to it see Mombushō Ishinryō Hensankai, ed., *Ishinshi* (History of the restoration), 5 vols.+Supplement (Tokyo, 1934-1941). This great work is a good factual account of the salient aspects of the restoration. For an interpretation based on the Marxist school of thought see Tōyama Shigeki, *Meiji ishin* (The Meiji Restoration; Tokyo, 1951.)

2. Sakata Yoshio distinguishes between *ōsei fukko* (restoration of imperial authority) and *ōsei ishin* (imperial renovation). Sakata Yoshio, *Meiji ishinshi* (History of the Meiji Restoration; Tokyo, 1960).

3. The first trials and experiments of the new government are described in Robert Wilson, *Genesis of the Meiji Government in Japan, 1868-1871* (Berkeley and Los Angeles, 1957). Some of the movements leading to the Meiji Restoration are described in Albert M. Craig, *Chōshū in the Meiji Restoration* (Cambridge, Mass., 1961), and Marius B. Jansen, *Sakamoto Ryōma and the Meiji Restoration* (Princeton, 1961).

4. The shogun's title, *sei-i tai shōgun* (barbarian-subjugating generalissimo), describes this secondary position: the shogun was the officer of state who bore the imperial commission to subdue the barbarians.

5. Herschel F. Webb, "The Mito Theory of the State," *Researches in the Social Sciences on Japan*, 4:33-52 (Columbia University, East Asian Institute Studies, 1957).

6. Yoshida Shōin, the Chōshū loyalist scholar, was one of the most explicit in defending the power of the emperor. The emperor, according to him, had absolute power over the life and death of each Japanese. The Japanese state belonged to one single person and the emperor's power embraced everything. "The state does not belong to one man alone. This is true in China, but in the land of the gods, it is not so." Yoshida Shōin stated that even in case of oppression the whole people could do nothing but offer their heads to the emperor. See Henricus Van Straelen, *Yoshida Shōin: Forerunner of the Meiji Restoration* (Leiden, 1952).

7. Ishii Ryōsuke does not like the term "restoration" because, he says, the Tokugawa had not obtained power from the emperor and could not therefore "restore" that power to the emperor. They had acquired power through military campaigns, not through imperial delegation. This reason, however, is

valid only for actual political power, not for the source of legitimacy. Ishii Ryōsuke, *Meiji bunkashi: Hōseihen* (History of Meiji culture: The legal system; Tokyo: Kaikoku hyakunen kinen bunka jigyō ka, 1954), II, 47.

8. Translation in Ike Nobutaka, *The Beginnings of Political Democracy in Japan* (Baltimore, 1950), p. 36.

9. Sakamoto's eight-point plan reads: "(1) Political power of the entire country should be returned to the Imperial Court, and all decrees should come from the Court. (2) Two legislative bodies, an Upper and Lower House, should be established, and all government measures should be decided on the basis of general opinion. (3) Men of ability among the lords, nobles and people at large should be employed as councillors, and traditional offices of the past which have lost their purpose should be abolished. (4) Foreign affairs should be carried on according to appropriate regulations worked out on the basis of general opinion. (5) The legislation and regulations of earlier times should be set aside and a new and adequate code should be selected. (6) The navy should be enlarged. (7) An Imperial Guard should be set up to defend the capital. (8) The value of goods and silver should be brought into line with that of foreign lands." This translation is taken from Jansen, *Sakamoto*, pp. 295-296.

10. McLaren, p. 2.

11. George B. Sansom, *The Western World and Japan,* rev. ed. (New York, 1958), pp. 318-320. Sansom does not accept the democratic interpretation of the Charter Oath. He concludes his analysis of the oath saying that the leaders may have thought it wise to hold the prospect of popular representative institutions as a distant goal, for there was apparent at that time a widespread if vague desire for reform which it was important not to disappoint.

12. Inada, I, 1-22. Inada gives a detailed account of the different drafts and revisions of this fundamental document.

13. *Ibid.,* I, 1. Yuri Kimimasa (1829-1909) was a Fukui samurai and a vigorous advocate of modernization after the coming of Perry. Besides taking part in the draft of the Charter Oath, he worked for the currency reforms, was a member of the Iwakura Mission, later became governor of Tokyo, *genrō* (elder statesman), and was finally made a viscount.

14. Fukuoka Kōtei was a bureaucrat of the Tosa han. After the restoration he served the new government in a variety of posts. He drafted the Charter Oath, supervised legal and educational reforms, was a member of the Privy Council, and was made a viscount.

15. Inada, I, 6.

16. Ishii, *Meiji bunkashi: Hōseihen,* p. 108.

17. *Ibid.,* p. 109.

18. The Seitaisho can rightly be called the first constitution of Japan. Though the leaders may have not understood it as a modern constitution, the Seitaisho was the fundamental law for the organization of the new government, and it prescribed clear limits and rules for the administration. Ernest Satow, interpreter and secretary to Harry Parkes, the British minister in Japan, calls the

Antifeudal National Unification

Seitaisho the "June Constitution." Ernest Satow, *A Diplomat in Japan* (London, 1921), p. 381. The text of the Seitaisho is in McLaren, pp. 8-10.

19. Ishii, *Meiji bunkashi: Hōseihen*, pp. 102-103.

20. Osatake Takeki, *Nihon kenseishi* (History of constitutional government in Japan; Tokyo, 1930), pp. 18-26. See also his *Nihon kenseishi taikō* (An outline of Japanese constitutional history), 2 vols. (Tokyo, 1938, 1939), I, 15-19. On the introduction of Western legal thought and terminology see MBZ, Vol. 13, which reproduces a few fundamental works of Nishi Amane, Tsuda Masamichi, Kanda Kōhei, and others.

21. *Ibid.*, XIII, 15-104. For the introduction of constitutional thought Tsuda's *Taisei kokuhōron* was particularly important. The work is divided into four books. In the first, after explaining the nature and aim of public law, Tsuda describes the essence of and the theories about *shuken* (sovereignty). Sovereignty is defined as the fundamental power without which there cannot be a state. The preservation of the country as well as the rights, peace, and prosperity of the citizens depend on this sovereignty. The divine rights theory, the social contract, and the system of direct and representative democracy are all explained in relation to the problem of sovereignty. The pros and cons of the separation of powers are also explained. The second book deals with the rights and duties of citizens, the third with the different forms of political systems, and the fourth with the problem of the fundamental law of the country. As Nishi Amane was responsible for philosophical terminology so Tsuda Masamichi was responsible for the introduction of the political terminology. Katō Hiroyuki borrowed heavily from Tsuda's *Taisei kokuhōron*.

22. Roger F. Hackett, "Nishi Amane: A Tokugawa-Meiji Bureaucrat," *Journal of Asian Studies*, 18:213-225 (Feb. 1959). See also Gino K. Piovesana, S. J., "The Beginnings of Western Philosophy in Japan: Nishi Amane, 1829-1897," *International Philosophical Quarterly*, 2:295-306 (May 1962).

23. McLaren, p. 8.

24. The Seitaisho, in its introductory sentences, reads: "All power and authority in the empire resides in the Dajōkan. By this means the difficulty of divided government is obviated. The power and authority of the Dajōkan is threefold, legislative, executive, and judicial. Thus the balance of authority is preserved among the various branches of government. The legislative branch cannot possess executive functions, nor can the executive branch possess legislative functions." These same ideas on centralization and unification of administrative power had already been presented by other leaders before the restoration. In 1867 the daimyo of Tosa had sent a memorial to the shogun: "The cause of this situation [disunion within and challenge from without] lies in the fact that the administration proceeds from two centers, causing the Empire's eyes and ears to be turned in two different directions. The march of events has brought about a revolution, and the old system can no longer be persevered in. You should restore the governing power into the hands of the sovereign, and so lay a foundation on which Japan may take its stand as the equal of all other

Notes to Chapter I

countries." Quoted in Ernest W. Clement, *A Short History of Japan* (Tokyo, 1936), p. 106.

25. Inada, I, 27-30. See also Satow, p. 377.

26. The Seitaisho states: "All officers shall be changed after four years service. They shall be appointed by a majority of votes given by ballot. When the first period for changing the officers of Government arrives, half of the present staff shall be retained for an additional space of two years, in order that there be no interruption of the public business. Such as cannot conveniently be dismissed, because they have won general approval, must be retained for a further period of years." Translation in McLaren, p. 10.

27. Ishii, *Meiji bunkashi: Hōseihen*, p. 112.

28. The Government Officials' Order brought about a reorganization of the central and local administrative structure. In fact this order led to the adoption of the ancient council of state system of government, which eclipsed the Western concept of a division of powers, as reflected in the Seitaisho.

29. Carl J. Friedrich, *Constitutional Government and Democracy*, rev. ed. (Boston, 1950), p. 10.

30. For a comprehensive discussion of the "public opinion" principle see Matsumoto Sannosuke, "Tennōsei hō shisō" (Legal theory of the imperial system), in Ukai Nobushige et al., eds., *Nihon kindai hō hattatsu shi* (History of the development of modern Japanese law; Tokyo, 1958-1962), X, 15-32.

31. Ishii, *Meiji bunkashi: Hōseihen*, p. 68.

32. McLaren, p. 31.

33. *Ibid.*

34. *Ibid.*, p. 30.

35. Ishii, *Meiji bunkashi: Hōseihen*, p. 68.

36. *Ibid.*

37. McLaren, pp. 32-33. It must be noted that Terajima Munenori, a Satsuma leader, had committed himself even earlier than Kido to the return of the han to the emperor. Prior to the restoration he had written in a letter to his daimyo, Shimazu of Satsuma, in December 1867: "The probable cause of military usurpations in the past being the feudal system, I believe that abolition of all feudal lords is the way towards a true Imperial Government. The way for you to be true to the principle of service to the Throne and to your belief in fidelity is to return your land and people to the Throne, and to take the initiative yourself in becoming a commoner." Quoted in Wilson. p. 91.

38. Hans Kohn, *The Idea of Nationalism* (New York, 1943), p. 3.

39. Rupert Emerson, *From Empire to Nation* (Cambridge, Mass., 1960), p. 214.

40. Karl Mannheim, *Man and Society in an Age of Reconstruction* (London, 1940), p. 44.

41. The conscription regulations were promulgated in January 1871. The preamble states: "No regard is to be paid to the social position of the people; men who are strong and serviceable are to be chosen." Translation in McLaren,

p. 17. The later decrees were even more radical than the conscription regulations; they destroyed the privileges of the samurai and brought about one of the most comprehensive changes in the traditional customs of Japan.

42. Before Yamagata, Ōmura Masujirō was responsible for the innovations in the military system. Ōmura had been a student of military science before 1868; he had commanded troops in the Chōshū *kiheitai* (auxiliary militia) during the restoration engagements and was an advocate of drastic military reforms after 1868. He had translated a German work on strategy in 1864, and realized that sweeping social reforms were necessary before a national army could be formed. He was assassinated by a samurai in late 1869. On Yamagata's political thought and action see Roger F. Hackett, "Yamagata Aritomo: A Political Biography," Ph. D. thesis (Harvard, 1955).

43. Ishii Ryōsuke, ed., *Japanese Legislation in the Meiji Era,* tr. and adapted by William J. Chambliss (Centenary Culture Council Series, Vol. 10; Tokyo, 1958), pp. 723-724.

44. The Satsuma Rebellion broke out in January 1877. To crush the rebellion the government mobilized over 65,000 men, including 56,000 infantrymen, 1,500 engineers, 310 quartermaster soldiers, and 7,000 police. The police were nearly all former samurai. See John R. Russell, "The Development of a Modern Army in Nineteenth-Century Japan," *Researches in the Social Sciences on Japan,* 6:48-54 (Columbia University, East Asian Institute Studies, 1959).

45. See Robert K. Hall, *Education for a New Japan* (New Haven, 1949), pp. 221-227. See also Ronald S. Anderson, *Japan: Three Epochs of Modern Education* (Washington, D. C., 1959).

46. This ambitious plan, however, could not be carried out in full. It was too big and costly, and it was introduced at a time when the new government was not yet quite firmly settled and had not succeeded in overcoming local prejudices. But to understand the ideology of the leaders the realization of the plan is of secondary importance.

47. Quoted in Kikuchi Dairoku, *Japanese Education* (London, 1909), pp. 68-69.

48. R. P. Dore gives a vivid description of the new utilitarian spirit pervading early Meiji Japan, especially in the field of education. See R. P. Dore, *City Life in Japan* (Berkeley and Los Angeles, 1958), pp. 191-207.

49. Condorcet argued that since all political and moral errors were based on philosophical fallacies, science, by dispelling false metaphysical notions and wrong prejudices, must lead men to social truth and progress. M. J. A. N. Condorcet, *Sketch for a Historical Picture of the Progress of the Mind,* tr. June Barraclough (New York, 1955).

50. Yamashita Tokuji, *Education in Japan* (Tokyo, 1938), p. 11.

51. Sansom, p. 456.

52. Kikuchi (p. 67) gives a characteristic example of the new educational trends in Meiji Japan: "Early in 1872 a girls' school was opened in Tokyo, where, besides ordinary subjects of common education, English was taught by

an American lady teacher. In June of the same year, the first normal school was opened in Tokyo, where methods of instruction in elementary schools were taught by an American teacher through the medium of an interpreter. In order to illustrate the spirit of those days, I may mention in this connection that the Minister of Education gave instruction to the American teacher that he was not to think of adapting his teaching to the Japanese, but was to teach just as he would at home."

53. On the economic development of Meiji Japan there are some outstanding works in Western languages. See G. C. Allen, *A Short Eonomic History of Modern Japan, 1867-1937* (London, 1946); William W. Lockwood, *The Economic Development of Japan* (Princeton, 1954); Henry Rosovsky, *Capital Formation in Japan* (Glencoe, Ill., 1961); Thomas C. Smith, *Political Change and Industrial Development in Japan* (Stanford, 1955).

54. Ishii, *Meiji bunkashi: Hōseihen*, pp. 77-84.

55. *Ibid.*, pp. 133-141.

56. *Ibid.*, p. 83.

57. Sidney D. Brown, "Ōkubo Toshimichi: His Political and Economic Policies in Early Meiji Japan," *Journal of Asian Studies*, 21:183-197 (Feb. 1962).

58. *Ibid.*, pp. 194-197.

59. This translation is taken from Hilary Conroy, *The Japanese Seizure of Korea, 1868-1910* (Philadelphia, 1960), pp. 47-49.

60. Ōkubo, who had himself opposed the invasion of Korea, decided in 1874 to put in motion the Formosan expedition as a sort of compromise with the samurai hotheads. He was fully aware of the possibilities of this campaign as a diversionary enterprise for restless samurai. *Ibid.*, p. 54.

61. Emerson, pp. 277-292.

62. The Jingikan was soon replaced by an office of lower rank, called the Kyōbushō (Board of Religious Instruction), under which a college of lecturers imparted and supervised ethical and religious instruction. This college was called the Daikyōin (College of the Great Doctrine). The fundamental principles of this doctrine were love of the country and reverence for the gods, the law of heaven and the way of man, and loyalty to the throne and obedience to the authorities. In order to spread this creed, no less than 7,247 government preachers were appointed, many of whom possessed no moral or intellectual qualifications for the task. Their success was very limited, and by 1877 the experiment of official intervention in religious propaganda, at least during the early Meiji period, came to an end. By 1877 the Kyōbushō was also abolished.

63. For the role played by the samurai class in the modernization of Japan, see Harry D. Harootunian, "The Progress of Japan and the Samurai Class, 1868-1882," *Pacific Historical Review*, 28:255-266 (Aug. 1959).

64. McLaren, p. 570.

65. Quoted in Dennis Austin, "Strong Rule in Ghana," *The Listener* (Jan. 25, 1962), p. 156.

66. David Apter, "Some Reflections on the Role of a Political Opposition

in New Nations," *Comparative Studies in Society and History*, 4:154 (1962).

II. GRADUALISM VERSUS RADICALISM

1. *MBZ*, IX, 344.
2. Friedrich, p. 35.
3. *MBZ*, I, 343-344. It seems necessary to introduce here a few terms frequently used during the early Meiji period—*bummei kaika:* "civilization and enlightenment," indicating the movement away from the past toward a deep study and a free borrowing of Western culture and Western ways of life; *kummin dōchi:* "joint rule by the monarch and the people," meaning essentially a system of constitutional limited monarchy; *kyūshinron:* "radicalism," representing the attitude of the people's rights movement, which advocated an early assembly and an immediate constitution upholding the principles of joint rule; *shōsōron:* the "too early" theory, the accusation leveled by the gradualists against the advocates of the immediate establishment of a constitution and a popular assembly. The gradualists defended their position by saying that the situation in Japan was not ripe for such a system of government and that the constitution and the assembly were "too early," or premature; *zenshinron:* "gradualism," accepted as the final goal of the restoration a constitutional form of government, but holding that Japan should go slowly, by degrees, toward this goal.
4. Uyehara, p. 63.
5. Sansom, pp. 378-441.
6. Ōkuma Shigenobu, "Speech in the House of Representatives, February 16, 1897," in Alfred Stead, ed., *Japan by the Japanese* (London, 1904), p. 219.
7. Watanabe Ikujirō, *Nihon kinsei gaikōshi* (Diplomatic history of modern Japan; Tokyo, 1938), pp. 38-40. On the Iwakura Mission see Marlene June Mayo, "The Iwakura Mission to the United States and Europe, 1871-1873," *Researches in the Social Sciences on Japan*, 6:28-47 (Columbia University, East Asian Institute Studies, 1959).
8. Quoted in Mayo, p. 31.
9. The Iwakura Mission was primarily interested in sounding out the various treaty powers concerning the possibility of revising the treaties. The Japanese were especially anxious to have the more obnoxious treaty provisions, such as the extraterritoriality clause, abrogated. A secondary objective was to observe and absorb the culture of the West. The total contingent of the mission reached 49 persons.
10. Mayo, p. 28.
11. Quoted in Sidney D. Brown, "Kido Takayoshi and the Meiji Restoration: A Political Biography, 1833-1877," Ph. D. thesis (University of Wisconsin, 1952), pp. 216-217.
12. *Shōgiku Kido-kō den* (The life of Prince Kido Takayoshi), 2 vols. (Tokyo: Kido-kō denki hensan kai, 1927), I, 72-73.
13. Ōe Shinobu, "Chūō shūken kokka no seiritsu" (The establishment of a

centralized state), in *Iwanami kōza*, XV, 55. See also Sidney D. Brown, "Kido Takayoshi (1833-1877): Meiji Japan's Cautious Revolutionary," *Pacific Historical Review*, 25:151-162 (1956).

14. *Kido Takayoshi nikki* (Diary of Kido Takayoshi), 2 vols. (Tokyo, 1932), I, 159.

15. Mayo, pp. 37-38.

16. See the text of Kido's observations in McLaren, pp. 567-577.

17. *Ibid.*, p. 568.

18. *Ibid.*, p. 574.

19. The two drafts are given in Inada, I, 212-228. George M. Beckmann, *The Making of the Meiji Constitution* (Lawrence, Kansas, 1957), pp. 100-110, gives a translation of "Dai Nihon seiki."

20. Inada, I, 195.

21. Beckmann, p. 101.

22. Inada, I, 199-200.

23. *Ibid.*, I, 200.

24. Beckmann, p. 102.

25. Osatake, *Nihon kenseishi taikō*, I, 309.

26. Inada, I, 198. In his diary Kido strongly stated that the final goal must be joint rule by the monarch and the people (*kummin dōchi*). He also said that this form of government implied the active participation of the people in governmental affairs. An initial, temporary despotic constitution was to be only the first step toward a real constitution of *kummin dōchi*. Kido also stressed the need for a constitution in order to prevent arbitrariness and selfishness in the administration of public affairs, pointing out that in any civilized country the people elect and control the public officials.

27. Inada, I, 204-205. Although Kido's proposal for the immediate proclamation of a constitution was not accepted, the administration nevertheless did make some innovations in order to adapt it to Western forms. Thus in November 1873 Itō Hirobumi and Terajima Munenori were placed in charge of research concerning the basic organization of the national government. When Itō, in connection with this research, sought the views of Kido, Kido, on November 20, 1873, wrote him a letter advocating once again the creation of a bicameral institution, in preparation for the eventual establishment of a real constitutional form of government.

28. See the translation of this document in Beckmann, pp. 111-119.

29. Inada, I, 210-212.

30. Beckmann, p. 112.

31. *Ibid.*, p. 117.

32. For the general background on the split of the Meiji leadership, see Robert A. Scalapino, *Democracy and the Party Movement in Prewar Japan* (Berkeley and Los Angeles, 1953), pp. 40-58. See also Conroy, pp. 18-77.

33. Ike, p. 56.

34. McLaren, pp. 427-428.

35. *Ibid.*, p. 430.

36. *Ibid.*, p. 445. See also George Akita, "Development of Parliamentary Government in Meiji Japan," Ph. D. thesis (Harvard, 1960), pp. 30-37. A revised version of this thesis will shortly be published in the Harvard East Asian Series.

37. *MBZ*, V. 93-94, 110-111. The Meirokusha arose in 1873, the sixth year of the Meiji era, and from this year took its name. It was conceived by Mori Arinori and Nishimura Shigeki. In February 1874, the Meirokusha started its own journal, *Meiroku zasshi*. The journal was published semimonthly from February to October; after November it appeared three times a month, and its circulation was said to have exceeded 3,000, a very considerable circulation for those times. On the Meirokusha see Kōsaka Masaaki, ed., *Japanese Thought in the Meiji Era*, tr. and adapted by David Abosh (Centenary Culture Council Series, Vol. 9; Tokyo, 1958), pp. 61-133.

38. *MBZ*, V, 62-63. The title of Mori's article is "Criticism of the Memorial on the Establishment of a Representative Assembly," and it appeared in the third issue of *Meiroku zasshi*.

39. *MBZ*, V, 63.

40. *Hyakuichi shinron* was published in 1874 in Tokyo. The title itself describes Nishi's attempt at finding a fundamental unity in human sciences. For a summary of Nishi's philosophical thought see Gino K. Piovesana, *Recent Japanese Philosophical Thought, 1862-1962: A Survey* (Tokyo, 1963), pp. 5-15.

41. *MBZ*, V, 66-67. Nishi saw as the fundamental problem of politics the equilibrium between order and change. According to Nishi, democracy solved the problem of change but lacked wisdom and order; aristocracy solved the problem of order and continuity but not that of change. Despotic monarchy was unpredictable because it could offer excellent rulers but also base tyrants. The best system, according to Nishi, was constitutional monarchy.

42. Katō Hiroyuki's political thought is examined in Tabata Shinobu, *Katō Hiroyuki no kokka shisō* (Katō Hiroyuki's theory of the state; Tokyo, 1939).

43. *MBZ*, III, 3-14.

44. Tabata Shinobu, *Katō Hiroyuki* (Tokyo, 1959), p. 72.

45. *MBZ*, III, 9.

46. Tabata, *Katō Hiroyuki*, pp. 72-74.

47. *MBZ*, III, v-vi. The text of *Rikken seitai ryaku* is in *ibid.*, pp. 17-26. In this work Katō borrowed heavily from Tsuda Masamichi, *Taisei kokuhōron*, published in Tokyo in 1868.

48. *MBZ*, III, 20.

49. *Ibid.*, III, 24-25.

50. *Ibid.*, II, 85-108. On November 19, 1881, Katō wrote a letter to Yamada Akiyoshi, Home Minister at the time, asking the government not to allow any new editions of *Shinsei tai-i* and his later work *Kokutai shinron*. He also sent letters to the newspapers asking for the suppression of these books because they no longer represented his ideas. The books had been the fruit of mistaken ideas

which were deleterious to society. Ōkubo Toshiaki, "Katō Hiroyuki," in Sakisaka Itsurō, ed., *Kindai Nihon no shisōka* (Thinkers of modern Japan; Tokyo, 1954), pp. 27-28.

51. Katō describes communism and socialism in these words: "Although there are some differences between the two, they are by and large similar. They are theories which propose to bring equality to all phases of the everyday life of the common people, including clothing, food, and shelter. The reason these schools of thought arose is this: if individuals were left to themselves, they say, there would arise distinctions between the rich and the poor, owing to differences of ability and effort. The rich would get richer, and the poor would become poorer. This would lead to the impoverishment of the entire world. They therefore propose that everything, including clothing, food, and shelter, and privately owned land, equipment, and industries be owned by the government." *MBZ*, II, 102; translation taken from Ike, p. 118.

52. Kōsaka, *Japanese Thought*, p. 92.

53. *MBZ*, II, 124-125.

54. *Ibid.*, II, 112. In the same chapter on the right of liberty Katō denied that the emperor had any special rights; he was a mere instrument of defense of the people's rights.

55. On Bluntschli's influence on Japan see Matsumoto Sannosuke, "Nihon kempōgaku ni okeru kokkaron no tenkai" (Development of the theory of the state in Japanese constitutional law), in Fukuda Kan'ichi, ed., *Seiji shisō ni okeru Seiō to Nihon* (Western Europe and Japan in political thought), 2 vols. (Tokyo, 1961), II, 167-176. It is often said that Bluntschli's ideas were responsible for the turn to conservatism made by Katō. But Bluntschli also had a very liberal side: he strongly defended the rights of the individual and the limitations of the power of the state. According to him, a modern state is one which recognizes the rights of everyone. Man has no property in man, for man is not a thing, but always a person with inalienable rights. The state is a legal political community, based on law and restricting its sphere of action to the political field without interfering in the religious, scientific, or artistic fields. The sovereignty of the state must be constitutionally limited. However, Bluntschli states also that the fundamental principles of the state are determined by history, and that the modern state regards itself as a person consisting at once of spirit (the national spirit) and of body (the constitution). It is interesting to note that Katō translated only the part of the *Allgemeines Staatsrecht* dealing with the organization of the state, where the general tone is more conservative than in the other parts.

56. The text of Katō's answer to the memorial of Soejima, Itagaki, and others is in McLaren, pp. 433-439.

57. *Ibid.*, p. 436.

58. *MBZ*, V, 70.

59. Kōsaka Masaaki, *Meiji bunkashi: Shisō genronhen* (History of Meiji culture: Thought and speech; Tokyo: Kaikoku hyakunen kinen bunka jigyō kai, 1955), p. 145.

Gradualism Versus Radicalism

60. *Ibid.*

61. *MBZ*, V, 108-110.

62. See Maruyama Masao, "Fukuzawa Yukichi no tetsugaku" (The philosophy of Fukuzawa Yukichi), *Kokka gakkai zasshi*, 61:129-163 (Sept. 1947); Maruyama Masao, "Fukuzawa ni okeru 'jitsugaku' no tenkai" (The conception of realism in Fukuzawa), *Tōyō bunka kenkyū*, 3:1-20 (Mar. 1947); Kōsaka, *Japanese Thought*, pp. 49-84.

63. *Fukuzawa Yukichi zenshū* (Collected works of Fukuzawa Yukichi), 21 vols. (Tokyo: Keiō Gijuku hensan, 1958-1963), IV, 9.

64. *Ibid.*, III, 123.

65. *Ibid.*, III, 128-129.

66. *Ibid.*, IV, 32.

67. *Ibid.*, IV, 30-35.

68. *Ibid.*, IV, 209.

69. *Ibid.*, IV, 192.

70. *Ibid.*, IV, 187.

71. Quoted in Kōsaka, *Japanese Thought*, p. 81.

72. This judgment of Fukuzawa on the riots in early Meiji Japan can be confirmed by the analysis of a typical riot in July 1873 in Tottori. The rioters were demanding the lowering of the price of rice, the banning of all relations with foreigners, the abolition of compulsory military service and of elementary schools, opposition to the reform of the calendar, and opposition to the order imposing the Western haircut. There were good reasons for these riots, but they alone were not sufficient to make the riots a symbol of progressive liberalism. At the same time they cannot be dismissed as simply reactionary phenomena. See Kōsaka, *Japanese Thought*, pp. 81-82.

73. In a comparison between the Tokugawa regime and the new Meiji government, Fukuzawa found that the Tokugawa *bakufu* had some elements of liberalism and freedom which were missing in the extreme concentration of power under the new system. He preferred the balance in the Tokugawa era, when political power had resided in the *bakufu*, spiritual power in the emperor, and economic power in the merchant class. Maruyama, "Fukuzawa Yukichi no tetsugaku," p. 135.

74. On Ueki and Nakae, see Ike, pp. 124-137. See also Hijikata Kazuo, *Nakae Chōmin* (Tokyo, 1958); Ishida, *Meiji seiji shisō*, pp. 292-315. On Ōi Kentarō, see Marius B. Jansen, "Ōi Kentarō: Radicalism and Chauvinism," *Far Eastern Quarterly*, 11:305-316 (May 1952).

75. *MBZ*, II, 186.

76. Ike, pp. 128-129.

77. Jansen, "Ōi Kentarō," p. 308.

78. Kawabe Kisaburō, *The Press and Politics in Japan* (Chicago, 1921). This work presents the English translation of many articles published during the middle and late seventies; of particular importance is Chap. 8, pp. 60-85. See also Ienaga Saburō, "Nihon ni okeru kyōwashugi no dentō" (The tradition of

Notes to Chapter II

republicanism in Japan), *Shisō*, No. 410:1109-25 (Aug. 1958). Ienaga gives a few examples of republican thought and violent opposition to the imperial system in which the emperor was called the thief of thieves whose power was based only on injustice.

79. *Saifū shimbun* (Jan. 19, 1876).

80. *Ibid*. (Mar. 14, 1876). Translation from Kawabe, p. 63.

81. *Hyōron shimbun* (Jan. 28, 1876). Translation from Kawabe, p. 68.

82. *Hyōron shimbun* (Jan. 28, 1876). Quoted in Kawabe, p. 69.

83. Horace Z. Feldman, "The Meiji Political Novel: A Brief Survey," *Far Eastern Quarterly*, 9:245-255 (May 1950). See also Okazaki Yoshie, ed., *Japanese Literature in the Meiji Era*, tr. and adapted by V. H. Viglielmo (Centenary Culture Council Series, Vol. 1; Tokyo, 1958), pp. 131-142.

84. Walter Fee, *The Transition from Aristocracy to Democracy in New Jersey, 1789-1827* (Somerville, 1933), p. 107.

85. Robert N. Bellah, "Values and Social Change in Modern Japan," *Asian Cultural Studies*, 3:51 (International Christian University, Publications III-A, 1962).

III. TOWARD A CONSTITUTIONAL GOVERNMENT

1. In September 1876, Prince Arisugawa, president of the Genrōin, had received an imperial rescript instructing the Genrōin to draft a constitution suitable to the Japanese situation, taking foreign charters as a guide. The "Nihon kokken an" of 1878 was the result of this imperial rescript. On the history of the Genrōin's drafts see Asai Kiyoshi, *Genrōin no kempō hensan temmatsu* (An account of the draft constitutions by the Genrōin; Tokyo, 1946).

2. Inada, I, 318. See also Ishii, *Meiji bunkashi: Hōseihen*, p. 122. The Genrōin prepared three drafts. The second one was presented in 1878 and had to be revised. The third draft was the revision of the second and was submitted in 1880, not differing in fundamental principles from the second one. The following discussion is based especially on the second draft. Inada, I, 305-316, reproduces the three drafts. Beckmann, pp. 120-125, gives a translation of the second draft.

3. This article is almost identical to the formulation of article 1 of the Meiji Constitution.

4. Inada, I, 308.

5. Inada has traced the origin of the various clauses of the Genrōin's draft article by article. He sees a particularly close relation between the constitutions of European continental monarchies and this draft. (He consulted the constitutions of Holland, Italy, Prussia, Austria, Spain, Portugal, Belgium, and England.) Inada, I, 321-332. When the emperor instructed the Genrōin to draft a constitution, he presented Prince Arisugawa then president of the Genrōin, with a copy of Alpheus Todd, *Parliamentary Government in England*, 2 vols. (London, 1867, 1868). Translations of Todd's book and other works on Wes-

tern constitutions were quickly prepared for the members of the Genrōin.

6. The provision of chapter II, article 2, reads: "When there is no legitimate male heir, the illegitimate sons shall succeed, with the younger giving precedence to the older."

7. Inada, I, 332-333.

8. Kaneko Kentarō received his LL. B. from the Harvard Law School in 1878. He worked with Itō Hirobumi in the framing of the Meiji Constitution, and was later a special envoy to the United States during the Russo-Japanese War.

9. Inada, I, 332. See also Ishii, *Meiji bunkashi: Hōseihen*, p. 123.

10. In a letter to Itō Hirobumi, written on December 21, 1880, Iwakura deplores the fact that the draft of the Genrōin was but an imitation of foreign constitutions, without any consideration for the Japanese *kokutai* and the peculiar circumstances of the Japanese nation. Inada, I, 335-336.

11. For a detailed analysis of the different opinions presented by the Meiji leaders see *ibid.*, I, 426-507. A translation of the opinions of Yamagata, Itō, Ōkuma, and Iwakura are found in Beckmann, pp. 126-150.

12. On Yamagata's political thought see Hackett, "Yamagata."

13. Beckmann, p. 126.

14. *Ibid.*

15. *Ibid.*, p. 127.

16. *Ibid.*, p. 129.

17. *Ibid.*, p. 130.

18. The text of Kuroda's opinion is in Watanabe Ikujirō, comp., *Nihon kensei kiso shiryō* (Basic historical materials on Japanese constitutional government; Tokyo, 1939), pp. 277-280. On Kuroda see also Scalapino, pp. 152-153.

19. The text of Yamada's opinion is in Watanabe, *Nihon kensei kiso shiryō*, pp. 281-284.

20. *Ibid.*, pp. 281-282.

21. *Ibid.*, p. 282.

22. Inoue Kaoru participated in the building of the new nation, working particularly in economic matters and foreign affairs. The text of Inoue's opinion is in *ibid.*, pp. 285-293.

23. Inada, I, 428-429.

24. A more detailed analysis of Itō's political ideas is presented in Chapter VI below.

25. From Itō's "Opinion on Constitutional Government," submitted in December 1880. Translation from Beckmann, p. 132.

26. *Ibid.*, pp. 132-133. Itō openly said that it was inevitable and desirable to establish *kummin dōchi*, but he also warned that changes had to be adopted gradually in order to prevent any serious modifications of the *kokutai*.

27. Text of Ōki's opinion is in Inada, I, 431-432. Ōki's exposition of the *kokutai* is very close to the propagandistic formulation expressed by the ultranationalists during the 1930's.

28. For a detailed analysis of the background of Ōkuma's ideas on the constitution and especially of his opinion see Joyce C. Lebra, "Ōkuma Shigenobu and the 1881 Political Crisis," *Journal of Asian Studies,* 18:475-487 (Aug. 1959). See also Nagai Hideo, "Meiji 14 nen no seihen" (The political crisis of 1881), in Horie Eiichi and Tōyama Shigeki, eds., *Jiyū minkenki no kenkyū* (Studies on the era of the people's rights movement), 2 vols. (Tokyo, 1959), I, 167-205. Akita, "Development of Parliamentary Government," pp. 68-131, gives a vivid description of the issues, personalities, and events related to the political crisis of 1881. Akita's description of the events of the period is one of the most objective.

29. Both Yano and Ono were strongly influenced by British constitutional principles. Osatake, *Nihon kenseishi taikō,* II, 567-568. Ono had been in England and America from 1871 to 1875 studying English constitutional law.

30. The translation of the whole text Ōkuma's opinion is in Beckmann, pp. 136-142.

31. Inada, I, 461.

32. Ōkuma's words recall Burke's definition of a political party: "Party is a body of men united for promoting by their joint endeavors the national interest upon some particular principle in which they are all agreed."

33. Lebra (pp. 480-482) describes the possible motivations of Ōkuma's behavior; pride, self-interest, commitment to the common good, and moderate liberal ideas could all exist together without necessarily being contradictory. Probably all these motivations were present, as often happens in political struggles. See also Akita, "Development of Parliamentary Government," pp. 96-99.

34. Tsunoda Ryusaku, William Theodore de Bary, and Donald Keene, eds., *Sources of Japanese Tradition* (New York, 1958), p. 560. It is worth noting that the platform of the Kaishintō (Progressive party) included the article: "Preserve the dignity of the imperial house and promote the happiness of the people."

35. Ōkuma's opinion was presented in March 1881, and was referred to the Dajōkan by the emperor in June of the same year. Prince Arisugawa, not heeding to a request by Ōkuma not to disclose the contents of his document to the other leaders, showed it to Iwakura and Sanjō. This fact is known by Iwakura's own admission in his diary. The reason for discovering the contents of Ōkuma's opinion was probably the simple fact that all other opinions had been discussed among the three leaders (Arisugawa, Sanjō, and Iwakura), and it seemed natural to discuss also Ōkuma's proposal, especially because it seemed to be very different from the others. Inada, I, 466.

36. Iwakura's documents are examined at length in Suzuki Yasuzō, *Kempō seitei to Roesler* (Roesler and the framing of the constitution; Tokyo, 1942), pp. 141-151. See the complete text of Iwakura's proposals in Watanabe, *Nihon kensei kiso shiryō,* pp. 324-337.

37. Beckmann, p. 144.

38. *Ibid.,* pp. 144-145.

39. On the distrust toward political parties it is interesting to see what Itō Hirobumi wrote in 1905, commenting on the political ideas of the govern-

ment leaders in 1881: "At that time we had not yet arrived at the stage of distinguishing clearly between political opposition on one hand and treason to the established order of things on the other. The virtues necessary for the smooth working of any constitution such as love of freedom of speech, love of publicity of proceedings, the spirit of tolerance for opinions opposed to one's own, etc., had yet to be learned by long experience." Ōkuma Shigenobu, ed., *Fifty Years of New Japan*, 2 vols. (London, 1910), I, 130.

40. Emerson, pp. 280-292.

41. Inada, I, 477.

42. *Ibid.*, I, 485-487. Translation in Beckmann, p. 59.

43. Suzuki Yasuzō, "Hermann Roesler und die japanische Verfassung," *Monumenta Nipponica*, 4:53-87, 428-453 (1941); Inada, I, 465-491.

44. Hermann Roesler and Inoue Kowashi played a leading role in the final formulation of the Meiji Constitution. As Suzuki implies in the conclusion, Roesler was probably responsible for the change from English constitutional ideas to German ones. Although the Japanese leaders were already inclined to adopt a more or less authoritarian constitution, they could not lightly reject English political ideas and practices. By his advice Roesler helped the Japanese leaders to posit well-founded reasons for their constitutional program.

45. The suspension of the Hokkaido colonization property sale was announced on October 12, 1881, the same day of Ōkuma's resignation, an attempt to placate popular indignation and to draw attention from Ōkuma's affair.

46. Following Ōkuma's dismissal, a total of 15 men resigned from government; all of them had been closely associated with Ōkuma, and most of them were graduates of Keiō University. Ōkuma's letter of resignation reads as follows: "Recently I have been suffering from rheumatism and can no longer perform my administrative duties. Consequently I wish to be relieved of my post." Quoted in Lebra, p. 486.

47. McLaren, pp. 86-87.

48. Probably the best commentary on the internal debate on constitutional government is that of Ōkuma: "What we should note is that from this upheaval the constitution was born. At this time no one in the cabinet objected to constitutional government, but there were differences in opinion on the date." Quoted in Lebra, p. 487.

49. Ishii, *Meiji bunkashi: Hōseihen*, pp. 295-299.

50. On Motoda Eifu see Donald H. Shively, "Motoda Eifu: Confucian Lecturer to the Meiji Emperor," in David S. Nivison and Arthur F. Wright, eds., *Confucianism in Action* (Stanford, 1959), pp. 302-333; Warren W. Smith, *Confucianism in Modern Japan* (Tokyo, 1959), pp. 68-88; Inada, I, 434-452; Ienaga Saburō, "Kyōiku chokugo seiritsu no shisō shiteki kōsatsu" (An ideological historical consideration of the making of the Imperial Rescript on Education), *Shigaku zasshi*, 56:1173-91 (Dec. 1946); Watanabe Ikujirō, *Nihon*

Notes to Chapter III

kempō seitei shikō (History of the making of the Japanese constitution; Tokyo, 1937), pp. 161-184.

51. Translation in Shively, p. 324.

52. The Seventeen-Article Constitution was issued in A.D. 604. Actually this "constitution" amounted to nothing more than a set of precepts for the ruling class, but it contained revolutionary doctrines of the greatest importance in Japanese history. It adopted Confucian ethical concepts and the centralized political institutions of China as the ideal in government. See the text of the Seventeen-Article Constitution in Tsunoda, de Bary, and Keene, pp. 50-53. The Taika Reform, which began in A.D. 645, involved a series of imperial edicts with the general purpose of strengthening the central government and imposing a unified administrative system. These edicts asserted the doctrine, "Under the heavens there is no land which is not the king's land. Among holders of land there is none who is not the king's vassal." In the place of the old political organization based on clan units was set up the systematic territorial administration of the Chinese, with local governors sent out by the court, centrally directed and executing a uniform law. See the text of some of the most important edicts, *ibid.*, pp. 71-78. The Taihō Code of 701-702 was the basic law of Japan until after the Meiji Restoration. In this code many Chinese institutions were taken over directly, and an elaborate bureaucracy was organized based on the merit system. *Ibid.*, pp. 81-87.

53. Shively, p. 324.

54. *Ibid.*, p. 326.

55. Inada, I, 446-447.

56. *Ibid.*, I, 447.

57. Shively, p. 325.

IV. THE DEBATE ON SOVEREIGNTY AND NATURAL RIGHTS

1. This division is taken from Ishii, *Meiji bunkashi: Hōseihen*, pp. 131-132. See also Shimoyama Saburō, "Jiyū minken undō" (The people's rights movement), in *Iwanami kōza*, XVI, 103-146. In this study Shimoyama examines the private draft constitutions. The Kōjunsha was a club organized by Baba Tatsui, Ōbata Tokujirō, Yano Fumio, and others. The society's inaugural ceremony was held in January 1880, at which time it was announced that the group professed allegiance to no single school of thought and was to be composed of intellectuals who represented different points of view, occupations, and backgrounds. The membership included officials, scholars, merchants, farmers, and artisans. For the role played by Baba Tatsui in the formulation of the Kōjunsha's program and for Baba's thought see Eugene Soviak, "The Case of Baba Tatsui: Western Enlightenment, Social Change, and the Early Meiji Intellectual," *Monumenta Nipponica*, 18: 191-235 (1963).

2. Inada, I, 375-382.

3. *Ibid.*, I, 380-381.

Sovereignty and Natural Rights

4. *Ibid.*, I, 381-382.

5. *Ibid.*, I, 390-400.

6. *Ibid.*, I, 401-425. See also Ike, pp. 132-134.

7. Inada, I, 402-404.

8. *Ibid.*, I, 405-406.

9. *Ibid.*, I, 352-362. The Chikuzen kyōaikai draft was very close to the Genrōin draft in that it also upheld a constitutional monarchy and gave very strong powers to parliament. It was based mostly on the constitutions of Spain, Portugal, Holland, Denmark, Italy, and Austria.

10. Ishii, *Meiji bunkashi: Hōseihen*, p. 132.

11. One finds also some relation to the United States Constitution; the right of habeas corpus is taken from it.

12. Inada, I, 388-389.

13. Watanabe, *Nihon kensei kiso shiryō*, pp. 335-336. This criticism was drafted by Inoue Kowashi at Iwakura's request. Kamishima Jirō, "Inoue Kowashi: kokka kikō no seisaku" (Inoue Kowashi: the formation of the state structure), in *Nihon no shisōka* (Thinkers of Japan), ed. *Asahi Jānaru*, 3 vols. (Tokyo, 1962-1963), I, 153-172. Kamishima points out Inoue's apprehension that Ōkuma Shigenobu's group—Yano Fumio, Baba Tatsui, and the other members of the Kōjunsha—might be entrusted with the formulation of the constitution, and that he might be deprived of all influence in the framing of the fundamental laws of Japan. Kamishima suggests that this was one of the motives for Inoue's violent attack on the Kōjunsha draft.

14. By this time the term *shuken* (sovereignty) was already widely used in the meaning of supreme power of the nation. Up to the mid-seventies, there had been talk of *kunken* (rights of the ruler), *minken* (rights of the people), and *kokken* (rights of the state), but the Western notion of sovereignty was often expressed by using the German *Souveränität* or the English "sovereignty."

15. Inada, I, 599.

16. *Ibid.*, I, 600-601.

17. *Ibid.*, I, 601. This editorial was probably written by Ueki Emori.

18. *MBZ*, II, 312-313.

19. *Ibid.*, II, 313-317.

20. *Ibid.*, II, 315.

21. The first article of the series was entitled "The Nature of Sovereignty and the Political Community." The quotation is taken from the introduction to this article. *MBZ*, II, 317.

22. *Ibid.*, II, 322-329.

23. *Ibid.*, II, 323.

24. In order to express more clearly the difference between *kunken* and *shuken*, *Mainichi* used the English word "prerogative" to amplify *kunken* and the German *Souveränität* to explain *shuken*. *MBZ*, II, 327-328.

25. *Ibid.*, II, 329-337.

26. *Ibid.*, II, 332.

27. *Ibid.*, II, 337-351.

28. Inada, I, 629-630.

29. Hijikata, pp. 101-102.

30. The journal *Ōbei seiri sōdan* (up to the sixth issue the title was only *Seiri sōdan*) appeared for the first time on February 20, 1882; the last issue was published in January 1884. The translation of the *Social Contract* started in No. 2 and finished in No. 45.

31. See also the article "Shuken no kai" (On sovereignty) in *Ōbei seiri sōdan*, No. 14 (Sept. 10, 1882). Inada, I, 636-637.

32. *Ibid.*, I, 639-644.

33. *Ibid.*, I, 639.

34. See *Fukuzawa zenshū*, V, 259-292.

35. All these works are reproduced in *MBZ*, Vol. 2. For a commentary on the debate on natural rights see Inada, I, 668-681.

36. *MBZ*, II, 371-372. The books Katō refers to were Bartholomäus Carneri, *Sittlichkeit und Darwinismus* (Vienna, 1871), and Otto Henne am Rhyn, *Allgemeine Kulturgeschichte*, 7 vols. (Leipzig, 1877-1879). Henne am Rhyn was a Swiss, not a German as Katō says.

37. *MBZ*, II, 362.

38. *Ibid.*, II, 366.

39. *Ibid.*, II, 375-380.

40. *Ibid.*, II, 380-385.

41. *Ibid.*, II, 383. At the end of *Jinken shinsetsu* Katō presented an impressive list of Western books used to prove his evolutionism. *MBZ*, II, 386-388.

42. *Ibid.*, II, 391-410.

43. *Ibid.*, II, 399.

44. *Ibid.*, II, 452. Baba's political thought is treated by Eugene Soviak, "Baba Tatsui: A Study of Intellectual Acculturation in the Early Meiji Period," Ph. D. thesis (University of Michigan, 1962).

45. *MBZ*, II, p. 467.

46. See Jackson H. Bailey, "Prince Saionji and the Popular Rights Movement of the 1880's," *Journal of Asian Studies,* 21:49-63 (Nov. 1961). Bailey examines the difficulties the Japanese intellectuals encountered in expounding the foreign ideas of freedom, self-government, etc.

47. Takeda Kiyoko, "Tennōsei shisō no keisei" (The formation of the imperial system ideology), in *Iwanami kōza*, XVI, 272-273.

48. For instance, in 1882 Ueki Emori was twenty-five years old; Nakae Chōmin was thirty-five, Ono Azusa twenty-nine, Yano Fumio thirty, and Baba Tatsui thirty-one. Nakae Chōmin expressed the gulf between generations in a very strong way: "These oldsters [the government leaders], boasting of the two or three great deeds they accomplished, to this day continue to cling to their managerial posts and maintain their right to leadership. Holding aloft their superannuated ideas, these oldsters want to inspire the young . . . Unfortunately, I say to them, your ideas like yourself have become old. They are

nothing more than antiques, curios . . . You, Sirs, are truly wise and are truly great commanders, except that today is a period of unprecedentedly great reform in all things in Japan; you are no longer fit for this. Your past is to be respected, your present is pitiable . . . What is called the country's well-being is something of which I probably understand little. However, I am a person who likes fresh, brisk, vernal-feeling air; I do not like stagnant, fetid swamp gases. Fresh air is produced by fresh, living things; superannuated things only produce stale gases." Kōsaka, *Japanese Thought in the Meiji Era*, p. 200.

49. Iwakura Tomomi was over fifty-five, Itō Hirobumi had already reached his forties, and Yamagata Aritomo was over forty-five.

50. Kōsaka, *Japanese Thought*, p. 220.

51. See Lookwood, pp. 503-592.

V. THE GERMAN INFLUENCE: ROESLER AND THE FRAMING OF THE CONSTITUTION

1. Suzuki, *Kempō seitei to Roesler;* Suzuki, "Hermann Roesler."

2. Shimizu Shin, *Dokuō ni okeru Itō Hirobumi no kempō torishirabe to Nihon kempō* (Itō Hirobumi's constitutional investigation in Germany and Austria and the Japanese constitution; Tokyo, 1939).

3. Inada. This often-quoted work offers the best collection of material available on this topic. The talks of Gneist, the lectures of Mosse and Stein, and the various drafts and documents of Roesler are examined in great detail.

4. Johannes Siemes, "H. Roesler no kempō riron ni okeru shakai hatten to rikkenshugi no kankei" (Social progress and constitutionalism in Roesler's constitutional theory), *Kokka gakkai zasshi*, 75:1-41, 181-202, 306-330, 418-424 (1962). Siemes has also published an article in German, "Hermann Roesler und die Einführung des deutschen Staatsrechts in Japan," *Der Staat*, 2:181-196 (1963). Siemes' contribution is especially important because he gives the philosophic and social background of many of Roesler's constitutional suggestions.

5. Suzuki, *Kempō seitei to Roesler*, p. 16.

6. On Roesler's life and work see Siemes, "Hermann Roesler und die Einführung des deutschen Staatsrechts in Japan," pp. 181-187.

7. Reinhold Lorenz, *Japan und Mitteleuropa* (Brünn, 1944), pp. 182-184.

8. Kaethe Mengelberg, "Lorenz von Stein and His Contribution to Historical Sociology," *Journal of the History of Ideas*, 22:267-276 (1961). In English one can only find occasional references to Stein in comprehensive texts on sociology and political science. No detailed analysis of his thought has yet been presented. Besides Mengelberg's article, see Herbert Marcuse, *Reason and Revolution* (London, 1941), pp. 374-388; W. A. Dunning, *A History of Political Ideas*, 3 vols. (New York, 1920), III, 377-386.

9. Marx wrote: "Stein shows that he had the right notion by stating that the

history of the state is inextricably interwoven with the history of the economy." Quoted in Mengelberg, p. 267.

10. These ideas were clearly expressed in Lorenz von Stein's *Geschichte der sozialen Bewegung in Frankreich von 1789 bis auf unsere Tage*, 3 vols. (Hildesheim, 1959). Stein dealt with the political, social, and ideological movements of the nineteenth century, which aimed to promote the welfare of the working class in an emerging industrial society.

11. Mengelberg, p. 274.

12. Rudolf von Gneist's legal political thought is presented especially in *Der Rechtsstaat und die Verwaltungsgerichte in Deutschland*, 2nd ed. (Berlin, 1879). See also Gneist, *The English Parliament*, tr. R. Jewery Shee (Boston, 1886); and Gneist, *The English Constitution*, tr. Philip A. Ashworth, 2 vols. (New York, 1886).

13. Gneist, *Der Rechtsstaat*, pp. 158-190. See also Gneist, *The English Constitution*, II, 350-359.

14. See Siemes, "H. Roesler no kempō riron," pp. 30-38.

15. Hermann Roesler, *Ueber die Grundlehren der von Adam Smith begründeten Volkswirtschaftstheorie* (Erlangen, 1871).

16. Hermann Roesler, *Das soziale Verwaltungsrecht*, 2 vols. (Erlangen, 1872, 1873). This book is being re-examined today in German social and political circles. Many of Roesler's thoughts on the necessity of some kind of "corporative" state in which the various "corporations" have their say in the administration of their professional problems have been adopted today in many countries.

17. *Ibid.*, I, viii-ix.

18. Roesler in opposition to Bismarck had advocated parliamentary government as the ideal system; he wanted a government according to laws consented to by the people. See Roesler, *Gedanken über den konstitutionellen Wert der deutschen Reichsverfassung* (Rostock, 1877), p. 25. Probably because of this opposition to some of Bismarck's political ideas, and also because Roesler had become a Catholic, Bismarck tried to dissuade the Japanese from hiring Roesler as an adviser.

19. The Meiji leaders had given Itō a detailed list of problems to investigate during his tour. He was asked to examine the position of the monarch, cabinet, parliament, courts, civil service, and their mutual relations. This list contained 31 points. See Watanabe, *Nihon kensei kiso shiryō*, pp. 352-355.

20. The whole period of Itō's tour is covered in Shimizu, *Dokuō ni okeru Itō Hirobumi no kempō torishirabe*. Inada, I, 565-596, follows Shimizu and adds a few newly discovered documents.

21. For the text of Itō's letters from Europe, see Watanabe, *Nihon kensei kiso shiryō*, pp. 356-368.

22. Inada, I, 573-576.

23. Watanabe, *Nihon kensei kiso shiryō*, pp. 361-365.

24. Shimizu, *Dokuō ni okeru Itō Hirobumi no kempō torishirabe*, pp. 341-439,

gives the transcription of Mosse's course as written down by Itō Miyoji.

25. Watanabe, *Nihon kensei kiso shiryō*, p. 356.

26. *Ibid.*, pp. 356-358.

27. Suzuki, "Hermann Roesler," *Monumenta Nipponica*, 4:440. See also Suzuki, *Kempō seitei to Roesler*, pp. 11-17.

28. Suzuki, *Kempō seitei to Roesler*, pp. 141-151.

29. Inada, I, 471.

30. Suzuki, *Kempō seitei to Roesler*, p. 148.

31. *Ibid.*, pp. 148-150.

32. Siemes, "Hermann Roesler und die Einführung des deutschen Staatsrechts in Japan," pp. 186-187.

33. The German text of Roesler's draft is in Suzuki, "Hermann Roesler," *Monumenta Nipponica*, 5:65-96.

34. The original copy of Roesler's commentary is in the Kokuritsu kokka toshokan (National Diet Library) among the papers of Itō Miyoji. The commentary, written in English when the constitution was still being discussed in the Privy Council, had to be revised in a few points according to the changes adopted in the final draft. Its title is "Commentaries on the Constitution of the Empire of Japan." This document is cited below as Roesler, "Commentaries"; the pagination follows the original document. The English of the quotations has been kept as in the original.

35. Roesler, "Commentaries," "Introductory Remarks," p. 5.

36. *Ibid.*, chapter 1, "The Emperor," pp. 5-6.

37. *Ibid.*, p. 5.

38. *Ibid.*, pp. 13-22.

39. *Ibid.*, pp. 15-16.

40. *Ibid.*, p. 16.

41. *Ibid.*, p. 18.

42. *Ibid.*, p. 19.

43. *Ibid.*, p. 10.

44. *Ibid.*, chap. 5, "The Judicature," p. 2.

45. *Ibid.*, pp. 10-12.

46. *Ibid.*, chap. 2, "Rights and Duties of the Subjects," p. 2.

47. *Ibid.*, pp. 28-29.

VI. THE NEW THEORY OF THE STATE:
INOUE KOWASHI, ITŌ HIROBUMI, AND THE CONSTITUTION

1. Ishii, *Meiji bunkashi: Hōseihen*, pp. 299-300.

2. Itō Hirobumi, "Some Reminiscences of the Grant of the New Constitution," in Ōkuma, *Fifty Years of New Japan*, I, 122-132.

3. *Ibid.*, p. 128.

4. *Ibid.*

5. *Ibid.*, p. 130.

Notes to Chapter VI

6. Inada, I, 697-704. For Iwakura's ideas on the peerage system see also Nagai Hideo, pp. 215-216.

7. Inada, I, 732-758.

8. *Ibid.*, I, 743-744.

9. *Ibid.*, I, 746.

10. Ishii, *Meiji bunkashi: Hōseihen*, pp. 303-304.

11. It is regrettable that so far there has been no detailed monographic study on Inoue Kowashi. Recently there have been two good articles: one by Tanaka Sōgorō, "Inoue Kowashi," in Konishi Shirō, ed., *Nihon jimbutsushi taikei* (Biographies of Japanese personalities), 7 vols. (Tokyo, 1959-1960), V, 224-251; the other by Kamishima Jirō, "Inoue Kowashi: Kokka kikō no seisaku" in (Inoue Kowashi: The formation of the state structure), in *Nihon no shisōka* (Japanese thinkers) ed. Asahi Jānaru (Tokyo, 1962-1963), I, 153-172. In other general works on the history of Meiji Japan there are frequent references to Inoue, but a detailed and systematic study of this influential bureaucrat is still missing. Inada Masatsugu reports many of Inoue's drafts and documents in his *Meiji kempō*. It is interesting to note what Nakae Chōmin had to say about Inoue Kowashi: "I have known only two men who examined deeply the problems at hand, without becoming arrogant and self-conceited, Inoue Kowashi and Shirane Sen'ichi. The late Inoue Kowashi was one of the few statesmen of our country who could think." Quoted in Kōsaka, *Meiji bunkashi: shisō genronhen*, p. 336. Watanabe, *Nihon kempō seitei shikō*, p. 151, states that in 1881 during the political crisis the only constitutional expert in the Meiji government was Inoue Kowashi. Watanabe also points out that many of Iwakura's and Itō's documents were drafted by Inoue.

12. Inoue's outstanding contributions were not limited to the constitution, but extended to the related laws of the two houses, the civil service system, the system of local administration, the military system, the framing of the imperial rescript on education, and the revision of the unequal treaties. In 1893 he became minister of education and pushed forward plans for technical education. He died on March 15, 1895.

13. Inada, I, 502. The whole tone of the letter is one of strong opposition to the Kōjunsha draft constitution and to Ōkuma's "radicalism." Shrewdly Inoue suggests to Itō that if he, Itō, wants to give up his position in government and build up a system like that of England—a monarchy in name but in reality a democratic republic—the only thing to do is to accept the Kōjunsha plan prepared by Fukuzawa and to set up a party cabinet. But, Inoue insinuates, if Itō wants to build a real monarchy like that of Prussia, then he must hurry up and frame a constitution based on the principle of a strong executive. Inoue's letter had the effect intended, and Itō openly broke with Ōkuma and rejected the English system of parliamentary government in favor of one closer to the Prussian system. The close partnership between Itō and Inoue goes back to this period of June and July 1881.

14. Kamishima, "Inoue Kowashi," p. 154.

The New Theory of the State

15. In *Meiji kempō* Inada publishes for the first time many of Inoue's letters, drafts, opinions, and answers to Itō's questions. Put together these documents amount to more than 250 pages. The best collection of Inoue Kowashi's writings is kept at Kokugakuin University library under the general title "Inoue Kowashi bunsho."

16. Printed in Murakami Shunsuke and Sakata Yoshio, eds., *Meiji bunkashi: kyōiku dōtokuhen* (History of Meiji culture: Education and morals; Tokyo: Kaikoku hyakunen kinen bunka jigyō kai 1955), III, 152.

17. *Ibid.*, pp. 147-155.

18. For a detailed description of the debate between Itō and Inoue and Motoda, see Watanabe, *Nihon kempō seitei shikō*, pp. 161-184. See also Warren W. Smith, pp. 73-86; and Ienaga Saburō, pp. 1173-91.

19. The Chinese character used for *kyō* in *kokkyō*, in different contexts, covers the range represented by the English words "education," "learning," "teaching", "doctrine," and "religion." To Motoda this range of meaning of the character was a single concept which had as its core Confucian moral training. The emperor had received the national teaching from the imperial ancestors and should propagate it among the people in his role as preceptor of the nation. This would bring uniformity of mind and a common purpose to the whole nation. Shively, p. 326.

20. W. W. Smith, pp. 84-85.

21. Inada, I, 434-435.

22. *Ibid.*, I, 449-451.

23. See especially the letter Inoue sent to Itō in July 1881. *Ibid.*, I, 501-503.

24. *Ibid.*, II, 142-150.

25. All the articles of the Meiji Constitution but one can be traced back to some article in European or American constitutions. The only exception is article 1, with its mythological implications.

26. Ishii, *Meiji bunkashi: Hōseihen*, pp. 304-305.

27. For the text of both drafts see Inada, II, 68-82.

28. Roesler's draft is divided into eight chapters and has 95 articles. See the German text in Suzuki, "Hermann Roesler," *Monumenta Nipponica*, 5:62-96.

29. Inada, II, 197-213. This draft is also called the "August Draft."

30. *Ibid.*, II, 213-247. Inoue insisted in this commentary that it was absolutely necessary to give broad powers to the diet. The right to censure ministers, the right to present petitions and to investigate the administration, and the right to propose legislative drafts were necessary, Inoue affirmed, for the perfection of the constitution, the happiness of the people, and the stability of the political system. Without these powers there would inevitably arise unrest and strong demands for a revision of the constitution. In this case, as in many other cases, Inoue again and again shows that it is not an easy task to label him a reactionary, a conservative, or a liberal. He was constantly thinking of building an efficient and stable form of government.

31. *Ibid.*, II, 247-267.

Notes to Chapter VI

32. *Ibid.,* II, 268.

33. Roesler always insisted that sovereignty was indivisible and that this indivisible power resided in the sole person of the emperor. He rejected the English system of parliamentary government, characterizing it as the absorption of state power by the rule of the majority party, in which the cabinet is an executive committee of the party and the monarch is excluded from any real governing. Roesler, "Commentaries," chap. 1, "The Emperor," pp. 5-6.

34. Inada, II, 311-329.

35. *Ibid.,* II, 330-347.

36. *Ibid.,* II, 413. The feelings of Itō Hirobumi in presenting the draft to the emperor are expressed in a letter to Sanjō of April 27, 1888.: "The constitution is an extremely important matter, and the fate of the Imperial House is closely linked to it. If one makes a mistake in this matter, it is like brewing disaster for a hundred years to come. Without entertaining any selfish purpose, in the belief that I was serving the emperor and my country only, I reached my decision." *Ibid.,* II, 411-412.

37. This is Beckmann's description (p. 78).

38. On the establishment of the Privy Council see Akita, "Development of Parliamentary Government," pp., 142-144.

39. Shimizu Shin, *Teikoku kempō seitei kaigi* (The council for the enactment of the imperial constitution; Tokyo, 1940).

40. There is no reference to Shimizu's work in Scalapino, Ike, or Beckmann.

41. Inada, II, 556-858. Writing twenty years after Shimizu, Inada was able to complete the documentation of this important phase in the formulation of the Meiji Constitution. These three hundred pages decicated to the discussions of the Privy Council probably represent the best contribution to the understanding of the ambivalent and ambiguous commitments of the Meiji leaders.

42. Shimizu, *Teikoku kempō,* pp. 87-89. See also Inada, II, 567-568. Before the session started a copy of the draft constitution and a document prepared by Roesler entitled "Shūsei iken" (Revision proposals) were given to each member of the Privy Council. Roesler in this document once again upheld his view that the executive had to be made as independent as possible from the diet. Many of his proposals were warmly supported by the ultraconservative members of the Privy Council. Inoue Kowashi and Itō Miyoji declared themselves against Roesler's extreme transcendentalism. Inada, II, 581-582.

43. Shimizu, *Teikoku kempō,* pp. 87-89.

44. Inada, II, 593. Mori Arinori had previously bèen the target of Motoda's attacks. In the Privy Council however, Mori and Motoda united against Itō in defense of a system of imperial absolutism. Both Mori and Motoda stressed the point that full sovereignty resided only in the emperor according to the principle of the *kokutai.* Nagai Michio, "Mori Arinori: Meiji kyōiku no kensetsusha" (Mori Arinori: The builder of Meiji education), in *Nihon no shisōka,* I, 137-152.

The New Theory of the State

45. Inada, II, 593-594.

46. Translation taken from Tsunoda, de Bary, and Keene, p. 667.

47. Inada, II, 628-629.

48. *Ibid.* The members of the Privy Council were designated by numbers; Mori was No. 14. Thus, Itō started his remarks by saying: "The theory of No. 14." In this translation Mori's name has been used instead for the sake of clarity.

49. Translation taken from Tsunoda, de Bary, and Keene, pp. 678-679.

50. Itō Hirobumi, *Commentaries on the Constitution of the Empire of Japan*, tr. Miyoji Itō, 2nd ed. (Tokyo, 1906), pp. 53-54.

51. Letter of June 20, 1890, quoted in Ienaga, "Kyōiku chokugo seiritsu no shisō shiteki kōsatsu," p. 1183.

52. *Ibid.*, p. 1181.

53. *Ibid.*, p. 1184.

54. Shively, p. 331.

55. Itō was also the first among the Sat-Chō leaders to advocate, after the promulgation of the constitution, the formation of party cabinets. In 1891 he presented his resignation from the government in order to dedicate himself to the organization of a political party. The emperor persuaded him to remain in the administration. See Watanabe, *Nihon kempō seitei shikō*, pp. 154-160.

56. Itō, *Commentaries on the Constitution*, p. 92.

57. *Ibid.*, pp. 92-93.

58. *Ibid.*, p. 93.

59. Itō Hirobumi, "Instructions Addressed to the Governors of Cities and Prefectures," September 28, 1887, in McLaren, p. 327.

60. In a speech to the prefectural governors on December 25, 1890, Yamagata said: "Necessarily, because administrative rights are the sovereign prerogatives of the Emperor, those who are given the responsibility of their exercise shall stand outside the various political parties." Quoted in Scalapino, pp. 153-154.

61. Translation in Ishii, *Japanese Legislation*, p. 386.

62. Inada, II, 657.

63. Ishii, *Japanese Legislation*, pp. 488-489.

64. Itō, *Commentaries on the Constitution*, p. 101.

65. *Ibid.*

GLOSSARY

Aochi Rinsō 青地林宗
Aoki Shūzō 青木周蔵
Arisugawa no Miya 有栖川宮

Baba Tatsui 馬場辰猪
bakufu 幕府
Bankoku kōhō 万国公法
bummei kaika 文明開化
bushi 武士
"Byakujaron" 闢邪論

"Chikujō iken" 逐条意見
Chikuzen kyōaikai 筑前共愛会
Chōshū 長州
Chōya shimbun 朝野新聞
chōzen naikaku shugi
　超然内閣主義

Daikyōin 大教院
daimyō 大名
"Dai Nihon seiki" 大日本政規
"Dai Nihon teikoku kempō"
　大日本帝国憲法
"Dai Nihonkoku seiten"
　大日本国政典
Dajōkan 太政官
"Doku Nippō kisha shukenron"
　読日報記者主権論

Etō Shimpei 江藤新平

fukoku kyōhei 富国強兵
Fukuchi Gen'ichirō 福地源一郎
Fukuoka Kōtei 福岡孝弟

genrō 元老
Genrōin 元老院
Giin 議院
"Goshijun-an" 御諮詢案
Gotō Shōjirō 後藤象次郎

hambatsu 藩閥
han 藩
Hirata Tōsuke 平田東助
Hizen 肥前
Hōchi shimbun 報知新聞
Hyakuichi shinron 百一新論
Hyōron shimbun 評論新聞

Inoue Kaoru 井上馨
Inoue Tetsujirō 井上哲次郎
Itagaki Taisuke 板垣退助
Itō Miyoji 伊東己代治
Iwakura Tomomi 岩倉具視

jakuniku kyōshoku 弱肉強食
Jingikan 神祇官

Glossary

Jinken shinsetsu 人権新説
Jinken shinsetsu bakuron
　人権新説駁論
Jinnō shōtōki　神皇正統記
Jiyūtō　自由党

kaigi　会議
Kaishintō　改進党
kambun　漢文
Kaneko Kentarō　金子堅太郎
kazoku kokka　家族国家
kempō　憲法
Kempō gikai　憲法義解
"Kempō sōan shūsei iken"
　憲法草案修正意見
Kempō zasshi　憲法雑誌
kiheitai　奇兵隊
Kihira Masami　木平正美
Kitabatake Chikafusa 北畠親房
Kiyoura Keigo　清浦奎吾
Kōchi shimbun　高知新聞
Kōeki mondō　交易問答
Kojima Iken　児島惟謙
Kōjunsha　交詢社
kōken　公権
"Kokka shukenron" 国家主権論
kokkai　国会
kokken　国憲
kokken　国権
"Kokken taikō"　国憲大綱
kokkyō　国教
Kokugaku 国学
kokutai　国体
Kokutai shinron　国体新論
Komatsubara Eitarō
　小松原英太郎
kōron　公論

kōtei　皇帝
kummin dōchi　君民同治
kummin kyōchi 君民共治
"Kummin kyōchi no setsu"
　君民共治ノ説
kunken　君権
Kuroda Kiyotaka　黒田清隆
Kyōbushō　教部省
"Kyōgaku taishi" 教学大旨
"Kyōiku-gi" 教育議
kyūshinron 急進論

Matsukata Masayoshi 松方正義
Meiroku zasshi　明六雑誌
Meirokusha　明六社
minken　民権
Minken jiyūron　民権自由論
Miyajima Seiichirō 宮島清一郎
Miyazawa Toshiyoshi 宮沢俊義
Motoda Eifu　元田永孚

"Naikaku shokken"　内閣職権
Nakamura Masanao　中村正直
"Natsushima sōan"　夏島草案
Nichi nichi shimbun　日日新聞
"Nihon kempō mikomi-an"
　日本憲法見込案
"Nihonkoku kokken-an"
　日本国国憲案
Nishi Amane　西周
Nishimura Shigeki　西村茂樹

Obata Tokujirō 小幡篤次郎
Ōbei seiri sōdan 欧米政理叢談
Ōi Kentarō　大井憲太郎
Okakura Kakuzō　岡倉覚三
Ōki Takatō　大木喬任

244

Glossary

Ōkuma Shigenobu 大隈重信
Ōmura Masujirō 大村益次郎
Ono Azusa 小野梓
Ōsaka mainichi shimbun
  大阪毎日新聞
ōsei fukko 王政復古
ōsei ishin 王政綱新

Rempō shiryaku 聯邦志略
Rikken seitai ryaku 立憲政体略
Risshisha 立志社
rōnin 浪人

Saifū shimbun 采風新聞
Saigō Takamori 西郷隆盛
Saionji Kimmochi 西園寺公望
saisei itchi 祭政一致
Saishōron 妻妾論
Sakamoto Namio 坂本南海雄
Sakamoto Ryōma 坂本龍馬
samurai 侍
Sanjō Sanetomi 三条実美
Sasaki Takayuki 佐佐木高行
Sat-Chō 薩長
Satsuma 薩馬
sei-i tai shōgun 征夷大将軍
Seiri sōdan 政理叢談
seitai 政体
Seitaisho 政体書
Seiyō jijō 西洋事情
Seiyō kakkoku seisui kyōjaku
  ichiran hyō 西洋各国盛衰強弱
  一覧表
"Shigi kempō-an" 私擬憲法案
shiken 私権
"Shikō kempō sōan"
  私考憲法草案

Shimeikai 紫溟会
"Shimmin kenri gimu"
  臣民権利義務
"Shimmin no bunsai"
  臣民ノ分際
shinsei 神聖
Shinsei tai-i 真政大意
shintōin 紳董院
Shirane Sen'ichi 白根専一
shizoku 士族
shōgun 将軍
shōnin 承認
shōsōron 尚早論
Shōtoku Taishi 聖徳太子
shuken 主権
"Shuken bemmō" 主権辨妄
"Shuken gairon" 主権概論
"Shuken no kai" 主権ノ解
"Shuken no shozai ikan"
  主権ノ所在如何
"Shukenron" 主権論
shūron 衆論
"Shūsei iken" 修正意見
Soejima Taneomi 副島種臣
Sōmō zasshi 草莽雑誌
Sūmitsuin 枢密院

Taihō 大宝
Taika 大化
Taisei kokuhōron 泰西国法論
Takada Sanae 高田早苗
Tanaka Fujimaro 田中不二麿
teiō 帝王
Teiseitō 帝政党
Teishitsuron 帝室論
Tempu jinkemben 天賦人権弁
Tempu jinkenron 天賦人権論

Terajima Munenori 寺島宗則

Tokugawa Keiki 徳川慶喜

Tōkyō Yokohama mainichi shimbun 東京横浜毎日新聞

Tōkyō yoron shinshi 東京輿論新誌

Tonarigusa 鄰艸

Torio Koyota 鳥尾小彌太

Tosa 土佐

Tōyō jiyū shimbun 東洋自由新聞

Tsuda Masamichi 津田眞道

Tsuda Sanzō 津田三蔵

Ueki Emori 植木枝盛

Yamada Akiyoshi 山田顕義

Yamawaki Ki 山脇巍

Yano Fumio 矢野文雄

Yochi shiryaku 輿地誌略

Yoshida Shōin 吉田松陰

Yūbin hōchi shimbun 郵便報知新聞

Yuri Kimimasa 由利公正

zenshinron 漸進論

INDEX

Index

Index

Index

HARVARD EAST ASIAN SERIES